Marketing Automation

Wiley and SAS Business Series

The Wiley and SAS Business Series presents books that help senior-level managers with their critical management decisions.

Titles in the Wiley and SAS Business Series include:

Business Intelligence Competency Centers: A Team Approach to Maximizing Competitive Advantage, by Gloria J. Miller, Dagmar Bräutigam, and Stefanie Gerlach

Case Studies in Performance Management: A Guide from the Experts, by Tony C. Adkins

CIO Best Practices: Enabling Strategic Value with Information Technology, by Joe Stenzel

Credit Risk Scorecards: Developing and Implementing Intelligent Credit Scoring, by Naeem Siddiqi

Customer Data Integration: Reaching a Single Version of the Truth, by Jill Dyché and Evan Levy

Information Revolution: Using the Information Evolution Model to Grow Your Business, by Jim Davis, Gloria J. Miller, and Allan Russell

Performance Management: Finding the Missing Pieces (to Close the Intelligence Gap) by Gary Cokins

For more information on any of the above titles, please visit **www.wiley.com/go/sas**

Marketing Automation

Practical Steps to More Effective Direct Marketing

JEFF LESUEUR

1807
WILEY
2007

John Wiley & Sons, Inc.

Library of Congress Cataloging-in-Publication Data:

LeSueur, Jeff, 1956–

Marketing automation : practical steps to more effective direct marketing / Jeff LeSueur.

p. cm.

Includes index.

ISBN 978-0-470-12542-7 (cloth)

1. Direct marketing. 2. Marketing–Data processing. I. Title.

HF5415.126.L47 2007

658.8′72–dc22

2007009240

To Alison and Alex, thanks for your patience

Contents

Preface

This book is derived from and motivated by a very successful ten-year period spent at BMG Direct, the direct marketing music club of Bertelsmann Music Group. During this period I witnessed, participated in, and contributed to profit growth from breakeven to over $80 million annually.

The growth was due without question to the combination of management, marketing, and customer interest; BMG rode the wave of the increasing popularity of the compact disc medium. But I stress the management and marketing aspects on equal ground with product interest. The company was effectively managed and marketing was very engaged in developing new views of customers, music, and promotions, addressing and implementing new presentations, new offers, and new channels for promotions and communications.

Challenges to continued profitability appeared around the same time as the CD purchasing wave began to peak: dramatically higher postage and paper costs, two of the largest cost drivers for any direct marketing business. Soon after these costs increased, the third cost factor—usage rights—also increased.

Faced with declining profitability, BMG Direct managed to continue earning profits at a relatively high level by focusing on the leverage provided by *customer information* and *marketing automation*. Three targeted marketing programs evolved. In the customer information was leveraged to identify least active customers first, to reduce promotion costs. Analytics were then applied to select less active customers more likely to respond to promotions, and target promotions directly to them. For the third marketing program, analytics were applied to select the most likely to respond from our best customers; specific—and incremental—promotions were created expressly for this group as well.

All three of these programs relied on leveraging customer information and automating the processes necessary to implement the programs on a timely basis: Any customer likely to respond was selected for a promotion within 30 days of the event that drove their selection. This demanded ease of access to customer information as well as response performance. Access and performance was based on a data warehouse implemented from the customer master file. As trial marketing programs evolved into production, the marketing selection processes were automated.

Results far surpassed expectations. As an example, we developed a process for selecting promotable customers that captured an incremental $4 million in profit—the goal for the year—in six months. "Incremental" profit was validated through ongoing response testing integrated with every promotion.

Leveraging customer information is a not a new story. The National Center for Database Marketing was founded in 1987. David Shepard and Associates first published their benchmark volume, *The New Direct Marketing: How to Implement a Profit-Driven Database Marketing Strategy*, shortly thereafter, in 1989.[1] However, the *practice* of using our customer information became itself a challenge. As the volume of customer-based marketing programs, modeling, and testing expanded, the process of accessing the information became a significant bottleneck: There were a lot more "marketers" asking for information and only a few *database* marketers who could access the customer database to build the lists that were the substance behind our success. We were unable to increase the ability of marketers to take a stronger role in the marketing process. Our solution then was to improve the system's response and effectively organize our customer information to improve our database marketing productivity.

This challenge—empowering marketers to plan and execute promotions—is the goal of marketing automation and the key behind fully leveraging marketing to increase profits. Software applications have advanced significantly in the past decade; more functionality is available

---

[1]Arthur M. Hughes, *The Complete Database Marketer*, Irwin, 1996, p. 61; David Shepard and Associates, *The New Direct Marketing: How to Implement a Profit-Driven Database Marketing Strategy*, 2nd Irwin Edition, 1995.

today, with more potential, to empower marketers to effect stronger, more responsive marketing programs. It is my expectation that this book will introduce that functionality and demonstrate—pragmatically—the benefits that can be derived from its application. Those benefits are people oriented; they empower marketers to effect more and more targeted campaigns, increasing value to customers as well as company profits.

Acknowledgements

Many people provided support and assistance in the preparation and completion of this book. From SAS I'd like to offer particular thanks to Andy Bober, Mark Brown, Jack Bulkley, Bryan Hendricks, Bryan Horne, Andy Ju, Brad Klenz, Keith Morgan, Carol Rigsbee, and Fred Volk for their help, support and encouragement. Also from SAS Sara Van Asch, Patrice Cherry, Margaret Crevar, Karen Day, Mark Filipowski, Terry Gilbert, Ed Harriss, Ralph Hollinshead, Douglas Liming, and Jeff McFall for very timely contributions.

From SAS Publishing thanks to Stephenie Joyner and Julie Platt for supporting the project to completion, and for making the SAS Marketing Automation suite available for development, and from Wiley thanks to Sheck Cho, Natasha Andrews–Noel, and Shelley Flannery for managing the project to completion.

Special thanks and acknowledgement is offered to Oracle Corporation for permission to use screenshots of copyrighted Oracle Software applications.

Special thanks and acknowledgement is offered to SAS for permission to use screenshots of copyrighted SAS Software applications.

Overview

This book covers a fairly broad range of business functions: operating financial management, marketing financial planning, information technology, customer information management, and the marketing process.

As noted in the Preface, the focus of the book is on increasing profits by improving the effectiveness of marketing. This is discussed on a purely pragmatic basis. *Customer relationship management* (CRM) as a concept is amply covered by a number of authors, notably Don Peppers and Martha Rogers, and Paul Greenberg.[1] The emphasis in this book is on the implementation details and particularly the financial return provided by more effective communication with customers.

Part One appropriately starts with a discussion of Operating Financial Management Statements. The *bottom line* in an operating financial statement is "net profit." Understanding the lines above the bottom line means understanding *profit*, and this is fundamental to learning how to leverage analysis of marketing investments so as to increase profit.

An Operating Financial Management Statement typically treats "marketing investment" as an expense. In this book the money spent by marketing in communicating with customers is considered an *investment*. As in any business the *return* on the investment is of greatest interest, how much money

---

[1]Don Peppers and Martha Rogers have authored several books, such as *The One to One Future: Building Business Relationships One Customer at a Time* (Judy Piatkus, 1994) and *Enterprise One to One* (Currency, 1996). Paul Greenberg's *CRM at the Speed of Light: Capturing and Keeping Customers in Internet Real Time* (McGraw-Hill, 2001) is now in its third edition.

is *earned* from this effort and allocation of available funds. Every business has competing needs for available funds; a well-managed business tries to get the best return from available alternatives. Analysis techniques for investment return and identifying poorly performing marketing investments are therefore demonstrated. One advantage of investing in marketing compared with other alternatives is that investment dollars can be moved easily from weak areas to strong areas in order to *improve investment return*.

Understanding profit and how it is calculated for analysis of *operating* financial statements is fairly straightforward, and, because the focus here is purely pragmatic, a complete analysis of all financial statements is *not* included. Sufficient information is provided to facilitate the discussion that takes place during most monthly business operating reviews: Revenue minus cost of manufacturing equals gross profit; gross profit divided by marketing investment equals return on marketing investment. Why is revenue down? Why are these costs higher? *How can we improve the return on our marketing investment?*

To flesh out the concept of "return on marketing investment," a financial spreadsheet is included that exemplifies how marketing investments can be expanded. The profit impact of an increase in communications per customer is demonstrated by example. The profit provided by new and more effective communications approaches a cumulative incremental impact of 20% to operating profit after marketing expense.

Part Two addresses the supporting infrastructure for more effective marketing, and the corresponding challenges for information technology and data warehousing. The increase in profit comes from spending marketing dollars more effectively by addressing more communications, promotions, and content to increasingly smaller audiences. *Targeted marketing* at this level depends on a reasonable amount of customer information being available *and easily accessible to marketers*. Software applications are at the core of "easily accessible." However, the information must exist and be accessible to these applications. Some businesses have millions of customers and tera-bytes of customer information: customer attributes, sales history, model scores, and segmentation. The organization and management of this information is both a significant challenge and fundamental to successful application of the principles discussed here.

Improving the effectiveness of marketing investment comes down to spen-ding less money per sale and communicating more often with customers.

This is an apparent paradox: How can less money be spent in marketing while at the same time increasing the contact frequency with customers? The answer is pragmatic and straightforward: by communicating more often with those customers most likely to respond, and not communicating as frequently with those least likely to respond.

Determining who is most and least likely to respond requires the application of analytical models derived from the history of current and prior customer activity. There are simple models and very complex models: Fully one-third of a customer email list never opened an email promotion over a three-month period; over one million people from a direct mail list never purchased in a year. Both of these observations could be the core of a simple model for *reducing* communications volume. However, what if an incremental promotion was offered to all customers who purchased in the last 30, 60, or 90 days? This is another simple model example that could be used to increase marketing effectiveness.

Given the availability of customer information, sales, and marketing history, predictive models can be developed and applied that highlight which promotions appeal to which groups of people. Incorporating predictive indicators—models—in the customer selection process is discussed toward the close of Part Two.

Part Two also addresses one of the critical roadblocks to improving return on marketing investment and increasing profits: the effectiveness of the people involved in developing marketing promotions and the process used to select the audiences to whom the promotions will be directed. It is a simple fact that there are many more marketers than people who can access customer information to develop a promotions list from a database, using standard database marketing tools. Empowering marketers to participate more fully in the marketing process—selecting the audience, scheduling execution of the list selection queries—can be accomplished using *campaign management* software applications. These applications strive to make it easy for marketers to access customer information and select customers for an increasing number of marketing communications.

All software vendors make a claim for "easy," with statements like "intuitive interface" and "powerful graphics." Because the overriding goal of this book is a realistic look at steps that can improve marketing effectiveness, a walk through of several marketing scenarios is done using a marketing automation software application together with customer data. Rather than invoke functionality as conceptual possibilities, a "show-me" approach highlights the reality of *marketing automation* as a software application. Screenshots taken from a marketing automation application are used at critical points in the marketing process to provide tangible examples. The software application used is called SAS Marketing Automation™. It is not the only marketing automation application available; however, it incorporates the fundamental capabilities of such applications and provides a good example of what marketing automation applications can do to improve the effectiveness of marketers.

The focus in this Part is not on exploring what SAS Marketing Automation software can do;[2] the focus remains on what functions marketing automation software can effect to facilitate the marketing process, and how marketers can take advantage of these functions in creating more communications to smaller audiences. This book does not provide a comparison of marketing automation applications just as it does not compare database technologies or hardware platforms. This book demonstrates how the investment in marketing automation can work to improve profits.

Part Three of the book addresses advanced topics and the corresponding software applications that implement incremental functionality. Incremental functionality includes managing contact frequency, optimizing communication decisions given resource constraints, effectively managing more models, and event-based communications.

The final topic of Part Three, and the last topic addressed in this book, is a marketing approach that I have termed *strategic marketing*. Marketing, even targeted marketing, typically approaches the process in a batch manner. A set of promotions are established that are repeated every year on a seasonal basis: Holiday and Post-Holiday Sales, Spring offerings, and Summer and Back-to-School Sales. All of these ignore the *life cycle* of the customer and company relationship. Addressing communications and promotions to the salient aspects of *relationship*—the beginning, the middle, and the (potential) end— creates an interesting marketing opportunity. Addressing this life cycle with

---

[2]Technology consulting firms such as Gartner and Forrester provide comprehensive and readable product comparisons. For more information, see Forrester Research (Boston, MA), www.Forrester.com. See also Gartner Research (Stamford, CT), www.Gartner.com.

appropriate marketing communications could prolong the relationship, generating higher profit per customer than more typical batch-based calendar campaigns.

Marketing automation applications can make a significant contribution toward customer life cycle marketing: These applications can be used to *proactively* establish customer communications targeting specific points in the customer life cycle. Proactively establishing these communications improves the timing of delivery, and improving the timing of marketing communications can increase response rates. Establishing a concept of the customer life cycle and crafting appropriate promotions is expected to lengthen the relationship and increase sales—and profit—per customer.

The primary topics of the book—marketing financials, marketing infrastructure, and marketing automation—emphasize the management of the marketing process in the context of the financial management of the business. This is not to suggest a subservient marketing position to financial management. It simply recognizes the overriding purpose of business process, which is to generate profit. The discussion emphasizes marketing management of marketing investments for recognizing and improving marketing's impact on the business.

PART ONE

Marketing Financials

CHAPTER 1

Profit and Loss Fundamentals

Business *profit and loss* (P&L) is an easy topic to introduce:

- Revenue – Expense = Profit.
- If Revenue > Expense, then Profit > 0; this is the goal.
- If Expense > Revenue, then Profit < 0, which is not Profit but Loss; this is to be avoided.

Achieving profit goals means winning the game, maxing out on the bonus, and going home from the office early while enjoying a sense of satisfaction. Missing the goals is frustrating and followed by even more work in an already-full day: *Managing* to achieve profit goals is very challenging.

Beneath the apparent simplicity of business profit and loss is a relationship that can be leveraged to increase profits. This relationship is fundamental to the business process, which means it can be leveraged now and in the future to provide a continual source of incremental profit and protection against loss. The relationship is

Gross Profit/Marketing Expense = Return on Marketing Investment

The relationship says that increasing the return on marketing investment will increase gross profit. Understanding and utilizing the relationship requires a solid understanding of the P&L—business profit and loss—which is the topic of this first part.

PROFIT AND LOSS GOALS: ACTUAL, FORECAST, PLAN, AND VARIANCE

"P&L" stands for profit and loss and "the P&L" is a reference to the *Management* Profit/Loss Statement presented monthly at business performance meetings. "P&L Goals" are monetary business targets captured in the operating business plan or forecast and the focus of discussion in performance meetings. Paying close attention to these figures, and managing to the "Plan" or "Forecast" is essential to achieving the targets, which is a significant—if not the primary—goal for management.

Management typically prepares a business plan in advance of a fiscal year. The business plan is presented to senior management for agreement and approval. This proposed business plan should contain sufficient detail to substantiate and defend the proposed goals—profit—as realistic and achievable.

The proposed profit goal may be adequate and accepted as presented. However, it may also be increased—"tasked"—by senior management: The business may be asked to provide a plan that is "more than" realistic and achievable, and be asked to meet the new goal. Large corporations with multiple divisions may need to ask their more successful divisions to reach a little higher to compensate for less successful divisions, in order to meet an overall goal for the corporation itself.

Once the business plan is accepted and the new year begins, it becomes "The Business Plan." Managing "to the Plan" involves recurring review of business conditions, revenue achievements, expense ratios, and a comparison of actual revenue, expense, and profit to revenue, expense, and profit in the Plan.

One focus of operational review meetings is the presentations that compare actual profit to Plan. Later in the year, particularly if the division is significantly ahead of or behind the plan, the focus may shift to a comparison of *forecast* revenue, expense, and profit.[1] The primary goal of the division in this case will then be to achieve the forecast, which could be higher or lower than the plan.

---

[1] A forecast is used to manage expectations: A large positive variance to a business plan early in the year, + 20% for Q1, for example, creates an expectation for similar performance (+20%) for the duration of the year. The forecast will clarify whether such an expectation is valid. A single large order or a shipment delayed from the prior year could create a one-time positive variance in Q1, which would set an invalid expectation for the remainder of the year. Management would need to communicate that this is a one-time variance; the forecast could be used for this purpose.

EXHIBIT 1.1   JULY P&L SUMMARY

$000	Actual	Forecast	Variance	Var%	Plan	Variance	Var%
July Profit	2,576	2,400	176	7.3%	3,000	(424)	−14.1%

The presentation of actual profit compared to the management goals can be seen in Exhibit 1.1.

Here there are two comparisons for July Actual Profit: Forecast and Plan. The first comparison is to Forecast; the company has earned $2.576 million for the month of July, while the forecast was for $2.4 million. Therefore they have a positive variance of $176,000, which is 7.3% above the forecast (176/2400 = 7.33%).

The second comparison for July Actual Profit is to the Plan, which was $3.0 million. July Profit is well behind the Plan: $424,000 or −14.1%.

The comparison in this example is for the month of July only. A business year is 12 months long; therefore a second performance comparison is made to year-to-date performance: From Exhibit 1.2, July Year-to-Date to Forecast is $176,000 ahead, the same figure for the month of July, while Year-to-Date Profit is ($2.524) million behind Plan.

Showing the same variance for both the month of July and July year-to-date against dismal performance in prior months (compared to Plan) suggests a forecast was prepared starting with the month of July. The forecast may have been requested by senior management to establish a new full year profit goal, as the plan does not appear achievable at this point. The forecast answers the question: If management admits to the fact the plan target is not achievable, what then is management's commitment for the year?

This same information is frequently presented in a bar chart (Exhibit 1.3), which makes the profit gap to business plan (year-to-date) more clear.

EXHIBIT 1.2   JULY P&L SUMMARY

$000	Actual	Forecast	Variance	Var%	Plan	Variance	Var%
July Profit	2,576	2,400	176	7.3%	3,000	(424)	−14.1%
July YTD Profit	18,032	17,856	176	1. 0%	20,556	(2,524)	−12.3%

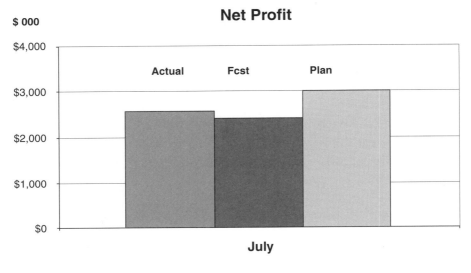

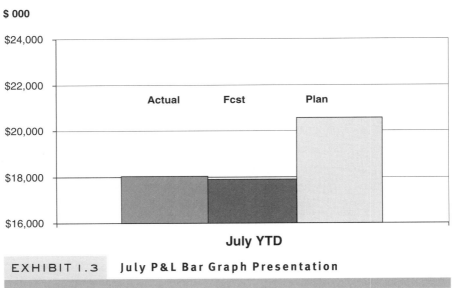

EXHIBIT I.3   July P&L Bar Graph Presentation

The remaining items to be shown to complete the management Profit view are the Full Year figures. Management will use the Forecast and Plan figures, together with the Year-to-Date Actual figures to present a Full Year view of expected company performance (see Exhibit 1.4).

EXHIBIT 1.4   JULY P&L SUMMARY

$000	Actual	Forecast	Variance	Var%	Plan	Variance	Var%
July Profit	2,576	2,400	176	7.3%	3,000	(424)	−14.1%
July YTD Profit	18,032	17,856	176	1.0%	20,556	(2,524)	−12.3%
Full Year Fcst	45,080	44,904	176	0.4%	51,027	(5,947)	−11.7%

A "Full Year Forecast" is based on the year-to-date actuals for each month, plus the forecast (or Plan) for each of the remaining months. For OurCompany, the full year forecast done prior to July incorporated actuals for January to June; therefore the only variance July YTD is attributable to the positive, $176,000 variance in the month of July (see Exhibit 1.5).

For the full year, comparisons will always be made back to Plan. In a large corporation consisting of many divisions, the plan becomes the basis for many longer-term investment decisions. Deviations from the plan can place additional risk on these decisions, which could make such decisions appear to have been ill advised. Negative deviations by a division such as OurCompany are expected to be recognized and quantified so that contingency plans can be considered. Contingencies can be as simple as

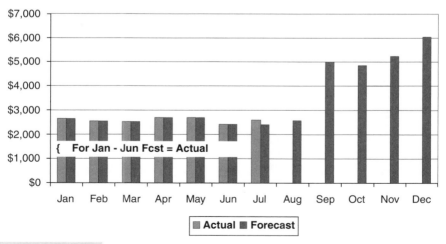

Actual - Forecast Profit, By Month

EXHIBIT 1.5   Monthly Profit/Loss Bar Graph

balancing a negative with a positive from another division that is experiencing better-than-plan performance. The Forecast formalizes commitment measures such as profit for such ongoing planning.

Returning to the Full Year picture, note that the July Year-to-Date Plan variance of −12.3% is greater than the variance for the Full Year Forecast comparison, which is −11.7%. This is because the positive variance of $176,000 in July is carried forward to the forecast for the *full year*. A full year forecast figure incorporates actuals to date, for purposes of comparison to Plan. Management has convinced their managers—a division President, a Board of Directors—that the forecast is *achievable*. Correspondingly, OurCompany management will be expected to *manage* to achieve it.

CHAPTER 2

Profit and Loss Component Details

The financial reporting (fiscal) year ends in December for OurCompany.[1] As of July the company is $2.5 million behind plan. Management has reforecast the year for each month to a significant level of detail, sufficient to convince the division president or board of its credibility and achievability. The details of the reforecast will help clarify how and why the company came to be so far behind plan. These details will also be surfaced in the monthly operating review, in a form shown in Exhibit 2.1.

Prior operating reviews would have highlighted the ongoing source of OurCompany's performance problems, assuming this was a recurring issue and not a one-time impact in a single month. That source of variance should be discernable from analysis of the statement above. Performance variance questions can often be answered by evaluating the figures under the Variance column in this report (Exhibit 2.1). The comparison to Plan is on the far right, the comparison to Forecast is in the middle. Note that the variance calculation intentionally uses a negative[2] value or percentage to connote a negative variance and "bad news"; a positive variance is therefore "good news."

In the top line, Revenue (also referred to as "Sales"), shows bad news of (5,304) or −$5.304 million. This means sales are significantly—minus

---

[1] It is not required that a fiscal year follow the calendar year.

[2] Negative numbers can be displayed with a minus sign "−19.4%" or in parentheses (3,874).

EXHIBIT 2.1   **JULY PROFIT AND LOSS DETAIL**

$000	Actual	Forecast	Variance	Var%	Plan	Variance	Var%
Revenue	21,968	21,694	275	1.3%	27,273	(5,304)	−19.4%
Returns	2,636	2,603	(33)	−1.3%	3,273	637	19.4%
Total Net Revenue	19,332	19,090	242	1.3%	24,000	(4,668)	−19.5%
Manuf Cost by Product							
Product A	5,055	5,101			4,775		
Product B	2,178	2,140			6,518		
Product C	1,465	1,362			980		
Total Manuf Cost	8,699	8,603	(96)	−1.1%	12,273	3,574	29.1%
Gross Profit	10,633	10,487	146	1.4%	11,727	(1,094)	−9.3%
Marketing	2,957	3,000	43	1.4%	3,200	243	7.6%
Overhead	5,100	5,100	–	0.0%	5,100	–	0.0%
Net Profit	2,576	2,387	189	7.9%	3,427	(851)	−24.8%

19.4%—below plan. Profit ultimately comes from sales (or revenue), and a proportion of sales should trickle down to the bottom line, a ratio known as "profitability." The large negative sales variance for OurCompany of −19.4% seems to be behind the corresponding large negative variance of −24.8% in profits. Further analysis will substantiate this, and in fact provide a clear explanation for the large variance in sales.

The following discussion will include details on most operating P&L line items, such as Returns, Inventory Provision, and Bad Debt. A marketer might question the relevance of this information for marketing purposes, questioning how "marketing automation" can involve or affect the bad debt or inventory provision, or the reverse. In fact both marketing success and lack of success contribute to many components of the P&L: Marketing can attract less qualified customers who do not pay their bills and increase bad debt. Marketing can create the wrong product expectation with customers and increase the amount of returned product, beyond expectations accounted for in the returns reserve. Marketing can fail to attract new customers or maintain existing ones, leading to a loss of market share and lower sales.

From a marketing automation standpoint, marketers with the capability to fine-tune their customer focus can reduce the volume of nonpaying

| EXHIBIT 2.2 | P&L DETAIL: REVENUE | | | | | | |

$000	Actual	Forecast	Variance	Var%	Plan	Variance	Var%
Revenue	21,968	21,694	275	1.3%	27,273	(5,304)	−19.4%

customers, test their presentation effectiveness, reduce aging inventory due for write-off or shipment to a discount wholesaler, and attract new customers to improve sales. The operating P&L details are very important to both marketing and marketing automation.

REVENUE

As Net Profit is the *bottom line*, Revenue is the *top line*. Revenue is income received from customers for products or services provided. Profit will be calculated after deducting business costs from revenue. Revenue is *not* the cash received from customers. "Cash" received or distributed is not monitored on a "P&L"; it is monitored on the balance sheet. *Revenue* is also a more general term than sales for income, as there are other sources of income besides product sales.

OurCompany shows revenue in July of $21,968,000 and a variance to plan of –$5,304,000, or 19.4% below plan (see Exhibit 2.2); $21,968,000 is a very large number and must be detailed further if management expects to understand and manage the similarly large and negative variance. Additional information should be available to management, detailing sales by region, sales by major account, and sales by product or product family. Anything less would weaken the support and credibility for the plan of $27,273,000. The plan would appear no more valuable than a guess, and similarly difficult to manage against.

Additional details on the sales variance source(s) will also help marketing assess how their efforts can be aligned or realigned for improvement.

RETURNS

Not all product sold is accepted and retained by customers; some product is returned. "Returns" are deducted from Revenue, which leaves Net Revenue (also recorded as Net Sales).

| EXHIBIT 2.3 | JULY P&L DETAIL: REVENUE AND RETURNS, NET REVENUE |

$000	Actual	Forecast	Variance	Var%	Plan	Variance	Var%
Revenue	21,968	21,694	275	1.3%	27,273	(5,304)	−19.4%
Returns	2,636	2,603	(33)	−1.3%	3,273	637	19.4%
Total Net Revenue	19,332	19,090	242	1.3%	24,000	(4,668)	−19.5%

At face value, lower sales should result in lower returns, and not surprisingly "Returns" for OurCompany July P&L shows a strong positive variance to plan of $637,000 (see Exhibit 2.3).

"Returns" noted here in the P&L are not the actual returns in the month of July; it is an estimate of returns based on sales in the month of July. Product returns can take place at almost any time after a sale. Accounting rules dictate that management should *recognize* (measure and record) accounting events such as sales and returns when the event occurs or a reasonable *expectation* can be established that the event will occur and is measurable. For sales, it is reasonable to record the sale when the product ships, not when the customer order is received, as any number of events can cause a delay in shipment, including cancellation of the order prior to actual shipment.

For Returns, past experience demonstrates that not all shipped product will be accepted by the customer, and past experience can be used to establish an *estimated* value for expected returns from sales in the month of July. The figure used to record returns represents management's *expectation* for eventual returns of product shipped in the month of July.

This figure will be estimated every month, and the estimate is done based on a *percentage* of sales. Therefore, if sales go down in a month, Returns will also go down and create a positive variance. For OurCompany, Revenue less Returns is Net Revenue; the −$5,304,000 Total Revenue variance for July is reduced by the $637,000 positive variance in returns for a Net Revenue variance of −$4,668,000.

Reducing the *actual* return rate in the longer term would enable more revenue to get to the bottom line and increase profits. More effective marketing could reduce returns and have a positive impact on profit. A lower return rate can have a particularly significant effect on a full business year, returning more dollars to profit in each of the 12 months that make up the business year.

EXHIBIT 2.4   RETURNS PROVISION

	Jan	Feb	Mar	Apr	May	Jun
Sales	1,000	1,000	1,000	1,000	1,000	1,000
Returns Provision (10%)	100	100	100	100	100	100
Cumulative Provision	100	200	300	400	500	600
Actual Returns		60	100	100	100	100
Net Returns Provision	100	140	140	140	140	140

In practice this is challenging. The returns expectation is an estimated rate applied to each month's sales. If the returns rate is 10% and sales are $1,000, then the estimate for returns in the month would be $100. Returns for that *specific* month could take place any time in, say, the next six months, based on prior experience. Therefore this amount of $100 is "banked" as a *provision* for returns in this month.

Every month a certain amount is banked for expected returns, using a constant rate, and the value of the provision increases: In the first month it is $100; $90 could be added the following month, and then $100 again in the third. The total provision is now $290.

If a customer makes an actual return of $10, the provision is reduced by this amount, $290 − $10 = $280. This approach can be maintained indefinitely; the returns provision will reach a stable value (see Exhibit 2.4).

The provision *balance* will be stable as shown in Exhibit 2.4 provided that actual returns are *less than* the expectation. If returns increase above expectations, as shown in Exhibit 2.5, the provision balance will decline, and

EXHIBIT 2.5   RETURNS PROVISION TOO LOW

	Jan	Feb	Mar	Apr	May	Jun
Sales	1,000	1,000	1,000	1,000	1,000	1,000
Returns Provision (10%)	100	100	100	100	100	100
Cumulative Provision	100	200	300	400	500	600
Actual Returns		80	140	140	140	140
Net Returns Provision	100	120	80	40	–	(40)

EXHIBIT 2.6   ACTUAL RETURNS DECLINE

	Jan	Feb	Mar	Apr	May	Jun
Sales	1,000	1,000	1,000	1,000	1,000	1,000
Returns Provision (10%)	100	100	100	100	100	100
Cumulative Provision	100	200	300	400	500	600
Actual Returns		50	80	80	80	80
Net Returns Provision	100	150	170	190	210	230

management will have to make an adjustment to increase the provision. In Exhibit 2.5 the adjustment will be required in June, where the provision balance is negative. This situation will also require management to increase the returns provision rate for future months. This would have the effect of reducing sales as well as profit.

To ensure the returns provision is consistent with actual returns, neither too low or too high, a periodic *audit* will be performed to determine whether the estimated return rate is consistent with actual experience.

Improved product quality, sizing, and marketing may all contribute to a long-term decrease in actual returns, and—if returns are less than expected—the audit may demonstrate the provision is *too* high and should be reduced. This situation is shown in Exhibit 2.6: Using six months' sales of $1,000, for example, assume an estimated return rate of 10%. The provision for six months' estimated returned sales would be $100. The audit report indicates an actual returns rate of 8%. The provision is 20% too high: 2%/10% = 20%. Therefore $20 would be considered an *excess* provision in every month, and accumulate.

After six months, the excess is $120. An excess provision for returns is in fact *revenue*, which has been held back from the P&L. Twenty percent will be returned to revenue in the month of the audit as a one-time *adjustment*. Revenue will therefore increase by 20% of the provision value of $100, or $20 for each month the estimate has exceeded actual returns. Assuming product costs are 50% of sales, the provision adjustment will result in a $60 increase in profits. The estimated rate will also decline in future months, providing an incremental benefit to each month, as long as returns can be maintained at the new, lower level. Hence an improvement in marketing effectiveness could lead to a long-term improvement in lower returns, providing an opportunity for long-term higher profits as well as a one-time adjustment to the provision for returns, which provides an immediate increase in sales and profit.[3]

On the darker side, a decline in quality or poor marketing could result in an increase in returns, which would have the opposite effect on sales and profit. Introducing a new channel such as Internet Marketing could have a similarly negative effect if actual returns are inconsistent with expectations. Remember that these expectations are incorporated in an *estimated* rate. It is very important to assess an appropriately conservative figure (a larger percentage) for estimated returns when a new business channel or product is introduced.

For OurCompany, with five months remaining in the year, a change in the returns rate could still be material (significant), but may not be justified. The expectation for returns is based on evaluation of actual returns over a relatively long period of time, say 12 months' sales plus 6 months for returns from that period, for a total of 18 months. Therefore adjustments to the returns rate are usually the result of a long-term trend.

MANUFACTURING COST

As might be expected, if the company is selling less product, Manufacturing Cost should also decline. This is obviously true for OurCompany, which shows a $3,573,000 positive variance to plan for manufacturing cost (see Exhibit 2.7).

Sales are *down* $5.3 million to plan and manufacturing cost is less by $3.57 million. If sales are so much lower than plan, is it possible that too much product was manufactured, and therefore manufacturing costs should be higher? This is a good question, but, as noted earlier, it is an accounting rule that Sales *and* Cost of Sales are recognized as *they occur in time*. Manufacturing costs are recognized at the same time the product *sale* is recognized.

That may seem an odd logic: The company could manufacture 100 items in the month of July but sell (*and ship*) only 80. How can manufacturing cost reflect only the cost for the 80 items shipped and not the remaining 20 items?

---

[3]For OurCompany, Sales—and Profit from Sales—will have been reduced by 10% every month for the past six months. If product quality improves and returns decline to 8% of sales, a one-time sales adjustment of $1.49 million would be made: 10% − 8% = 2% × $140 million (Sales) = $2.48 million. If gross profit is 60% of Sales, the one-time profit increase is $2.48 million × 60% = $1.49 million.

EXHIBIT 2.7   JULY P&L DETAIL MANUFACTURING COST

$000	Actual	Forecast	Variance	Var%	Plan	Variance	Var%
Revenue	21,968	21,694	275	1.3%	27,273	(5,304)	−19.4%
Returns	2,636	2,603	(33)	−1.3%	3,273	637	19.4%
Total Net Revenue	19,332	19,090	242	1.3%	24,000	(4,668)	−19.5%
Total Manuf Cost	8,699	8,603	(96)	1.1%	12,273	3,574	29.1%

One expectation could be that these 20 "extra" items will be sold next month, and their cost will be recognized at that point in time, and not when they were actually manufactured. This seems inconsistent with the accounting rule just introduced, that of recognizing the cost when the event occurs. Even if the product is sold next month, how is the cost to manufacture this month recognized and "moved" to next month?

In fact, the "cost" to manufacture the additional items this month is not a cost at all. "Extra" product manufactured this month is *held in inventory* for sale next month. "Inventory" is an asset—it retains its value for a period of time. If wages and materials to fabricate the additional, unsold product totaled $100, then Inventory Value will increase by $100. The $100 could have come from Cash, which is another asset: Inventory can increase by $100 and Cash decrease by the same amount; total assets remain the same. Therefore, even if too much product were manufactured as a result of a decline in sales, the "cost" to manufacture these unsold items will be measured and reflected in *Inventory.*[4] Therefore, it is not surprising that the business shows a positive variance to Plan for Manufacturing Cost of $1,826,000: Less product was sold.

CHANGES IN INVENTORY VALUATION

As noted above, inventory retains its value *for a period of time.* Eventually unsold items can and will become out of date and difficult if not impossible to

---

[4]Inventory is not measured or recorded using the P&L form; it is measured and recorded using the Balance Sheet form. On the Balance Sheet, Inventory will take several forms, from Raw Materials to Finished Goods. If 100 units are manufactured and 80 shipped out, the remaining 20 will be recorded in the Balance Sheet as Finished Goods. These 20 units would be expected to ship in a later month.

sell at their original price. Selling these items may require significant price reductions, and some may not sell even with drastic reductions. In the previous example just discussed, inventory increased by $100, with the *expectation* it will be salable at previous values.

If these expectations change, if the inventory becomes out of date, its inherent value will be less than the assets (cash) used to manufacture it. Summer items manufactured in the spring and not sold by July may not be ordered again until the following year or may never be ordered. Such items could remain in a box in a company warehouse until disposed of; however, accounting rules for inventory *valuation* require that the company revalue inventory periodically, and *scrap* (write off[5]) inventory that is unlikely to sell above cost.

The company can quite literally "scrap" such product by throwing it away, or it can be sold at a large discount to a discount wholesaler, for example. In that case, the $100 in inventory must be reduced in value. This reduction in inventory value is a cost and will be found in the P&L. Sometimes this cost is included with "Manufacturing Cost." An estimate will be made for the value of Scrap Inventory based on prior experience, and any difference between cost and the discounted value will be included in Manufacturing Cost.

GROSS PROFIT

Gross Profit represents the profit remaining from Revenue after adjustment for Returns and Manufacturing Cost of 4%. OurCompany shows a July variance in Gross Profit of −$1,855,000 or −13% to Plan.

The proceeds of product sales after manufacturing cost—Gross Profit—must be used to pay for marketing, overhead, corporate taxes, and investor dividends; however, only the first two of these are recorded in the management operating P&L.

---

[5]A *write-off* refers to a loss that the company records when an asset's value is reduced to zero. Inventory is frequently revalued based on its marketability. Product that is determined to be no longer marketable at original value will be written off and the company will recognize the difference between the new value ($0.00) and the old value as a loss. Past experience will dictate that some inventory is always scrapped or written off eventually. Based on this expectation, the company will record an *allowance* for future scrapped inventory by recording an estimated loss every month, referred to as an *inventory provision for scrapping*. This is very similar to the Returns provision based on expected returns from sales.

Marketing Expense

Marketing Expense is the next line in the management P&L, and Our-Company shows a small $43,000 positive variance to Plan, meaning Marketing Expenses are less than Plan, and therefore a positive contribution to the Profit variance.

Although Marketing can be considered a discretionary item, and management can have considerable control over marketing expenditures, there may be immediate as well as long-term penalties from ad-hoc, short-term reductions in marketing activity. Pulling a print advertisement from *BusinessWeek* or *Parade* may mean the page position is lost to a competitor at a future date; reductions in successful marketing activities can be associated with measurable loss of sales in the future. Therefore, while a reduction in marketing expense this month could provide an immediate benefit for profit this month, it could become a just-as-significant loss in sales in the following months.

Overhead

The final operating expense item is Overhead. Overhead includes salaries and departmental expenses, travel expenses, office rent, electricity, training, nonmanufacturing personnel–related expenses, and bad debt.[6] Overhead varies primarily with the number of employees working for the company and significant changes in the company's office space situation. Changes in these expenses are fairly small, and consistent with long-term growth, even with health-care expenses growing more rapidly.

If OurCompany were to look at overhead as a source of cost savings, there would be minimal possibilities. Significant changes in expense for office space are infrequent, and it is customary for a company to pay a severance allowance, even allowing for earlier—and excess—severance provisions, so

---

[6] Neither Revenue nor Returns represent what people paid (or promised to pay) for the product. Revenue represents what was shipped, (i.e., the fulfillment of an Order). What people pay for Product Received is Cash; what they promise to pay when the product is ordered is called a Receivable. Both Cash and Receivables are components of a financial statement—the Balance Sheet—but they are not part of the P&L. Cash that is not received is an expense called Bad Debt, and it is part of Overhead. Further information on the relationship between Marketing and Bad Debt is provided in the section titled "Revenue, Payment and Bad Debt."

reducing the number of employees does not necessarily lead to an immediate reduction in expense. In fact severance costs and or changes in rental agreements can be recognized (*accrued*)[7] immediately, leading to a short-term *increase* in overhead expense when compared to prior months.

As a result, it should be surprising if the overhead expense for the month varied significantly from the plan, and in this case it does not, showing a zero variance.

REVENUE, PAYMENT, AND BAD DEBT

As noted earlier, revenue does not represent what people paid or promised to pay for the product that the company shipped in response to an order. The promised payment is recorded as an asset on the Balance Sheet called a *Receivable*, which is somewhat similar to Inventory. When payment for the order is *received*, the Cash asset increases and the total receivable is reduced by the same amount.[8] Revenue continues to represent what was *shipped* as the fulfillment of an Order.

---

[7]An *accrual* is an accounting term that refers to a future expense that is known, not yet paid, but recognized as an expense because there is certainty it will be paid. A net increase in expense accruals will result in an increase in expenses. In the case of severance payments, the company will sign an agreement that identifies the severance benefits (e.g., months of salary and medical) at the time of separation.

[8]To complete the picture, and without delving too deeply in the balance sheet, Receivables and Cash are both Assets for a company. *Asset* usually conjures a positive image, and accounting Assets are definitely positive for a business; most Assets represent tangible value for the business. Other Assets include inventory, raw materials for manufacturing, and buildings and equipment that the business owns, for example. However, the business may have borrowed money to purchase Assets, including buildings, of course, but also inventory. The borrowed funds are recorded as a Liability. If the company borrowed $10 million to purchase a building, the balance sheet will record the building as a $10 million Asset and the bank loan as a $10 million Liability. These two values "balance,". Assume the company also borrowed $1 million to build product that it sold for $2 million, a profit of $1 million. The loan would be recorded as a $1 million Liability, and the manufactured product as $1 million Inventory before it was sold. After it was sold—for cash—the company would show $1 million Cash, and a new category called Equity would show $1 million. Again the Balance Sheet "balances."

Just as there are expectations for returns justified by past experience, there are expectations for some shipments that will never be paid for. A provision for unpaid orders, known as *bad debt*, is established in the same way that a provision for returned product is established.

This provision can be estimated in a more elaborate fashion than that for returns. The accounting system keeps track of the number of days between shipment and nonpayment. A bill that has gone unpaid for six months is less likely to be collected than a bill that is only 90 days old. An accounting process is established called *Aging of Receivable*; increasing proportions of the amount owed—the payable—are estimated as bad debt according to how long the amount has gone unpaid. A bill that is 12 months old could be recorded as 100% bad debt, for example, while a bill 180 days past due could be provided for at 50%. Experience can provide a guide as to appropriate amounts. The longer a bill goes unpaid, the higher the proportion that is added to the provision.

Each incremental provision amount is recorded as a reduction of income already included in the P&L. Remember that revenue is recorded when product is shipped and a proportion flows to profit. If some of that revenue is never received as cash, then profit must be correspondingly reduced. This reduction in income is known as Bad Debt, and is part of Overhead.

If an old unpaid bill should suddenly be paid, the previously expensed amount—which could be 100%—could be reversed by reducing the Bad Debt Provision. The previous expense would also be reversed and profit increased.

The provision for bad debt is also relevant to marketing. Part of a successful marketing effort is to improve on the proportion of customers who pay for product or services received. New customers who do not pay have a twofold impact: the loss recognized as bad debt for non-payment, and the accompanying loss from the expense of acquiring that customer.

Managing marketing expense as an investment involves estimating the gains—as well as the losses—relative to each marketing dollar spent, relating that directly to the profitability of the customer, and not just the revenue received. Profitable customers will be those who consistently pay for their purchases.

VARIANCE TO PLAN

This completes a review of the July operating report titled "July P&L for OurCompany." The primary reason for the reduced profit to Plan of −$824,000 is reduced sales of 19.4%. Management has reforecast the year and expects to maintain the reduced level of sales. Small changes have been made in marketing and overhead expense, but no fundamental changes have apparently been planned or agreed to. Effectively management has accepted lower sales and a shortfall in profit for the year, which probably also means management and employee bonuses are not to be expected. This is unfortunate, as OurCompany has a performance-oriented bonus plan, paying as much as 25% for an equivalent increase in profit over plan.

CHAPTER 3

Managing the P&L

Managers manage to targets that are derived from the P&L. A Regional Sales Manager is responsible for revenue in a specific region, Operations is responsible for product cost, and the Marketing Manager is responsible for marketing expense.

The importance to Profit of managing to targets can be illustrated by comparing the entries in the P&L in the form of ratios. At the outset of this discussion on the P&L a ratio for profit to marketing expense was said to provide an important measure. To understand and appreciate this measure it is necessary to examine similar measures—ratios—for the components of the P&L. These ratios are discussed below for the July P&L of OurCompany, and shown in bold in Exhibit 3.1.

In this example, Returns represent 12.0% of Revenue, which is simply the returns value divided by total revenue. Note that the percentage is consistent for Actual, Forecast, and Plan, while the values themselves are different. Recall from our earlier discussion that Returns are estimated every month based on a rate projected from prior experience. Unless a significant difference in products or sales channels is noted or anticipated, it would not be surprising to see the same rate applied for estimated returns against Actual, Forecast, and Plan sales. If differences in the rates do exist, they will highlight underlying differences between Plan and Forecast *expectations* compared to actuals.

The ratio for Net Revenue is shown in the figure as "100%," meaning Net Revenue is divided by itself. This has no inherent meaning but serves to highlight the *base* of the ratios shown below Net Revenue: The P&L components below Net Revenue will be compared to Net Revenue, and not to Total Revenue.

EXHIBIT 3.1   JULY P&L DETAIL MARKETING, OVERHEAD, AND NET PROFIT

$000	Actual	%	Forecast	%	Plan	%
Revenue	21,968		21,694		27,273	
Returns	2,636	12.0%	2,603	12.0%	3,273	12.0%
Total Net Revenue	19,332	100.0%	19,090	100.0%	24,000	100.0%
		–		–		
Total Manuf Cost	8,699	45.0%	8,603	45.1%	12,273	51.1%
Gross Profit	10,633	55.0%	10,487	54.9%	11,727	48.9%
Marketing	2,957	15.3%	3,000	15.7%	3,200	13.3%
Overhead	5,100	26.4%	5,100	26.7%	5,100	21.3%
Net Profit	2,576	13.3%	2,387	12.5%	3,427	14.3%

The ratio for Manufacturing Cost is shown as a consistent 45% of Net Revenue for Actual and Forecast. For Business Plan Manufacturing cost is 51.1% of Net Revenue, substantially higher than Actual and Forecast. A difference of this magnitude would be worth further review to understand its source. The higher rate may suggest a different expectation for product mix between the Business Plan and the Actual/Forecast. A fundamental question is whether the 45% Forecast cost ratio is sustainable for the year, compared to the higher Plan value. As Manufacturing Cost is a significant driver for profitability, there will be significant pressure on manufacturing to maintain this lower rate to support the final profit figures.

Note that Actual Marketing *expense* of 2,957 is lower than the Plan value of 3,100, but the *percentage* for Actual Marketing expense to Net Revenue is higher: 15.3% for Actual compared to Plan of 12.9%. Recall that July Sales are significantly lower in July compared to Plan. Since the percentage is a ratio of two numbers, if the denominator—Net Revenue—gets smaller and the numerator—Marketing expense—stays the same, the ratio of numerator to denominator gets larger. Hence the percent of Net Sales—15.3%—is significantly higher than the Plan of 12.9%. As discussed earlier, reducing Marketing expense based on a decline in Sales may not have desirable effects in the longer term. As an alternative, management could make short-term changes in the *timing* of Marketing expense by moving some programs out a month or so to reduce next month's costs and improve profits. This may be useful in the final months of the year, but for OurCompany, beginning its third quarter, it only delays the inevitable and risks future sales in the current year.

The ratio for Overhead expense shows the same higher proportion to Net Revenue as Marketing expense: The lower sales in July increase the proportion of Overhead from 21.7% of Net Sales in the Plan, to 26.4% of Net Sales in Actual. Improving profit by adjusting overhead expense may have limited scope: Salaries, rent, and utilities are not easy to change quickly.

And last, the Net Profit ratio to Net Revenue is a full percentage point less than Plan for July: 13.3% compared to 14.3%. Note further than the *expected* results for July—the forecast of 12.6%—was almost another percentage point lower still compared to Plan. Again, this is due entirely to the lower sales in the month.

Some worthwhile questions can be asked and answered using these ratios. For example: How far can Net Sales decline before Net Profit is zero?

$$\$2,576/55\% = \$4,684 \quad \text{or } 21\%(\$4,684 \text{ is } 21.3\% \text{ of } \$21,968 \text{ Revenue })$$

How significant a change in operation costs can the business survive? Only a small increase in product cost—15%—is sufficient to eliminate almost half the profit:

$$15\% \text{ of } \$8,699 \text{ Product Cost} = \$1,305 \quad \text{or } 44\% \text{ of } \$2,957 \text{ Net Profit}$$

If manufacturing costs increase 30%, net profits would decline to 0:

$$2,576 \text{ (July Profit)}/8,699 \text{ (Manufacturing Cost)} = 29.6\%$$

Changes of this magnitude may be unusually high and perhaps unlikely in isolation, in the short term. But *why should they be held in isolation?* An 8% increase in operating costs *in combination with* a similar decline in sales revenue would just as effectively reduce profits to zero.

To this scenario add a reasonable increase in Overhead, say 10%, which could easily come from a change in office space, salary pressures, and particularly medical and health benefits cost increases. This combination of not unlikely events would put this company into a loss.

Managing the P&L means making business changes that improve the various component ratios of expense to revenue. Improving the ratios means higher profits. The adjustments cannot be arbitrary and must respect the accounting rules; a manager cannot arbitrarily decide to use a higher or lower returns ratio or manipulate marketing expense on a whim. The ratios and their underlying values provide important visibility to business activity and the magnitude of influence that different categories of expense and revenue exert on profit and profitability.

Managing the P&L also means having access to sufficient detail to understand primary business factors. "Revenue" shown so far in the P&L reports is the total of all revenue. It's not very illuminating, and summary figures like this provide little support to management trying to understand and improve business profitability. Breaking Revenue down into product families or categories will demonstrate *product profitability*, and may highlight products that are more or less profitable than others. With pressure on OurCompany to improve net profit, product profitability measures may suggest reallocation of effort to increase sales of more profitable products, decrease manufacturing cost of more costly product, or increase prices.

From the Product Sales detail (Exhibit 3.2) it is easy to determine why Manufacturing Cost for Plan was proportionately higher than Actual and Forecast: Relevant figures have been highlighted in Exhibit 3.3. Sales for Product B ($12,000,000, see first boxed figure) were expected to account for half of total sales of $24,000,000, and Cost for Product B was expected to be 54.3% of net revenue (second boxed figure), significantly higher than the Plan cost for Product A, which was estimated at 50.3% (figure at right of arrow). The higher proportion of Product B expected in sales, plus the

EXHIBIT 3.2   JULY P&L: REVENUE BY PRODUCT

$000	Actual	%	Forecast	%	Plan	%
Revenue	21,968		21,694		27,273	
Returns	2,636	12.0%	2,603	12.0%	3,273	12.0%
Net Revenue by Product						
Product A	11,234		11,335		9,500	
Product B	4,356		4,280		12,000	
Product C	3,742		3,475		2,500	
Total Net Revenue	19,332	100.0%	19,090	100.0%	24,000	100.0%
Manuf Cost by Product						
Product A	5,055	45.0%	5,101	45.0%	4,775	50.3%
Product B	2,178	50.0%	2,140	50.0%	6,518	54.3%
Product C	1,465	39.2%	1,362	39.2%	980	39.2%
Total Manuf Cost	8,699	45.0%	8,603	45.1%	12,273	51.1%
Gross Profit	10,633	55.0%	10,487	54.9%	11,727	48.9%

EXHIBIT 3.3   JULY P&L: REVENUE BY PRODUCT, HIGHLIGHTING
KEY FIGURES

$000	Actual	%	Forecast	%	Plan	%
Revenue	21,968		21,694		27,273	
Returns	2,636	12.0%	2,603	12.0%	3,273	12.0%
Net Revenue by Product						
Product A	11,234		11,335		9,500	
Product B	4,356		4,280		12,000	
Product C	3,742		3,475		2,500	
Total Net Revenue	19,332	100.0%	19,090	100.0%	24,000	100.0%
Manuf Cost by Product						
Product A	5,055	45.0%	5,101	45.0%	4,775 →	50.3%
Product B	2,178	50.0%	2,140	50.0%	6,518	54.3%
Product C	1,465	39.2%	1,362	39.2%	980	39.2%
Total Manuf Cost	8,699	45.0%	8,603	45.1%	12,273	51.1% ←
Gross Profit	10,633	55.0%	10,487	54.9%	11,727	48.9%

higher relative cost compared to product A, combine to drive the total cost ratio in the Plan to 51.1% (far right Total Manufacturing Cost figure), compared to current Actual of 45% (figure in oval).

Further review (Exhibit 3.3) shows that lack of Product B sales in the Actual account for most of the Plan variance in Sales: The expected (Plan) sales were 12,000 for July, compared to Actual of only 4,356. The shortfall in Product B sales of almost $8,000,000 is only partly offset by higher actual sales of Products A (+$1,700,000) and C (+$1,200,000).

While sales of Product B are significantly less than Plan, the corresponding higher product cost for B contributes a positive variance to Manufacturing Cost. As sales of Product B are lower, so too are manufacturing costs. The Actual manufacturing cost ratio of 45% compares favorably to the Plan ratio of 51.1%.

This breakdown of sales by product provides two significant points in favor of the achievability of the forecast for the year: The large variance in sales is explained by a shortfall in a specific product, and the lower manufacturing cost ratio in the forecast is explained by lower sales of the higher cost Product B. Presumably year-to-date sales experience for Products A and C supports their levels in the full year forecast. And assuming stability of their manufacturing cost components—labor and materials—the forecast manufacturing rate of 45% seem similarly achievable.

By increasing the level of detail in the report and providing visibility to sales and cost of sales by product, a significant cost variance is explained, new information is available to explain the sales shortfall, and two products are identified that have low and lower cost of sales.

A logical step would be to increase marketing for products A and C to improve profits and the profit ratio. Allocating more marketing effort to Product B would have less effect: The impact of increasing sales for Product B would produce lower relative profits compared to similar increases for A or C.

Less obvious areas for managing the P&L also exist: the Allowance for Returns, Allowance for Scrap or Excess Inventory, and the Allowance for Bad Debt. In some businesses, these allowances are considered a "cost of business." The rates (ratios to Net Revenue) are small, and it can be difficult to make substantial improvements that have a material effect on the business without a correspondingly high cost to make the changes. For example, the inventory allowance may be quite small—less than 3%—making any material impact from improvement difficult.

A second option for excess inventory could be making use of a new alternative marketing outlet or channel for selling excess inventory; this could have a more significant profit impact over reducing the scrap rate itself.

Using existing marketing channels for discounted product may be less desirable. Providing existing customers with discounted product has the negative effect of introducing a lower profit substitution for current, higher profit product on the shelf. While scrap inventory levels would be reduced from the discount sales, existing product sales could be replaced by cheaper alternatives, reducing net sales as well as profits and profitability.

Analyzing actual product returns could lead to business changes that reduce returns and improve net revenue. Identifying and cataloging the reasons for returns may highlight common causes that can be addressed through more effective marketing and product presentation, so customers no longer make a purchase that does not match their expectation.

Analysis of individual customer return rates could identify some customers with significantly higher returns than others. However, analysis of sales by customer would need to parallel this analysis to create a combined Net Sales by Customer picture. This would ensure that high-volume customers—who may have reasonable return *rates* but relatively high return *volume*—are not negatively affected by efforts to reduce their returns activity.

Allowance for bad debt is an important factor, and for some heavily direct mail–based customers a very important factor. Where bad debt can be demonstrated to be common to customers who share particular attributes, marketing efforts can be adjusted to manage lower bad debt levels. This is a delicate subject, raising issues of "profiling" or "redlining," where ethnic attributes or geographic areas are highlighted and used for exclusion. Other techniques exist to improve payment ratios that are less broad-brush in excluding likely good customers.

It is at least conceivable that the provision amounts mentioned earlier for returns, inventory, and bad debt could be overstated by some amount, and management could gain a short-term benefit from more finely tuned provision rates. One measure of positive financial management is the ability to manage these rates, being conservative when business is positive, in order to provide some relief when business conditions are less positive. As noted earlier, however, the impact of fine-tuning provision rates provides only a one-time benefit, and goes against the original purpose of the provisions themselves, to cover eventual returns, nonpayment, and excess inventory. If the provisions are not conservative, actual and negative changes in the business conditions driving these factors could create a situation where the provisions themselves are insufficient to cover changes in actual experience.

Analysis of the ratios above is a strong step toward managing the P&L and business more effectively. Perhaps the most advantageous step is more simply the addition of business detail. As noted earlier, detailing sales by product mix for OurCompany (Exhibit 3.3) provided visibility to Manufacturing Cost variances and Sales variances, and suggested where marketing could be directed to improve profits and profitability. Detailing Manufacturing Cost by component can provide similar benefits in highlighting where manufacturing design efforts could be allocated to improve profitability and reduce manufacturing cost.

The key is access to information and the ability to organize it into manageable pieces. The goal is to provide answers to questions that should be raised in the monthly review meetings. Details for explaining both positive and negative variances are appropriate and essential to management decision making.

For OurCompany an obvious question is why Product B sales are so far below Plan. This could be due to:

- **Pricing.** The price is too low, reducing revenue and margin; or the price is too high, reducing volume.
- **Volume.** Manufacturing was unable to meet demand.
- **Distribution.** The product is not on the shelf and available for sale.
- **Quality.** Returns could be significant due to a quality issue.
- **Marketing.** The right customers may not be the focus of marketing efforts.
- **Engineering, research and development (R&D), marketing, or all three.** The product does not meet customer needs.

Manufacturing cost for Product B could be relatively higher due to:

- **Higher setup costs.** Low unit volume or poor engineering.
- **Higher material costs.** Low unit volume, or suppliers did not meet original cost estimates.
- **Higher labor costs.** Low unit volume again; product is harder to manufacture, rework.

Unexpected costs could be higher due to:

- Higher-than-expected returns
- Higher-than-expected scrapping rate
- A large adjustment to inventory value on the balance sheet[1]

---

[1] A case in point: Inventory scrap rates should be based on a ratio of sales to manufacturing. If shipments routinely approximate 95% of manufactured product, then the scrap rate could be based on the 5% difference. However, the level of inventory must be constantly refreshed against the scrap excess inventory balance based on the scrap rate. A business that does not monitor inventory in the warehouse risks finding "excess inventory" at an audit, which must be *written off* as unsalable. The balance of excess product to be written off could exceed the balance (*reserve*) created as an offset. Any difference is returned to the P&L. A positive difference— Reserve greater than Write-off—would be a gain in the P&L; a negative difference—Reserve less than Write-off—would be a loss in the P&L, and would normally be recorded to Manufacturing Cost.

- Higher-than-expected bad debt experience
- Health-benefit costs
- Reorganization costs
- Legal costs
- Building maintenance costs
- Accounting adjustments[2]
- Corporate assessments[3]

Having access to information that provides good answers on a timely basis means decisions—and better decisions—can be made to improve the business. Having access to more information comes with a caveat. Two of the more difficult questions then become:

1. What does that number mean?
2. How do you know?

Presenting detailed information that supports figures in the operating P&L is particularly subject to these questions. The continued credibility of the presenter, whether from Operations, Finance, Marketing, or Management, depends on positive and consistent response to questions like this. Moreover, effective management of the P&L must be based on factual and accurate information that is understood and understandable.

---

[2]Accounting adjustments are manual entries into the accounting system to correct prior entries. These corrections could be due to errors or simply be larger than usual adjustments to account for business activities that are not correctly represented in the automated accounting system.

[3]A *corporate assessment* is a cost allocation from one business division to another, and commonly an allocation of overhead expense from a business entity that services other business entities. For example, a business might share information technology (IT) resources administered by a single IT department. The IT-related costs would be allocated (assessed) as a monthly fee to all service users. It happens that the Plan allocation amount is not sufficient to cover the total IT costs, and the value of the assessment changes. "Corporate Assessment" is also associated with the overhead costs for "Headquarters," management that is responsible for total company management, but is not directly associated with product sales. Some businesses find reason to allocate these costs to the reporting businesses that do have sales and profits.

This problem is particularly acute when the source of the information used to support the P&L is derived from other sources. Earlier description of "the P&L" noted that it is derived from the accounting statements. These statements in turn are often driven by legacy systems that are updated based on operational systems, and manual (journal) entries made to the accounting system based on operational reports that can be inconsistent or out of date. Operational reports may not be complete and can be misinterpreted. Mistakes can be made in the transcription of information or in the interpretation of the information provided: It can be incomplete or simply wrong—the right number in the wrong place.

The combination of detailed information, opaque definition of terms, obfuscation from primary sources, and practices of deriving information from secondary or tertiary sources creates a challenging situation for managers in a position of defending credibility. Consequently, "What does that number mean?" and "How do you know?" could best be avoided by *minimizing* presented information. Therefore it should not be surprising when some managers in fact eschew detailed information in order to maintain an appearance of control, and engage in the similar practice of controlling information (silo effect) in order to maximize influence, which has about the same result.

Instead of following the practice of the anecdotal ostrich, the challenge can be met head on by organizing the information, however complex, and clarifying areas of confusion. The benefit is clarification for all management, and improved business management through informed decisions.

There is one more area that can benefit from both more and better information, and which marketers can use to directly impact profits for both the short and long term. This is particularly advantageous when business conditions are the most challenging.

Assume OurCompany has easy access to business information and that knowledgeable people have provided explanations for all P&L variances. Actual profit for OurCompany is still 15% below plan for the month, and has been for the past several months. Since this is now the beginning of third quarter and goals for the year are clearly in jeopardy, the most important question is not "How do you explain this?" or "Was the plan over stated?" or even the unspoken "Is the business in control?" The important question is "What are you going to do about it?"

Managing marketing expense to targets in a difficult or competitive sales market is very challenging. A reduction in marketing expense is easy to measure and hits the bottom line immediately, in a positive way, while the negative impact is more long term and less easy to quantify directly. However, a decrease in product visibility and corresponding loss of market share and revenue may be harder and more expensive to restore than the short-term benefit provided by a "small" reduction in marketing expense.

This can be more damaging if the business needs to spend *more* on marketing in order to foster growth in a competitive arena. With pressure to put more money to net profit and the competing need to be competitive, some method must exist for determining where to spend less money, *as well as where to spend more.* The ability to measure *return on marketing investments* is the concept behind *marketing financials.* In situations where the return is measurable, marketing financials will identify how much to spend and where to spend it.

CHAPTER 4

Measuring Marketing Effectiveness

Marketing activities for OurCompany may follow a tried-and-true investment strategy: "We always advertise with them"; "This is a good publication"; "Everyone else is in this magazine"; "This publication is very popular." Management relies on traditional marketing methods and lacks the ability to focus more unique marketing offers and campaigns to smaller groups of people. Their customer information—transactions, payments, products purchased—is finely detailed but buried in the company's financial transaction system. They have a general knowledge of the customer distribution by state, but no ability to characterize differences in customers by state or within state according to their purchase activity.

Lacking other means of discrimination, simply increasing marketing expense could lead to improved sales. Using the financial values from the P&L, a ratio of marketing expense to net revenue can be created as a place to start in assessing the potential impact of increased marketing activity.

As indicated in Exhibit 4.1, for July, OurCompany Marketing expense was $2,957,000 and Net Revenue was $19,332,000. The ratio of Revenue to Marketing expense suggests the Revenue associated with every marketing dollar:

$$\$19,332,000/\$2,957,000=\$6.54^{1}$$

For each marketing dollar spent, OurCompany Revenue = $6.54. For $3,000,000 in Marketing then, there is an expected $3,000,000 × $6.54 in Revenue, or $19,613,000, very close to the July Actual of $19,332,000.

---

[1]This figure is rounded up from $6.537707.

EXHIBIT 4.1   **JULY P&L RATIO ANALYSIS, MANUFACTURING COST, AND MARKETING EXPENSE**

$000	Actual	%	Forecast	%	Plan	%
Revenue	21,968		21,694		27,273	
Returns	2,636	12.0%	2,603	12.0%	3,273	12.0%
Total Net Revenue	19,332	100.0%	19,090	100.0%	24,000	100.0%
		–		–		
Total Manuf Cost	8,699	45.0%	8,603	45.1%	12,273	51.1%
Gross Profit	10,633	55.0%	10,487	54.9%	11,727	48.9%
Marketing	2,957	15.3%	3,000	15.7%	3,200	13.3%

However, the real focus is profit, and it would take some work to identify the incremental profit associated with $6.54 in incremental revenue, so a more useful ratio would describe directly the incremental profit associated with each dollar of marketing expense (Exhibit 4.2).

This could take the form of Net Profit per Marketing expense except for the intervening Overhead figure; therefore a more accurate measure is the Gross Profit contribution from Marketing:

$$\$10,633,000/\$2,957,000 = \$3.60$$

Each marketing dollar contributes $3.60 in gross profit from sales. Therefore $3,000,000 in marketing expense can be expected to generate $3,000,000 × $3.60 = $10,788,000, very close to the $10,633,000 for

EXHIBIT 4.2   **JULY P&L RATIO ANALYSIS, NET PROFIT**

$000	Actual	%	Forecast	%	Plan	%
Revenue	21,968		21,694		27,273	
Returns	2,636	12.0%	2,603	12.0%	3,273	12.0%
Total Net Revenue	19,332	100.0%	19,090	100.0%	24,000	100.0%
		–		–		
Total Manuf Cost	8,699	45.0%	8,603	45.1%	12,273	51.1%
Gross Profit	10,633	55.0%	10,487	54.9%	11,727	48.9%
Marketing	2,957	15.3%	3,000	15.7%	3,200	13.3%
Overhead	5,100	26.4%	5,100	26.7%	5,100	21.3%
Net Profit	2,576	13.3%	2,387	12.5%	3,427	14.3%

OurCompany July Actual gross profit. However, the $3.60 in Gross Profit "cost" $1.00 to achieve; therefore the true marketing contribution is $2.60.

On this basis it would seem fairly straightforward to invest more money in marketing, since for every $1.00 in marketing there appears to be $2.60 returned to Net Profit from Gross Profit (after marketing expense).

However, if the company elected to use existing marketing channels, it is likely that sales results would be *marginally less* than they are currently, assuming the company has allocated its marketing budget in a reasonably efficient way. That means that for every incremental marketing dollar spent, sales—and profit—would not be expected to increase by the same level they are at currently. The *incremental* contribution would be *less than* the ratio of $2.60 profit for each incremental $1.00 in marketing.

How much less? And how much more profit could be generated? Would it not be true that any incremental profit over cost of marketing would be beneficial, potentially justifying an unlimited marketing budget?

Marketing is just one contributor among several whose combined efforts generate OurCompany profits. The company only theoretically has access to unlimited funds for investment, and all participants are in competition for a piece of that budget. Again theoretically speaking, the net result of competition for funds should generate the best results for OurCompany, and marketing must demonstrate equal or higher benefit to merit a higher budget, their "budget" being marketing expense represented in the business plan.

The ability to "demonstrate equal or higher benefit" generally is based around experience, which creates a Catch-22: how to demonstrate the merit of a higher budget if the increase is expected to be based on experience.

For these reasons it is difficult to expect a windfall increase in the marketing budget. Instead, marketing will need to *reallocate their existing budget for more effective results* from marketing activities.

Assume that a good portion of the company's customers, perhaps 75%, are returning customers. Assume the same proportion—75%—of marketing expense is directed toward servicing and maintaining those customers. Any incremental marketing expense would be used to attract new customers.

In real dollar terms, if OurCompany could add $1,000,000 to marketing each month, the gain would be $2,600,000 in profit. That is double what the company currently earned in the month of July.

Is it possible to add new customers for the same cost as maintaining existing customers? It is a truism that adding new customers is more expensive than maintaining existing customers. Is it possible that the existing maintenance cost could be decreased without losing existing customers? In other words, can the existing marketing budget be *better allocated*, to retain the best customers, maintain existing sales, and free up some funds to be allocated toward acquiring more new customers?

Finally, can the added marketing expense be allocated to positive (profitable) marketing programs without adding more people and increasing overhead expense? This is the management challenge for OurCompany: how to increase marketing expenses and gross profit without adding more people and increasing overhead expense. And it is precisely the target for marketing automation.

Analyzing Marketing for Efficiency

Part of the challenge will be evaluating the existing marketing expense to confirm its effectiveness. Successful analysis could identify poorly performing marketing activities, whose funds could be better used elsewhere, in either increasing sales from existing customers or acquiring new customers. Evaluating existing marketing expense may also identify marketing activities with unusually high response or effectiveness, suggesting that additional investment in these marketing offers or channels may be profitable. By reducing the expense in less profitable areas and increasing investment in more profitable activities, the effects of marketing expense can be amplified to produce more profit per dollar spent.

This is an important point. Theoretically any business plan that can demonstrate a positive return greater than the cost of money should have no difficulty acquiring additional funds for investment. The same should be more true, theoretically, from inside a company that has a positive orientation toward new investment.

This ignores the implicit risk that all new investments bear: Inside the company or outside the company money for investment is difficult to acquire; incremental funding is not arbitrarily allocated by management or investors. There are competing proposals and the decision process can be involved and protracted. Furthermore, businesses are constrained by size: A small business with $10 million in revenue will not generate enough excess cash internally to justify a $5 million advertising budget, nor will it have the financial justification to acquire that much cash from investors. Therefore, the ability to generate incremental funding *internally*, by allocating existing expenses better, can provide a valuable contribution to growth.

As the internally generated funds lead to better performance, the improved performance will provide justification for increasing total budget in the next and future years. This is exactly how BMG Direct was able to increase revenue from $200 million to over a billion dollars. It did not happen in one or two years or even three. It took five years of constant improvement and a constantly expanding marketing budget. The first year's success becomes a step up into the second year, with each successive year building on the demonstrated success of the prior year.

A parallel experience evolved in the development of BMG Direct's telemarketing program. Initial telemarketing experience was based on an almost generic selection of customers. Response was profitable and acceptable, but telemarketing a quarterly volume of 750,000 customers taxed existing resources; it became nearly impossible to increase telemarketing activity in order to generate more profit.

This situation was resolved after telemarketing lists were refined to eliminate tens of thousands of customers who were identified through modeling as least likely to respond. The capacity saved by not calling these customers was used to increase the calling effort against those more likely to respond, resulting in significantly higher profits at lower cost.

In perspective, the results from reallocating marketing expense for Our-Company to more profitable avenues can be surprisingly effective. Assume 20% of the existing "maintenance" marketing effort of $2,366,000 could be demonstrated to generate no sales at all. This enables a significant savings in the marketing budget: 20% × $2,366,000 is $473,000. This amount alone could reduce the Plan Profit shortfall of $852,000 for July by more than 50%.

This analysis also shows that the current marketing effort is more effective than the initial analysis: Each marketing dollar generates $4.50 in Gross Profit, not $3.60 as first calculated.

If these funds could be applied to acquiring new customers who contribute the same average value—$4.50—the incremental Gross Profit generated would be $2.1 million; $2.1 million additional profit is an 83% increase—nearly double—over OurCompany July Net Profit.

Is the total effect of this reallocation of marketing expense therefore $473,000 saved plus $2.1 million incremental gross profit? No, the $473,000 has been "reinvested" in more profitable areas to generate incremental gross profit, so the effect on profit for OurCompany is the profit of $2.1 million contributed by the new investment less the cost of $0.473 million to make the investment.

This example epitomizes the goal for marketing automation: to improve the allocation of marketing expense to grow revenue and profit. The example outlined above will be continued, to demonstrate how this is done.

MARKETING COST DETAIL

Managing marketing expense in the context of the P&L requires a deep collection of numbers representing the costs of the various components in each of the channels. The costs can be fairly simple and easy to collect (e.g., the number of emails per penny plus setup costs), to fairly involved for direct mail. To understand the cost of marketing in order to improve efficiency it is essential to accurately and consistently collect all marketing communication costs, and make this information easily accessible for analysis.

For direct mail–based promotions, the cost components are:

- Creative cost for the effort of designing and fashioning the components for each promotional piece
- Paper and envelope for each inserted piece
- Print setup fees
- Printing cost
- Insertion cost
- Sorting cost (for sorting by mail delivery route)
- Freight delivery to primary mail distribution points
- Postage

Telemarketing costs are less complex:

- Telematching

- Setup fees
- Calling costs

For email-based promotions the costs are:

- Creative
- Setup
- Delivery

The arrangement of costs for analysis will be aided by a number of ratios. The first would be the collection of all costs on a per-thousand-piece basis. This enables direct comparison of promotions with different cost and distribution bases. An expensive mail piece with a small distribution will become even more expensive when compared with a less expensive piece delivered to a larger audience. Similarly, the costs of different channels can be compared directly when presented on a per-thousand-recipients basis.

Second, costs can be summarized into two categories, nonrecurring and recurring. "Nonrecurring" costs are incurred for each campaign, recurring costs for each piece in the campaign. Both are reexpressed as cost per thousand, again to enable direct comparison between campaigns and channels. Recurring and nonrecurring costs are also combined as total cost and total cost per thousand.

Third, the cost of the list can be added. List costs can be presented in several ways. Total cost and cost per thousand are both valid, as is the *net cost* after accounting for names that are already on the house list. A typical floor value will be 85% of total cost, meaning the least number of names that must be paid for will be no lower than 85% of the total list, even though the source list may net out far less after comparison to the house list.

If a business ships prior to payment, bad debt costs can be important to include in the cost equation. However, true bad debt costs are not known for some time in the future, as much as a year or more. In the interim, an assumption or expectation must be established for each promotion, using a similar, prior promotion as a substitute. This approach has an inherent risk; therefore analysis of bad debt trends should supplement the decision on the choice of a bad debt rate to assume for each promotion.

Finally, several analytical ratios are computed and maintained for monitoring promotion performance. Techniques for effectively managing the ratios are discussed in Chapter 6 on marketing financials. These ratios, by marketing channel, are:

- Cost per promotion
- Response
- Value of the sale

For companies investing millions of dollars in marketing every month, this approach involves an extensive level of detail and definitive presentation; therefore one of the key components of a marketing automation system is the systematic and automated acquisition of the information as well as automated reporting to provide marketers immediate visibility to results. To fully manage marketing investments requires consistent and accurate comparison of *each investment* along a number of attributes. Access to all marketing component costs will improve understanding of the success and failure of each investment, and support the effort to identify weakly performing promotions, as well as the identification of more profitable avenues for further investment.

In the long term, an understanding of the sensitivities of these component costs enables a greater awareness of what external events could affect the ongoing business expectations. For example, if paper costs are 30% of the direct mail budget, and direct mail comprises 25% of the total budget, a long-term increase in paper costs of 20% will result in a 1.5% increase in the total advertising budget. In turn this may result in some promotions becoming less cost effective, meaning they no longer make a profit, or as much of a profit as other promotions. In response to an increase in paper costs, other channels or marketing investments may become more attractive. It is equally useful to know the important ratios for the cost components. Knowing the setup fees dictates the floor for volume mailings. Knowing response rates by vendor ensures anomalies are identified early. Knowing the alternative envelope insertion fees ensures promotional content remains competitive.

CUSTOMER PROFITABILITY

Just as Gross Profit represents the difference between Revenue and Cost of Goods Sold, average profit per customer must be adjusted for the cost of acquisition. There are several ways to calculate this ratio. One such approach will demonstrate the impact of debtors and why the P&L is so important to managing marketing expense.

Assume a particular marketing promotion cost $100,000 to produce and deliver, and acquired 10,000 new customers. That is an average cost per customer of $10.

Assume each customer purchases products in a year equivalent to $40 Revenue and $20 Gross Profit. The difference is the Cost of Goods Sold. That is a return of $200,000 profit based on the $100,000 investment in marketing to acquire these customers. The ratio of Gross Profit per customer to cost of acquisition is 2 to 1; $20 Gross Profit is a 100% return on the $10 cost to acquire that customer. Net profit after marketing cost is $100,000.

Now assume 10% of the people do not pay for their purchases. The *net profit* of $100,000 will be reduced as follows:

$$10\% \text{ of Expected Revenue of } \$400,000 = -\$40,000$$
$$\text{Cost to Collect (some effort is made)} = -\$2,500 \text{ ($2.50 per person)}$$
$$\text{Total Loss} = -\$42,500 \text{ or } \$4.25 \text{ per person}$$

The initial $20 recognized in Gross Profit per person from this promotion is reduced by $4.25 or greater than 20%. The net gain after marketing cost of acquisition is reduced by *43%*: $100,000 less $42,500.

It is not uncommon to organize customer acquisition marketing separately from customer maintenance marketing. In such a case, *acquisition marketing* is measured according to the "number of bodies brought in" relative to the expense of acquisition. Measurement that does not include sales performance as well as payment performance for new acquisitions will eventually lead to declining sales and rising bad debt, as the impact of nonpayers accumulates over time.

CHAPTER 5

Measuring Return on Investment

The more generalized financial analysis of *investment return* involves analysis of investments whose return is measured over a period of years, not months. Significant investments involving large sums will need to take into consideration the cost of money. Financial analysis of investment return is part of corporate investment proposals, particularly capital investments that involve the purchase of buildings, machinery, and equipment, as well as businesses. An investment in *marketing automation* capability involves a similar initial investment followed by an expected return, and will likely require a similar proposal and analysis of investment return. This analysis will be different from *marketing investment return*, the return on individual marketing promotions, which can be summarized with the simple ratio of gross profit to marketing cost, since the return will take place most often within 12 months.

INVESTMENT RETURN VERSUS MARKETING INVESTMENT RETURN

The measurement of financial investment return is an analytical exercise based on the value of the investment—the cost to purchase the building, relative to the expected profit that the investment (the building) will generate. The investment itself is not directly a cost visible in the P&L under normal circumstances. Purchasing long-term assets such as machinery or buildings, in accounting terms, is directly visible in the Balance Sheet, an exchange of Cash or other assets for "Machinery, Plant and Equipment," another asset. At the time of purchase, the Cash balance in the Balance Sheet would decline, say by $1,000,000, and Machinery, Plant and Equipment increase by $1,000,000.

Accounting rules do not require that the "cost" of a building or other assets be recognized in the P&L in the same way that Manufacturing Costs are recognized. However, accounting rules do recognize that the value of an asset will decline over time. As noted earlier for Inventory, whenever the value of an asset is reduced, the difference between the new value and the prior value is recognized as a cost to the business. In the case of assets, the reduction in value is known as *depreciation* and is recorded as a cost in Overhead. Because this depreciation is a cost to the business, there must be a tangible and measurable profit associated with the investment, and the cumulative value of the profit associated with the investment must be greater than the investment itself, for the investment to be profitable.

The *excess* in value of this profit over the investment is the *return* of the investment, what it pays back to the business. With competing opportunities and proposals for business investment, management looks for the investment with the largest return for the business, the investment that has the highest likelihood of generating the largest excess profit over the investment cost. The investment purpose is typically captured in a proposal, and the proposal includes one or more financial schedules demonstrating the expense and profit of the investment over time. The cumulative excess value can be reexpressed as a percentage return on the value of the investment, similar to investing in a certificate of deposit. A typical corporate investment proposal will need to demonstrate a much higher return value than the 5% associated with a certificate of deposit, to justify the risk associated with the investment. Returns of 25% and higher would be more appropriate.

The cost of depreciation is allocated over "the life of the asset." The "life" (in years) of various assets, for accounting purposes, is available in standardized tables. There are also several depreciation methods besides a constant depreciation, most of which involve formulas for accelerating the depreciation expense (higher expense in the first years, lower in later years). For our purposes depreciation will be assumed to be constant; that is, the annual depreciation cost of the initial investment is equal to the investment value divided by the number of years of life of the asset.

The cost of investing in a computing system such as for marketing automation can be similarly treated over a period of time (*amortized*), in recognition of its lifespan as an asset. The total cost of the system—hardware, software, and implementation—can be combined to create the asset value itself. The lifespan for accounting purposes would typically be three to five years, although the asset itself could be effective for much longer.

Once depreciated, there is no further "cost" for the asset reflected in the P&L, other than "maintenance." Therefore, with an expectation that an asset is acquired to play a role in generating profit, once the asset is depreciated, its profit contribution is to some extent "free," without cost (other than maintenance).

Management can also take a more aggressive approach to amortizing[1] the investment, and choose a shorter period in which to recognize depreciation of the asset, assuming the business has an excess of profit available to absorb the expense, or a similar reason for recognizing a higher expense over a shorter period of time.

In an extreme case, the accumulated investment in the system—its value as an asset—could be reduced to zero in a single accounting period, particularly if the investment is recognized as a failure, to provide little or no longer-term benefit. In such a case, the large, one-time negative impact to net profit would be recognized in company P&L statements, and could jeopardize achievement of the business plan, with a corresponding reflection on management in their failure to achieve the plan. This represents a risk for any large and long-term investment.

The analytical exercise of estimating the investment return, however, is based on *estimates* of the cost for the asset being invested in, and the *expected* profit the investment will generate. The goal for the exercise is to justify the investment in a proposal form, to demonstrate it has a positive long-term impact to profit, to identify risks that could reduce the expected profit, to measure the long-term profit impact against inflation and alternative, less risky investments, and to facilitate the ability of management to compare alternative investment proposals. At any time a company will have a finite access to investment funds, and there will be competing projects of merit. Analyzing investment return will help determine which of the competing investments is best for the business.

---

[1]*Amortize* means "recognize over time."

Several alternatives exist for presentation of investment return, and each will be briefly presented here. Many companies use a formula approach for analysis based on a concept known as the *present value (PV) of money*. The perspective of long-term present value–based presentations does not account well for the higher level of uncertainty associated with longer-term investments. Some managers prefer a shorter-term, "cash-based" or "payback period"–based proposal that emphasizes short-term profit and how fast the investment recovers its total value. The presentation of marketing financials in Chapter 6 follows this approach. However, investment proposals are generally based on preestablished forms in order to standardize presentation for ease of comparison. Supporting information such as shown in the presentation of marketing financials related to investment in marketing automation can provide support to the standard investment proposal forms.

Presentation and analysis of investment return is known commonly as *return on investment* (ROI). It is not uncommon to evaluate competing investments based on the ROI, and businesses can establish minimum ROI rates for investment proposals, known as "hurdle rates." Any proposal of a particular type must meet a certain minimum rate in order to be considered. The ROI is presented as a percentage, so the comparison of various proposals can be very simple, on the surface.

PRESENT VALUE OF MONEY

Underlying an ROI calculation is the concept of *present value of money*. Simply stated, the present value of money recognizes that cash loses value over time due to inflation. The longer the time period, the higher the loss in later time periods: $100 today is worth less in a year due to inflation, and worth still less in two years, three years, and so on. There is also an opportunity cost: $100 cash today could be invested in risk-free government bonds and be worth $105 in a year's time.[2] The cash value of a building with a 40-year time horizon would therefore have a high cost due to the present value of money.

---

[2]Approximate. The government bond rate fluctuates with perceived inflation and demand for money.

The present value of money also adjusts investment returns for the timing of their respective profit flows: Some investments may provide a larger return later in time. Due to inflation, later returns are worth less than earlier returns; two investments with the same return but in different years are not worth the same when adjusted for the present value of money. Assuming a 5% inflation rate, the discount in the first year is 5%, in the second year 10.25%, and in the third year 15.7%. *Discount* means $100 profit earned in the second year is discounted by 10.25% to become $90.70; $100 in the third year would be discounted by 15.7% to become $86.40. Hence earlier profits are worth more than later profits for the purpose of the investment analysis.

There are significant investment opportunities for available cash that are less risky but not central to a company's business. The expectation of stockholders and business management is that the company's products and management expertise will generate the highest value for investors over time. Management in fact is entrusted with access to corporate funds expressly to generate long-term value that is higher than government bonds or similar monetary investments. The risk of management investments should be mitigated (reduced) by management's acquired expertise in their market, their company, and their knowledge of what the people in the company can do, in other words, their ability to manage the business.

Inside the company, there are competing proposals for the profitable investment of available cash. The company, through stock, bonds, or bank loans backed by company assets, will have access to additional funds, up to a point, in order to finance a number of investments having potential for long-term profit. In order to measure the impact of the time value of money, the future cash flow of these investments is discounted by the expected interest rate. Only if the initial outflow—the investment—is less than the expected discounted income generated by the investment—the return—is the investment considered to be worthwhile.

Each proposal will be expected to generate income over a number of years. One of the challenges in evaluating competing proposals is to recognize the timing of profit. One proposal may forecast $1,000,000 profit in Year 3, another in Year 2. Intuitively the second proposal seems better, as the income is expected earlier. As noted above, this intuitive observation is backed by analysis based on *discounting* the expected profit from each investment by a consistent factor, such as the rate of inflation or the government bond rate. In this way, long-term profit streams with different timing are evaluated in a consistent manner, and simultaneously the company can compare the profit potential against the time value of money.

Exhibit 5.1 provides an example of a proposal drafted for investing in a new manufacturing plant. The cost is $1,000,000 in Year 1, and the expected annual profit is shown in the exhibit.

Exhibit 5.1 provides two lines of figures. The first line is management's forecast of expected profit from the investment in the manufacturing plant. In Year 2 the plant is just coming online and profits are small, $100,000. In Year 3 profit increases to $300,000, and in Year 6 the peak of profitability is achieved: $1,200,000 that is expected to be earned annually for the duration of the plant's utility. The profit numbers are assumed to include adjustment for all plant-related expenses, but should not include expenses that would exist if the plant were not purchased.

In the second line the profit numbers are discounted for the time value of money, using a rate of 5%. In Year 2, the discounted value of $100,000 is $95,238. The figures from Year 6 to Year 9 demonstrate clearly the impact of time on value: In today's dollars, $1.2 million earned in Year 6 is worth only $940,231; $1.2 million earned in Year 7 is worth only $895,458. The discounted value is worth less and less the further out the return takes place.

Increasing the discount rate from 5% to 10% shows an even more dramatic reduction in the value of future year profits (see Exhibit 5.2).

In Exhibit 5.2, $1.2 million in Year 6 is now worth $745,106, almost $100,000 less than the prior example, and only 62% of the forecast value of $1.2 million in Year 7.

The value of investment comparisons made using present value can be seen by comparing Investment A (Exhibit 5.2) which has a $6.8 million total profit over 8 years, with a similar investment that generates the same profit earlier in time. See Investment B (Exhibit 5.3).

Graphically presented, the higher value of the latter investment is obvious (Exhibit 5.4).

Investment B achieves a net (discounted) total value greater than Investment A by achieving its payback period more than a year earlier

EXHIBIT 5.1   RETURN ON INVESTMENT: PRESENT VALUE OF MONEY

	Investment	Profit from Investment							
	Year 1	Year 2	Year 3	Year 4	Year 5	Year 6	Year 7	Year 8	Year 9
Profit Forecast $	(1,000,000)	100,000	300,000	600,000	1,000,000	1,200,000	1,200,000	1,200,000	1,200,000
Discounted at 5%	(1,000,000)	95,238	272,109	518,303	822,702	940,231	895,458	852,818	812,207

Total Value, 8 Years, Discounted at 5%

4,209,067   421% Return

EXHIBIT 5.2   RETURN ON INVESTMENT: INVESTMENT A

	Investment	Profit from Investment							
	Year 1	Year 2	Year 3	Year 4	Year 5	Year 6	Year 7	Year 8	Year 9
Profit Forecast $	(1,000,000)	100,000	300,000	600,000	1,000,000	1,200,000	1,200,000	1,200,000	1,200,000
Discounted at 10%	(1,000,000)	90,909	247,934	450,789	683,013	745,106	677,369	615,790	559,809

Total Value, 8 Years, Discounted at 10%

3,070,718   307% Return

EXHIBIT 5.3   **RETURN ON INVESTMENT: INVESTMENT B**

| | Investment | | | | Profit from Investment | | | | | |
	Year 1	Year 2	Year 3	Year 4	Year 5	Year 6	Year 7	Year 8	Year 9
Profit Forecast $	(1,000,000)	600,000	800,000	900,000	900,000	900,000	900,000	900,000	900,000
Discounted at 74%	(1,000,000)	545,455	661,157	676,183	614,712	558,829	508,027	461,842	419,857

Total Value, 8 Years, Discounted at 10%

3,446,062   345% Return

Discounted Profit for Two Investments

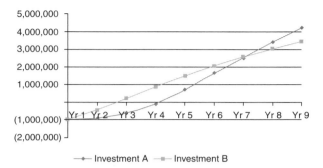

EXHIBIT 5.4   Return on Investment by Period

than Investment A. Investment B is intuitively more favorable than Investment A, and the discounted rate presentation supports this. And, even though less annual profit is generated by Investment B in the later years, the discounted return increased from 307% to 345%, creating a present value of future profit $3,446,062, almost $400,000 higher.

If management is reviewing these financial projections as competing proposals for the same $1,000,000, the second proposal is stronger, in terms of discounted profit, than the first. And this is consistent with the intuitive belief that the earlier recognition of profit is more valuable.

INTERNAL RATE OF RETURN

An alternative measurement technique extends the discounted future profit technique and is called the *internal rate of return* (IRR). In this measurement, a discount rate is estimated that discounts the profit values to match the investment value of ($1,000,000) in Year 1. The resulting rate, expressed as a percentage, can be used not only to compare investments, but also to compare with a company-established minimum, known as a "hurdle rate." Investment proposals that fall below the hurdle rate are not considered without extenuating circumstances. The hurdle rate can be set arbitrarily high, or different rates can be used according to the perceived risk of differing investment classes. Investing in fixed assets could be considered less risky than investment in a new business, and have a correspondingly lower hurdle rate.

EXHIBIT 5.5 RETURN ON INVESTMENT: INTERNAL RATE OF RETURN = 48%

	Investment	Profit from Investment							
	Year 1	Year 2	Year 3	Year 4	Year 5	Year 6	Year 7	Year 8	Year 9
Profit Forecast $	(1,000,000)	100,000	300,000	600,000	1,000,000	1,200,000	1,200,000	1,200,000	1,200,000
Discounted at 48%	(1,000,000)	67,408	136,316	183,776	206,467	167,010	112,579	75,887	51,154

Total Value, 8 Years, Discounted at 48%
597 0% Return

IRR 48%

EXHIBIT 5.6 RETURN ON INVESTMENT: INTERNAL RATE OF RETURN = 74%

	Investment	Profit from Investment							
	Year 1	Year 2	Year 3	Year 4	Year 5	Year 6	Year 7	Year 8	Year 9
Profit Forecast $	(1,000,000)	600,000	800,000	900,000	900,000	900,000	900,000	900,000	900,000
Discounted at 74%	(1,000,000)	344,828	264,236	170,842	98,185	56,428	32,430	18,638	10,711

Total Value, 8 Years, Discounted at 74%
(3,702) 0% Return

IRR 74%

Assume the hurdle rate for OurCompany is 35%. Do either of the above examples, Investments A or B, meet a hurdle rate of 35%?

In the first case, the IRR is computed as 48% (see Exhibit 5.5). This value is based entirely on the figures in the first line, the Profit Forecast, including the initial investment value of $1,000,000, portrayed as a negative value. No assumption is made about the discount rate; however, for clarification of the concept, the IRR rate has been added to the spreadsheet as the discount rate to demonstrate the effect. Notice that the Total Value of the discounted is very small, $597, and the Return is 0%. This example demonstrates that the IRR rate of 48% will discount the future profit flow to match the initial investment value of $1,000,000, creating a net return of zero.

In the second case, the IRR is higher, 74%, because higher profit occurs earlier in time (see Exhibit 5.6).

The same $6.8 million return is presented in two ways, the second proposal with earlier profit recognition than the first.

Both financial presentation approaches—PV and IRR—utilize a concept of discounted future profit; however, the IRR more aggressively values earlier returns (profit in this case) by more heavily discounting later returns.

As it happens, both approaches exceed the hurdle rate of 35% for OurCompany, and the second "proposal" rate of 74% significantly exceeds that of the first because the earnings from the investment are captured earlier.

INVESTMENT RETURN AND MARKETING AUTOMATION

Investment return is particularly important to marketing automation, as most companies will engage the project of marketing automation on paper at the outset, as an investment proposal. Investment in marketing automation is not as generally recognizable as an investment in a manufacturing plant or new equipment to support lower-cost manufacturing. The initial paper proposal, including the analysis of investment return, will likely face greater scrutiny.

The first question is often simply *Does this investment make sense?* The answer can be drafted in the form of an *Analysis of Investment Return*, the same as investing in a building, based on a discussion of the return on marketing investments as captured in the marketing financials worksheet in the next chapter.

CHAPTER 6

Marketing Financials

The previous discussion of the P&L and investment return was necessary in order to develop the concept of *marketing financials* in the context of the P&L and investment return. The ability to improve the allocation of marketing expense to grow revenue and profit depends on the ability to identify and measure the return for each marketing investment.

The fundamental concept behind marketing financials was introduced in the discussion in Chapter 4 on measuring marketing effectiveness. Marketing effectiveness is represented by the ratio of Profit (Gross) to Marketing Expense.

For review, OurCompany invested about $3 million for Marketing activities in July. The $3 million was allocated between maintenance of existing customers and acquisition of new customers. Analysis of the maintenance investment determined that 20% or $473,000 was not effective, generating little or no sales or profit. OurCompany was able to reallocate these funds to more profitable marketing opportunities, which had two effects: It increased the net return for maintenance marketing activities from $2.60 for every marketing dollar to $3.49, and established an incremental profit of $2,127,000 for OurCompany, nearly 83% increase in total Net Profit, using the month of July as a benchmark. The incremental profit may not have accumulated in a single month but it is nonetheless a substantial gain. (See Exhibit 6.1.)

The underlying assumption in this analysis, and fundamental to the successful development and application of marketing financials, is the ability to identify the return—gross profit from product revenue—and the all-in cost for each marketing investment. Because the gross profit from sales can be

EXHIBIT 6.1   MARKETING INVESTMENT RETURN BASED ON REALLOCATED BUDGET

	Marketing	Sales	Ratio	Gross Profit	Ratio	Net Ratio
Maintenance	2,366	17,575	7.43	8,507	3.60	2.60
Acquisition Revised	591	4,339	7.34	2,127	3.60	2.60
Maintenance	1,892	17,575	9.29	8,507	**4.49**	**3.49**
Reallocated Funds	473					
Incremental Profit	2,127					

estimated fairly easily from revenue based on product margin estimates, it is essential to be able to attribute revenue for each marketing investment—to be able to say "this marketing action created this response."

For example, revenue based on direct marketing methods such as telemarketing should be easily available; product orders generated from the telemarketing calls must be recorded with an indication of the source, the call, and the vendor. Without this information, the return on the telemarketing activity cannot be measured, and the ongoing investment in telemarketing cannot be justified. The expectation from the analysis is that marketing will be able to reallocate marketing investments from poorly performing sources to better performing sources. Therefore, the attribution of revenue based on the marketing investment as a source is fundamental to the development of effective marketing.

As noted in the analysis of the detailed P&L for OurCompany in July, the components of the P&L determine the profit of the company, and knowing the components—*having access to information about the P&L that is broadly understood*—enables the company to manage the P&L to Business Plan targets. The same rationale applies to analyzing the return for each marketing investment. Without a similar level of detail as shown in the company management P&L, marketing will not be able to fully manage or optimize the marketing investment.

MARKETING FINANCIALS EXAMPLE

The example shown in Exhibit 6.2 uses a comparison of the cost, revenue, and profit generated by two marketing channels: *direct mail* and *telemarketing*. At face value, these channels appear identical, both having a marketing cost of $250,000, similar returns, and a profit of $50,000. The profit shown is net of

EXHIBIT 6.2   COMPARISON OF MARKETING CHANNEL REVENUE

$ooo	Marketing Cost	Sales	Returns	Profit
Direct Mail	250	2,000	500	50
Telemarketing	250	2,000	460	50

the cost to fund the marketing activity. If OurCompany were to increase use of either channel, this information might suggest the two channels are the same.

Analyzing the sales mix indirectly by adding volume, price, and cost by item sold shows that profit per unit is higher for the telemarketing channel, but slightly lower on a percentage basis (see Exhibit 6.3). Profit per unit for telemarketing is $9.50 ($25.00 – $15.50) or 38% compared to $8.00 or 40% for direct mail. Still, the figures are sufficiently similar to suggest both channels are effectively the same.

After adding the Number of Contacts for each channel, the information becomes more useful for determining which channel might be more effective at driving revenue and acquiring new customers: Telemarketing contacts were significantly lower than direct mail (i.e., 150 versus 250) and Profit *per contact* was more than 50% higher, $0.33 versus $0.20 for Direct Mail. For every contact in telemarketing, more than one and a half contacts would be required through direct mail to generate the same profit volume (see Exhibit 6.4).

This does not suggest that direct mail is ineffective; it is simply less effective. To complete the picture, the actual response volume and response rates are added, which shows that more units per order are generated from direct mail, while the response rate and unit margin is better for telemarketing. To accommodate the additional columns, less relevant information has been removed (see Exhibit 6.5).

The same analysis can (and should) be applied to each individual marketing promotion for each channel. The volume of information

EXHIBIT 6.3   MARKETING CHANNEL REVENUE AND PROFIT
PER UNIT

$ooo	Marketing Cost	Units	Price	Sales	Returns	Unit Cost	Profit	Profit/ Unit
Direct Mail	250	100	20.00	2,000	500	12.00	50	40%
Telemarketing	250	80	25.00	2,000	460	15.50	50	38%

EXHIBIT 6.4   MARKETING CHANNEL RATIOS INCLUDING PROFIT PER CONTACT

$000	Marketing Cost	Units	Price	Contacts	Sales	Returns	Cost	Profit	Cost/ Contact	Profit/ Contact
Direct Mail	250	100	20.00	250	2,000	500	12.00	50	1.00	0.20
Telemarketing	250	80	25.00	150	2,000	460	15.50	50	1.67	0.33

EXHIBIT 6.5   MARKETING CHANNEL RATIOS WITH RESPONSE RATES AND PROFIT PER CONTACT

$000	Marketing Cost	Contacts	Response Rate	Units	Sales	Profit	Price	Margin/ Order	Cost/ Contact	Profit/ Contact
Direct Mail	250	250	10%	100	2,000	50	20.00	32.00	1.00	0.20
Telemarketing	250	150	20%	80	2,000	50	25.00	25.33	1.67	0.33

generated is very high and presentation logistics must be resolved systematically to make the information easily accessible on a timely basis. The collection of the information and generation of reports requires automation, and is a fundamental component of a marketing automation system. The reports themselves are also somewhat challenging to develop, because of the level of detail and because the cost and performance measures are not the same for each channel. Email performance measures include response and rates for "Opens" and "Click-Thrus," while telemarketing reports will include response measures for "No Answer," "Bad Number," and "Refused." All channels incorporate "Opt Out" measures as well, to identify trends in the proportion of customers who wish no longer to be contacted on specific channels.

RETURN ON MARKETING INVESTMENT REPORT

Using direct mail as an example, mail costs, insertion and postage, are broken out to facilitate understanding the financial return for each campaign (see Exhibit 6.6). This is a fairly detailed view of the costs and return on marketing investment for a direct mail campaign, called simply *Communication A*. The second column identifies the Communication ID, which

EXHIBIT 6.6   RETURN ON MARKETING INVESTMENT REPORT

Our Company Direct Mail Campaign Results (March Campaigns at 21 weeks)

Communication	CommID	Volume	Offer	Non Recurring Act/CPM	Media Act/CPM	Postage Act/CPM	Insertion Act/CPM	Total Campaign Cost/ CPM	Orders/ OPM	Sales/ SPM	Aug Order	Net Profit/ PPM	RMI
Communication A	Comm001	1,234,000	Offer A	9,519	185,100	283,820	86,380	564,819	61,700	1,727,600	28	271,339	48%
				7.71	150.00	230.00	70.00	458	50	1,400		220	

ensures each communication can be uniquely identified in the reporting system. The volume for the campaign was 1,234,000 people. Depending on the company and product, marketing campaigns can be associated with specific "deals," called *offers*; the offer for this campaign is noted simply as "Offer A." Wireless phone offers can be quite complex: one- and two-year commitments, varying number of minutes, number of phones, type of phone, family plans, text messaging packages, and so on. It would not be uncommon to have a single campaign with multiple offers to subgroups within the campaign. If that is the case, each offer-specific group would need to be identified so the performance could be compared between the offers for the same campaign as well as across campaigns.

In the next column, Nonrecurring costs summarize costs per campaign that are unrelated to the volume of a promotion. These costs include Creative costs in developing the promotional materials and packaging (envelope), letter shop setup fees, and other one-time expenses. Nonrecurring costs are divided by the total volume and reexpressed in the second line of the report as CPM, which is cost per thousand recipients in the campaign. Using a common denominator to reexpress the cost and response values enables campaigns to be compared to a standard as well as to each other.

Recurring costs are detailed in the next several columns, and each of these costs is in turn reexpressed in the second line in cost per thousand (CPM). Recurring costs are those costs that are related to the volume of the campaign, and include the cost of the materials or "media," postage, and insertion cost (the process of packaging the printed material into the envelope). Recurring costs are directly related to the volume of the campaign; nonrecurring costs are fixed, regardless of the total campaign volume.

Recurring and nonrecurring costs are combined for Total Campaign cost (presented in CPM:

Nonrecurring Cost (CPM)	7.71
Media	150.00
Postage	230.00
Insertion	70.00
Total Cost (CPM)	457.71 (rounded above to 458)

Response details include the number of Orders, Total Sales for these orders, both reexpressed per thousand in the campaign, an average order value, and Net Profit, which is Net after the cost of the campaign. Total Sales were generated of $1,727,600. The gross profit provided by these sales depends on returns and manufacturing cost, which can be estimated using figures from the P&L and standard costs per product. For OurCompany the actual P&L returns rate of 12% will be used, and the product mix for this campaign example will be assumed to match the average manufacturing cost available from the P&L, which is 45%. Therefore the net profit contribution for this campaign is:

$$\$1,727,000 - \text{Returns}(12\%) - \text{Manufacturing Cost}(45\%) - \text{Campaign Cost}$$
$$\$1,727,000 - \$207,240 - \$683,900 - \$564,819 = \$271,041$$

The last figure in the report is labeled "RMI" (return on marketing investment). This is a percentage ratio of Campaign Net Profit to Total Campaign Cost, where profit is net of the campaign cost. RMI is similar to ROI, but there is no accounting here for the time value of money; the duration of time is too small to be relevant. Remember that the time value of money is used for analysis of long-term investments; the "cost of money" over 21 weeks would not be material (would have a small and irrelevant impact).

At this point it should be clear how the preceding detailed discussion of the P&L components is related to the analysis of campaign profitability. Campaign response information—the number of responses and their revenue—has been combined with the cost components derived from the P&L to estimate the profit generated by the campaign. This in turn has been used to calculate a return, as a percentage, on the cost of the campaign. Capturing and reporting this information on a per-campaign basis enables comparison of results over time, including comparison between channels (e.g., email, direct mail) and comparison to a Marketing Campaign Plan.

A marketer might ask why this information is not directly available from 'the finance department'. The financial system will capture incremental revenue and costs on a time-based dimension, using months and years. Campaigns take place without a fixed monthly reference point; in fact, campaign results will frequently accumulate across months. This makes information from the financial system difficult to relate back to marketing promotion activities. The costs for a campaign may be captured in March, for example, while the response takes place unevenly from March through June, July, or later.

This issue can lead to inconsistencies between the financial view of the business, taken month by month and reflected in the operating P&L, and marketing's view, based on campaign results. The business may be showing a shortfall in profits against plan, while marketing campaigns continue to be profitable. There must be a Marketing Campaign Plan that supports the financial plan, so that performance of marketing promotions can be measured against a plan that is consistent with the financial business plan.

Note the title for the report identifies the campaign as a March campaign "at 21 weeks." This means the campaign was initiated (mailed) in March, and these results, reported in July, are cumulative sales and profit after 21 weeks.

Responses for this campaign—sent direct mail—could continue to accumulate for many months; however, there would be an expectation that later responses would be small. For this report and campaign, "21 weeks" could be considered "100% complete" for purposes of analyzing the return on the marketing investment.

This concept can be expressed graphically. Exhibit 6.7 shows an idealized accumulation of responses by day, which appears to peak at 8,000 in week 8, and falls off gradually for the next 12 weeks. It is clear from Exhibit 6.7 that the volume of daily responses becomes very small after 19 weeks.

Exhibit 6.8 reexpresses the same figures on a "percent complete" basis, showing the cumulative percent of total responses acquired over time. It

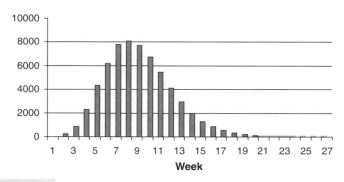

Campaign Response by Week

EXHIBIT 6.7   Campaign Response by Week

Cumulative Response Percent

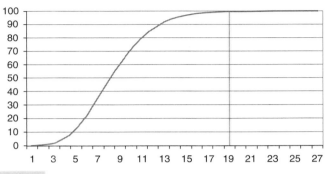

EXHIBIT 6.8   **Cumulative Campaign Response by Percent Complete**

forms an S-shaped curve. From this exhibit, the volume of response at 19 weeks is nearly 100%; therefore 21 weeks seems acceptable as a point to measure total response.

Returning to the direct mail campaign (Exhibit 6.9), 1.234 million pieces were mailed and the total cost was $564,819. After 21 weeks the communication has generated $1.728 million sales and $271,339 profit, for an RMI of 48%—not an unreasonable return after 21 weeks' time.

When additional campaigns are reviewed in the same report, the volume of figures can be difficult to digest quickly or easily (see Exhibit 6.10). This is where the reexpression of the per-campaign figures on a per-thousand-recipients basis is useful. Trying to compare campaign costs directly has to take into account the volume of people mailed. The largest campaign in this example (Communication B) had the second lowest total cost ($878,993), while the smallest campaign (Communication C) had the second highest cost ($1,179,891). The highest net profit campaign (Communication D, $2,928,256) was also not the largest campaign, which was campaign Communication B with a distribution of 2,045,000. Using the common denominator of Campaign Volume means the costs, sales, and profit for each of these marketing efforts can be compared directly.

On this basis, the most expensive campaign is Communication C, with a CPM (total cost per thousand) of $2,554. The least expensive campaign is Communication B, with a CPM of $430.

EXHIBIT 6.9 COMMUNICATION A RETURN

Our Company Direct Mail Campaign Results (March Campaigns at 21 weeks)

Communication	CommID	Volume	Offer	Non Recurring Act/CPM	Media Act/CPM	Postage Act/CPM	Insertion Act/CPM	Total Campaign Cost/CPM	Orders/ OPM	Sales/ SPM	Aug Order	Net Profit/ PPM	RMI
Communication A	Comm001	1,234,000	Offer A	9,519	185,100	283,820	86,380	564,819	61,700	1,727,600	28	271,339	48%
				7.71	150.00	230.00	70.00	458	50	1,400		220	

EXHIBIT 6.10 MULTIPLE COMMUNICATION COMPARISON

Our Company Direct Mail Campaign Results (March Campaigns at 21 weeks)

Communication	CommID	Volume	Offer	Non Recurring Act/CPM	Media Act/CPM	Postage Act/CPM	Insertion Act/CPM	Total Campaign Cost/CPM	Orders/ OPM	Sales /SPM	Aug Order	Net Profit/ PPM	RMI
Communication A	Comm001	1,234,000	OfferA	9,519	185,100	283,820	86,380	564,819	61,700	1,727,600	28	271,339	48%
				7.71	150.00	230.00	70.00	458	50	1,400		220	
Communication B	Comm002	2,045,000	OfferA	13,958	251,535	470,350	143,150	878,993	75,665	2,042,955	27,	109,798	12%
				6.83	123.00	230.00	70.00	430	37	999		54	
Communication C	Comm003	462,000	OfferA	12,417	169,554	900,900	97,020	1,179,891	55,440	1,995,840	36	(213,904)	−18%
				26.88	367.00	1950.00	210.00	2,554	120	4,320		(463)	
Communication D	Comm004	873,00	OfferA	8,656	272,376	960,300	157,140	1,398,472	279,360	8,939,520	32	2,928,256	209%
				9.91	312.00	1100.00	180.00	1,602	320	10,240		3,354	
Total Direct Mail		4,614,000		44,549	878,565	2,615,370	483,690	4,022,174	472,165	14,705,915	31,	3,095,489	77%
				9.66	312.00	566.83	104.83	872	102	3,187		671	

The most profitable campaign is Communication D, with a PPM (profit per thousand) of $3,354. Further review clarifies why this effort performed best: The OPM (orders per thousand) is 320, more than six times Communication A and three times Communication C. Additional detail on the recipients would probably help in understanding why Communication D performed so well and Communication B performed so poorly.

All four campaigns had fairly large orders and similar order sizes; however, Communication C did not make a profit. The RMI is −18% and Net Profit is −$213,904. This is a curious result, given the high sales figure of $1,995,840 and the highest average order size of $36. With further analysis the poor profit performance is clear: The Campaign Total Cost per thousand is $2,554, almost double the best performing campaign. All campaign component costs for Communication C significantly exceed communications A, B, and D. Nonrecurring cost per thousand is triple the next most expensive campaign, Media cost is more than double A and B, and postage is 8 times—almost 9 times—higher than A and B, and almost double Communication D. Clearly the mailing costs (in hindsight) far exceeded the ability of this promotion to generate corresponding sales to cover these costs.

If the campaign costs for Communication C were more similar to D, the communication would have been profitable. Using the per-thousand figures makes this calculation easy: The difference in CPM for C and D is $2,554 − $1,602 or a positive impact of $952. Adding this value to the present PPM of −$463 creates a positive PPM of $489, which would be a positive 19.1% RMI. Not a fantastic result, but positive nonetheless. If Communication C were repeated, management might advise targets more consistent with Communication D.

While the figures alone cannot explain the underlying reason for even particularly large differences, management has a significant advantage in pursuing those reasons, based on this level of detail, in order to learn from mistakes and capitalize on opportunities. Analysis of campaign results from this level of detail easily enables identification of poorly performing channels and promotions, and how much of the marketing budget can be reallocated to more successful opportunities, as well as what the more successful opportunities are. The details enable an estimate of expected performance to be made and, over time, provide a historical record of previous performance for use as benchmarks and for providing trend analysis. The historical information also provides the basis for developing the marketing investment plan for successive years.

Integrating the marketing RMI analysis with the operating plan review of the business can also provide an understanding of otherwise-unexplained sales performance fluctuations. If the response peak of a campaign is expected between 8 and 12 weeks, and the campaign execution is delayed by a few weeks, that response peak will move out in time, affecting sales results for the previous period. If that sales peak were to have fallen in the final two weeks of a month, moving those sales to the next month could result in a significant drop in the sales of the prior month, and an equally unexpected and large increase in sales of the succeeding month. Knowing of a delay in a specific promotion well in advance of the month for expected results, and knowing its expected value and anticipated timing, provides management foresight into the sales fluctuation well in advance of its occurrence. When the P&L is presented for discussion at the operating meeting, marketing would be well prepared to explain a potentially significant sales variance, as well as predict its reversal in the following month. Timely information prevents purposeless firedrills and misguided efforts to supplement missing sales that may simply appear next month. The same firedrill is avoided in the following month when the sales variance goes in the opposite direction.

INCREASING MARKETING INVESTMENT

With these reports in hand, management not only has the ability to reduce or eliminate investment in underperforming marketing activities, management now has the visibility and control to increase marketing investment in those areas demonstrated to be performing well. Investment can be increased to the point where incremental investment produces no noticeable incremental increase in profit.

This does not suggest "keep spending until RMI goes to zero." Each incremental dollar invested in a strong performing activity must be compared to the incremental change in sales and profits. If an incremental change cannot be measured, then further increases are not justified.

The risk from increasing investment can be mitigated by testing incremental changes to subsets of the market, rather than the entire market. This is again a benefit provided by a comprehensive marketing investment reporting capability, which is part of a well-executed marketing automation investment. Testing multiple marketing vehicles in multiple markets becomes much easier to do if collection and reporting of response information is automated and formatted to provide clear signals of success or failure.

MEASURING RESPONSE

Similar reports to the previous example can be generated for any marketing effort, such as telemarketing and email as well as television, newspaper, and magazine. However, these reports carry an implicit assumption that the sales attributed to each marketing communication were in fact driven by that communication. Response to telemarketing is most directly and easily recorded, because the customer is talking directly to a sales agent who is recording exactly the response of the recipient. The direct response connection means the revenue from orders received can be attributed to the marketing effort with confidence.

However, the connection between marketing communication and recipient and orders from direct mail, email, and particularly television, radio, and magazines is more tenuous. Analysis of the financial impact of marketing investments requires some confidence in the attribution of sales. A common approach might be to ask customers "Where did you hear about us?" For the customers, the response could be based on their most recent memory of an advertisement, but now may be almost exclusively based on follow-up research using the Internet. Their response to "Where did you hear about us?" will therefore be commonly "the Web" because that was their most recent experience. Follow-up surveys may help in determining brand identification, but do not necessarily provide the immediacy and accuracy provided by direct sales vehicles. With the marketing information displayed as above, limited ability to allocate sales results directly to the promotion vehicle generating the sale may lead to unsubstantiated investments in otherwise valuable channels.

Direct channel promotion codes can be used effectively to identify advertising effectiveness. Promotion codes can be tied to special offers accompanying a sale of standard product, an incremental discount, or a cross-sell opportunity. If a channel bears a significant proportion of the marketing budget allocation, the small incremental cost incurred to facilitate identifying the source of sales results will substantiate the continued investment.

Another approach is available. Instead of testing response to a promotion by focusing on recipients, a holdout sample of people can be selected who will *not* receive the communication, mail, or magazine insert. In turn the responsiveness of the people who did receive the marketing communication is compared to that of the holdout sample. The difference in sales between the two groups is referred to as the *lift provided by the communication*. A positive (or negative) lift is attributed to the marketing effort and the incremental sales allocated accordingly in the management reports.

Response measurements differ by marketing channel and there are several very useful response measurements that are not directly sales related. For example, recipient response to email communications can be tracked when the email is opened,[1] known as the *open rate*. Each email will also have several "hot links" embedded in words or pictures that bring the recipient who clicks on them to the company web site. These "click-thrus" can be tracked. More sophisticated web-site monitoring can also be used to track recipients who visit the web site even though they did not use the email to click through. Forwarding actions can also be monitored by tracking opens and click-thrus from people whose email ID and recipient codes do not match the "new" recipient.

This information can be applied in several ways primarily to improve response and lower cost. Open and click-thru rates can be compared for several emails to determine how to improve subject line and content. The rates can also highlight recipients who are nonresponsive over an extended period of time, which may be intentional or signal a confrontation with a spam filter.[2]

---

[1]Until a few years ago, "open" rates were problematic, as some email users maintained a preview pane that would send a "false positive" open signal. The email was opened by the preview pane, and the user did not necessarily read it. Later, Microsoft modified Outlook so the pictures were not automatically opened. This effectively eliminated the "false positive," but also reduced total opens, as some users would skip downloading the pictures. It is the picture download that triggers the open signal.

[2]Spam filters are a positive contribution to everyone's Internet email experience; however, the filters do make it more difficult for legitimate email marketing. Recipients who do not show responsiveness through opens or click-thrus may be getting filtered. One approach to confirm this would be to correlate the open and click-thru rates against the server address. Another approach is building a strong email presence through email marketing services and organization.

In telemarketing, while response is easy to capture, there are additional response parameters of significant interest. While telemarketing legislation has dramatically reduced the use of telemarketing as a channel in the mainstream, it remains an acceptable communication channel for many businesses contacting existing customers. Monitoring the following rates can demonstrate increasing or decreasing effectiveness: telematching rates, the proportion of potential recipients who do not have a phone number on file, "Bad Number" rates, where the intended recipient in fact does not have the phone number on file, "No Response" rates, and "Opt Out," "Do Not Call," or "Cancel" rates. All of these can provide insight into the quality—as to potential responders—of the list used in a marketing communication.

FORECASTING RESPONSE

Once the measurement criteria have been identified, and the components of cost and response are accessible on a regular basis, the historical information can be used to project results. This is done in any normal business planning cycle. Expectations for next year are necessarily based on this year's and prior years' results, for both revenue and cost.

A more refined forecast can be done to identify results for current promotions, with a level of reliability to be determined. The benefit of a more refined forecast for the short term is the same as knowing the cost components of any promotion: better control over the P&L.

Business planning is typically year by year. January's results might be tremendous but do not affect the prior year (assuming a calendar-based cycle). By forecasting forward current promotions, planning for contingencies—poor results—can be accomplished in time to make a difference in the current fiscal year.

LONG-TERM RETURN ON MARKETING INVESTMENT

In the short term, measurement of return on marketing investments is direct: An investment of $100 is estimated[3] to generate $330 in revenue. Using the

---

[3]Estimation or attribution of revenue to marketing investments is critical to the ability to measure the contribution of marketing to revenue.

figures from the P&L above, this will produce $165 gross profit, net $65 after the marketing investment, or 65% return.

$330	Revenue
30	Returns
$300	Net Revenue
135	Product Cost
165	Gross Profit
100	Marketing Expense
65	Net Profit (before Overhead)[4]

In the long term, consider the impact of continued spending by new customers attracted by the initial investment of $100. Their spending would be harder to identify but not impossible. This could increase the total *incremental* profit by 10% or more, further justifying the original increase in marketing expense.

For most companies engaged primarily in direct marketing, systems have evolved that can identify and measure the profit contribution from nearly every marketing vehicle and channel. BMG Direct evolved a system that could identify and measure customer profitability *for five years*. This presents an interesting financial analysis challenge: How are the financial return goals for customer acquisition balanced with the ongoing marketing maintenance goals for the same customer profitability? It would appear that long- term measurement would justify higher investment, but the maintenance effort could not use the same customer activity to justify its own marketing activity.

---

[4]The reference to "Net Profit before Overhead" is similar to "Net Profit" without an adjustment for overhead expense. In this example, there should not be any adjustment to the net proceeds of this marketing investment, as no incremental overhead costs should be necessary. A different example might consider, for example, the potential gains from a marketing investment in a web site. Developing a website would likely include additional headcount to generate content for the site as well as manage the site.

CHAPTER 7

Improving Response: Modeling and Analytics

Once marketing management reports are available that facilitate analysis of profitable marketing activities and detail the responsiveness of recipients on other parameters, the goal is to improve the effectiveness of these communications in generating a positive response, in other words, to increase response and reduce cost. As noted earlier, the ability to reallocate funds from lower-performing investments to higher-performing investments has a significant potential for dramatically increasing growth in sales, profits, and profitability.

Marketing analytics involves segmentation of the customer population into groups with some commonality. One dimension common to these groups is their propensity to respond to particular promotions. Not everyone responds in the same way to marketing communications and marketing channels. Based on information—response—to previous marketing promotions, predictive models may be able to identify customers more or less likely to respond to future promotions along specific channels. From these predictive models, those least likely to respond can be eliminated from the promotion population, representing a cost savings. Modeling response will not generate a perfect solution. There will be some opportunity cost from the use of models: Some people will be removed from the list as likely *not* to respond, who would otherwise have been responsive and made a purchase. Nonetheless, promotional cost could be reduced by 20 to 30% while sacrificing less than 5% of the responders.

Therefore, the next step after weaker-performing communications are weeded out is to improve the response to existing campaigns, by developing response models. Response models are developed by comparing the attributes of responders to nonresponders and determining by association whether some of these attributes are different between the two groups. The differences associated with responders can then be used to select similar people who are—by induction—more likely to respond to similar communications, promotions, and offers. The attributes common to nonresponders can similarly be applied to identify people who are not likely to respond to new and similar communications.

The process of assessing the strength of these attributes in predicting response and nonresponse is known as *modeling*. Using basic as well as very sophisticated modeling techniques, communications can be directed to people more likely to respond. This will reduce the total volume of most marketing efforts, a significant source of cost savings. The cost savings from successful modeling can be applied to other marketing opportunities. The goal is not to reduce the marketing budget, but to reallocate it for business growth.

In the context of the modeling process, the expense of the marketing communication is known; the response or response value is uncertain. Modeling will provide an assessment of the likelihood of a response. The assessment can be expressed as a number between 0 and 1, a probability of response, which conveniently enables an evaluation technique for determining who should be selected for a particular promotion or marketing communication.

The evaluation technique is very simple: The probability of response generated by the model, a number between 0 and 1, is multiplied times the average profit per order. The probability is a figure generated by the model for each person in the list. Each person will have a different number according to the attributes used in the model. If the result is greater than the cost to send the direct mail piece or make the telemarketing call to this particular person, they should be selected to receive it. The calculation of a probability and a response value is known as an *expected value*. If the expected value of a response is greater than the cost to make the contact, through direct mail, telemarketing, or other channel, then the expected value is said to be *greater than breakeven*.

Any individual in a prospective list whose expected value is greater than breakeven represents a potentially profitable recipient. Not every recipient selected in this way will respond, and some potential recipients who are not selected may have in fact responded very favorably. These two groups will reduce the profit potential from modeling. However, if the model is effective, the profits generated and cost saved will substantially exceed the costs and lost opportunity associated with the other two groups.

The next step is to choose the breakeven probability to be used in selecting people for a particular communication. This value is calculated by dividing breakeven profit—the cost of the promotion—by the most likely profit per order. For example:

Promotion Cost	$1.50
Breakeven Order Profit	$1.50
Average Order Profit	$5.00
Response Breakeven	30.0% = 1.50/5.00

To test this, multiply the average order profit of $5.00 by the breakeven response value of 30%. The result is $1.50, the same as the promotion cost. If only those people are selected whose probability of response is greater than 30%, then our expected results for the promotion—profit—will be positive.

An underlying assumption is that there are people who have a probability of response greater than 30% in the population. That is a key feature of a good model: a broad distribution of values, some high and some low, but not all low or high. It must be able to discriminate the audience, that is, to provide everyone a distinct value that is not the same as or close to everyone else.

There are some circumstances where consistently low-response likelihood would be very desirable, in choosing "least likely" responders instead of "most likely" responders. An example was mentioned in an earlier chapter of a large group of people—more than a million—who had continued to receive promotions from a direct mail company and had not purchased in more than a year. If the company decided to mail this group much less frequently, it would be useful to have a model that would predict those likely not to respond. A potential 'predictor' variable could be "Number of Days Since Last Purchase." The challenge would be to identify the right point where the number of days since last purchase provides a strong indication of the breakeven point for the promotion, below which it is not profitable to make a contact. The model could be effective enough to identify people who may never purchase again, but this more extreme step would not be

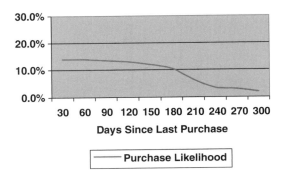

EXHIBIT 7.1   Response by Days Since Last Purchase

justified without further information demonstrating how effective such a decision would be.

Based on analysis, Exhibit 7.1 shows the score curve of value to "Days Since Last Purchase." It displays a significant falloff in purchase rate between 180 and 210 days since last purchase. With this information a test could be devised to promote a group of people with a Last Purchase from 150 to 250 days, and create a holdout sample of similar people who will not receive a promotion. Analysis of the response from both groups can be used to identify the best Days Since Last Purchase value that signals a high likelihood to *not* respond.

Future promotions can do two things with this information: Standard promotions can use this value as a cutoff, reducing the campaign volume as a cost savings. A *second* promotion can be created specific to those *below* the cutoff point, which attempts to motivate a purchase using a discount, customer-specific information, or a reiteration of the company's products and product benefits. Further analysis of responders will demonstrate if the new promotion is effective, and support additional models to further improve results.

Similar analysis can support other types of customer differentiation, identifying potential lost customers or customers likely to respond to an up-sell, cross-sell, or other prior purchase–related offer. The important contribution of analytics—modeling—is the ability to refine the audience selection to a volume that is cost effective and profitable. Without the application of analytics, a campaign would have to be directed at all or most customers who more loosely fit the criteria of the promotion. More targeted campaigns—campaigns with specific promotional goals—which are directed to a *less* targeted audience will almost by definition generate lower response rates, which means the campaigns will not be as effective and may in fact generate too little response to be profitable.

Assume a particular promotion will be guaranteed attractive to 10,000 people and the value of an order is $100, representing a profit potential of $1,000,000. The 10,000 interested people exist in a population of 10 million and there is no other information available to identify any of the 10,000 from the rest of the population. If I choose any one person at random, the likelihood that I choose one of the 10,000 is extremely low, just 1/10 of 1%. This parallels the concept of a response rate, and 1/10 of 1% is a very low response rate under most circumstances. Assume the cost of a bare-bones promotion for this product is $0.25 per person: Promoting to all 10 million people will cost $2.5 million. The expected profit for the promotion will be

$$0.1\% \times 10,000,000 \times \$100 = \$1,000,000$$
$$- \text{ Promotion Cost } \$2,500,000 = -\$1,500,000$$

The promotion creates a net loss of $1,500,000. Under these circumstances, the potential $1,000,000 gross profit represents a *significant* forgone opportunity.

The application of modeling could aid the identification of this group of people, providing a method of discriminating likely responders from nonresponders, enabling a dramatic reduction in the campaign volume, from 10,000,000 to something within the range of profitability. Cutting the cost of the campaign by $2,000,000 would require a volume reduction of 4/5 or 8,000,000 recipients. Provided sufficient information is available for modeling the population, it is at least worth the effort, given the scale of the opportunity.

Hence, the use of modeling gives rise to the possibility of increasing the number of communications to customers:

- More frequent communications to smaller groups
- More effective choice of communication channel, improving response
- More complex communication timing based on scheduling and automated delivery, including trigger-event scheduling and delivery based on response or nonresponse

The process of modeling can be used to expand marketing activities, creating more—and more varied—communications, again to smaller groups of people. Modeling can be used to further a good marketing idea by creating the ability to focus the idea to the right people.

More frequent communications to smaller groups of people creates a challenge in the marketing process downstream from the audience selection process, the challenge of managing selection, execution, and results analysis of many more promotions. Marketing automation, with its ability to facilitate and manage a high volume of varied communications, provides the platform from which many good marketing ideas, targeted to predictively responsive audiences, will be successful in generating incremental profits. The ability to support more and more varied marketing activities is a fundamental capability provided by marketing automation.

The new and incremental marketing activities will be expected to be targeting smaller groups of people, and therefore the net gain for each new activity will be smaller than the mainstream marketing activities currently active. However, the cumulative effect will be very material to profits, as will be demonstrated in the Marketing Financials Worksheet. This worksheet, which is presented in Chapter 8, will tie together the incremental marketing benefits so far presented, and provide a baseline for a marketing investment proposal.

REDUCED BUSINESS RISK

The acquisition of marketing investment information and the development of marketing campaign profitability information improve the budgeting process, performance reporting, and the organization's ability to respond to changing economic situations. It improves a manager's understanding of the business processes supporting product sales, and their understanding of fluctuations in sales activity month to month. Marketing campaign information improves a marketer's understanding of how their customers respond to promotions, and therefore their ability to improve promotions and target product promotions to appropriate customers. The culmination of this understanding should be better business decisions and fewer mistakes. Better understanding of the business reduces business risk.

This is a reasonable enough assertion but not easy to quantify. A business may have a profit goal of $25 million, against which a risk of achievement could be estimated as 10% or $2.5 million. Expanding information by improving the systems and process infrastructure, as well as enhanced productivity of marketers and analysts alike, could mitigate this risk by 20% or $500,000.

While the logic may *seem* reasonable, substantiating such a figure is challenging. A company may be able to identify specific circumstances in which additional information might have prevented a poor investment. The value (loss) associated with the investment could in turn be used to substantiate the impact of risk reduction.

CHAPTER 8

Creating a Marketing Financials Worksheet

The earlier discussion of business P&L created a view of marketing profitability by equating marketing activities directly to gross product sales and gross profits and incorporating business costs to create a marketing profitability ratio. In the discussion of P&L components and marketing, suggestions have been made as to how improved understanding of marketing campaign performance, together with modeling to develop more targeted campaign audiences, could improve the return on marketing investments.

Managing the information associated with each marketing promotion and managing the ability to generate more and more targeted promotions are both significant components of a marketing automation system. It provides an infrastructure supporting access to the information necessary to evaluate the progress and contribution of marketing activities to business profits. The infrastructure—systems comprised of hardware and software including data management capabilities—will be discussed in detail beginning with Chapter 9.

Acquiring and implementing the necessary infrastructure that provides these capabilities can be a significant investment. Hence there is a need to fund such an investment, and, as noted earlier, business funding for such a project is in competition with other business projects; an investment proposal will be required that demonstrates the return on such an investment.

Therefore, a marketer must anticipate preparation of a business investment proposal to include a presentation of ROI. The proposal must substantiate the return in terms financial management can understand and accept, as well as demonstrate a strong positive return that is competitive against other proposals.

Such a proposal is of great interest for a marketer. It quantifies many marketing activities in terms of their financial benefit and cost, it provides a baseline of promotional returns between channels, it can set a baseline of expectations based on current performance, as well as substantiate expected gains in the future based on increased marketing activities. Establishing the content behind new marketing activities can be the impetus for new and creative marketing concepts that find their potential implementation more achievable, using a testing approach, where previously larger populations would have generated too much risk to try new marketing ideas.

A detailed example of a financial worksheet appropriate to supporting such a proposal is developed in this chapter. Reasonable numbers are included that will demonstrate a not-unreasonable 20% improvement in gross profit. This increase in profit is in turn incorporated into a hypothetical business investment proposal, including the ROI based on both PV and internal ROI methods.

Worksheet Basics

The goal of the worksheet is to substantiate and demonstrate the incremental profit that can be generated from an investment in marketing infrastructure (*marketing automation*). The worksheet is based on current campaign costs per channel and current campaign profitability. The costs and revenue of current campaigns are projected forward as the basis for revenue and costs associated with the additional campaigns expected to be possible with an improved infrastructure. Total gain is based on a combination of cost savings and incremental investment in additional marketing promotions. Expected gains for the incremental promotions are conservatively adjusted by an "effectiveness" factor, to account for an assumed marginal decline in response. Response may in fact be better, but a conservative factor provides an allowance for what may be speculative information. This again speaks to the Catch-22 aspect of such a proposal.

The complete worksheet is presented as Exhibit 8.6. To simplify the presentation, each section of the worksheet is discussed individually in the next several pages. The worksheet begins with the company's present *annual gross profit*, which in this case is $250,000,000. The company has 20,000,000 customers and a current annual marketing budget of $165,000,000.

The next section of the worksheet details the current allocation of the marketing budget across marketing channels, including average circulation, cost, and profit, by promotion and channel. The specific amounts by channel are not important, as the campaign averages are used to estimate the incremental costs and benefits.

Using these per-campaign averages, the final section of the worksheet details the incremental promotions expected based on exploiting the capabilities provided by the marketing automation system. Each type of promotion, the number of such promotions, and their incremental profit is estimated. At the bottom line the total increment is calculated and compared to the initial gross profit before the application of a marketing automation system.

The worksheet is structured in a way that makes tuning it easy, using adjustable values of:

- Campaign circulation
- Cost per campaign
- Campaign response
- Value per response

These are the basic components of the *return on marketing investment*.

As noted above, an additional factor is added, called *effectiveness*. This factor is applied to each incremental marketing activity as a measure of how it compares to the current average response. In this example, a comparable effectiveness is estimated at 50%. This says that the incremental campaigns will only achieve 50% of the response of the average campaign.

One of the expectations or assumptions in this example worksheet is that the company will continue to use the same channel mix in their new promotions moving forward. This assumption is not unreasonable, and it does make the calculations simpler, enabling the use of a simple "average response and value" across all marketing channels for the incremental campaigns. This assumption could be modified as required, increasing or decreasing utility of specific channels.

The company in this example presently allocates the marketing budget across direct mail, telemarketing, email, and direct sales channels, and the worksheet includes the annual circulation for each channel. On an annual basis each customer is contacted about five times: The company generates 96,800,000 total contacts to its 20,000,000 customers. Most contacts are through email (47,000,000) and direct mail (43,200,000), with only 4.2 million contacts through telemarketing and 2.4 million contacts through direct sales.

The company delivers approximately 200 unique communications per year to its customers through these channels, and there is an average of 484,000 people in each campaign. On average, the response rate is 3.6% based on response from all four channels. The value (gross profit) of a response varies dramatically by channel, from $35.00 through direct mail to $125.00 for direct sales contacts. In this example, direct sales contacts also generate a very high response, nearly 50%, which drives total gross profit of $120,000,000, nearly 50% of total gross profit. This has a significant effect on the average value per response, which is $73.00 (gross profit of a response, not revenue).

As a proposal, the expected *future* channel mix must be confirmed to ensure that an appropriate baseline figure is assumed in the analysis. This value will be applied to *all* incremental marketing activity attributed to the investment. If this company were to anticipate growth in primarily direct channels, yet continued to maintain a higher average response value in the analysis, then the proposed gains would be grossly exaggerated. The investment proposal will establish new performance expectations, and no clearer red flag can be raised than a future decline in plan response rates and value, following a proposed increase carefully recorded in the investment proposal. If the direct sales channel is eliminated in this example, the average response value declines to $52.87 (still substantially supported by the high volume and value of responses from the email channel, which represents 70% of the remaining total).

Each campaign on average generates $1.3 million gross profit, less campaign costs of $1,710.00 per thousand or a net contribution to overhead of $429,950 per campaign (average). For this company, net profit after marketing costs is $85,990,000, which can also be calculated based on 200 campaigns multiplied by $429,950 profit (net) per campaign.

The average number of contacts per customer is 4.8, meaning each customer on average is contacted about five times per year, and the total number of unique campaigns or communications is 200. The goal for marketing—and this worksheet—is to demonstrate how to increase the frequency of contact while reducing the total cost of each campaign. Currently the cost per contact is $1.71 (rounded), which is calculated by dividing the total marketing cost of $165,350,00 by the total number of contacts, which is

$$\$165,350,000/96,800,000 = \$1.7082 \text{ or } \$1.71$$

As noted in Chapter 7, "Improving Response: Modeling and Analytics," one of the prime areas for improvement is the efficiency of all campaigns, reducing the volume while improving response by modeling the audience and contacting those customers most likely to respond.

Specific sections below discuss the incremental impact of each improvement to marketing capability brought about through marketing automation. Basically incremental campaigns are engendered that create incremental profit.

Additional communications may not perform as well as current campaigns, assuming that current campaigns have been optimized for better targeting of recipients. Room for error in modeling is also recommended. Therefore, all incremental campaigns are given an "efficiency factor" to adjust response and value down to more conservative levels. In other words, if existing campaigns (optimized) generate a 10% response worth $50, an incremental campaign with an efficiency of 50% will generate only half the response, or 5%, but retain the same response value. To be conservative, the spreadsheet assumes only a 50% efficiency for incremental campaigns.

MODELING IMPACT (ANALYTICS)

The foremost expected benefit of modeling is to reduce the total circulation volume without undue impact on response. Experience demonstrates that some models can achieve 30 to 40% reduction in total volume while retaining 95% of the total response. A more conservative approach might be to assume a 20% reduction in volume for one in four campaigns. In this example the savings is calculated as follows:

$$(200 \text{ Campaigns} \times 25\%) \times (20\% \times 484,000) \times \$1.7082$$

In our example this would represent a savings of $8,267,688.

Modeling may similarly be able to identify new opportunities that otherwise would have been unprofitable. Recall the example of 10,000 potential customers within a total population of 10,000,000. If modeling can highlight these customers, with some level of accuracy, a new marketing opportunity is created. These opportunities would be more targeted and therefore lower in total volume and total response than current campaigns; hence the incremental impact could be half that of a normal campaign, equivalent to $215,000 net profit per campaign. In the worksheet, four such campaign opportunities are assumed in any year, noted as "Additional Opportunities," with an incremental contribution of $859,900.

The total impact of modeling is therefore $8,267,688 savings plus $859,900 for new campaigns, a subtotal of $9,127,588.

CAMPAIGN MANAGEMENT

The next category for incremental marketing activity is labeled "Campaign Management" in the worksheet. In this section the effect of *personalization*, the impact on customer attrition, process improvement, and improved timing of customer contacts, will be quantified.

Experience has shown that personalization, including channel selection, can achieve an incremental response. Personalization is fostered by improvements in customer information and its accessibility for marketers in tailoring campaign contact. The effect of personalization in the worksheet is estimated as a 5% lift on half of the existing promotions:

$$\$429,950 \times 5\% \times (50\% \times 200)$$

Personalization would provide $2,149,750 incremental profit (net).

IMPROVED RELATIONSHIP IMPACT

Using campaign management to automate delivery improves the timing of customer messaging and delivery. Higher levels of personalization combined with automated delivery through campaign management improve the customer dialogue and are central to customer relationship management (CRM). All of the above should contribute to a longer and more effective—higher value—relationship with the customer, which in turn means increased revenue. One method for quantifying this impact is to assume

EXHIBIT 8.1	IMPROVED RELATIONSHIP IMPACT

Customers	20,000,000
Total Annual Purchases	3,444,000
Purchase Per Cust	0.1722
Lifetime	0.6888
Value Per Purchase	$73
Percent Increase	5%
Percent of Customers	25%
Annual Total Impact	$3,141,750

an overall increase in purchase volume per customer, not on an annual basis but on a lifetime basis.

In this example the customer lifetime is assumed to be four years. Total customer purchases based on responses over four years are 4 × 3,444,000 responses, just under 14,000,000. An annualized increase of 5% for every customer would be (4 × 3,444,000) × 5%/4 years, which is the same as a simple 5% increase in annual gross profit ($13,087,200). A second approach can be based on a per-customer average purchase volume in a lifetime. In this example, if at least 25% of 20,000,000 customers were to increase their purchases by 5%, using the same average purchase value, the total annual profit value would be $3,141,750. (See Exhibit 8.1.)

IMPROVED DELIVERY INFRASTRUCTURE

Automating delivery through marketing automation means that additional campaign opportunities exist in the form of follow-up responses, for example. The tools themselves afford the ability to carry increased frequency of communication. If these incremental opportunities are combined, marketing will be able to deliver additional promotions with existing resources. This can occur in several areas: The infrastructure provides delivery automation that improves operations' productivity, enabling more campaigns to be executed in the year. Planning facility creates an opportunity for follow-up on responsive—and nonresponsive—customers. Planning and delivery facility enables a higher contact rate—not necessarily to all customers, but to those demonstrating an interest.

The combined impact of campaign management exceeds $1,000,000 gain in the year, as follows:

Automated Delivery: 4 Additional Campaigns × 50% Volume = $859,000

Follow-up Response: 3 Additional Campaigns × 50% Volume = $644,925

Increased Frequency: 2 Additional Campaigns × 50% Volume = $429,950

Total Impact   9 Additional Campaigns   = $1,933,875

PRODUCTIVITY

While some increase in productivity would be necessary to achieve the above incremental campaigns, the improved infrastructure can provide a further lift from its ability to empower marketers to act on more ideas targeting unique customer groups. Productivity in this case is not a potential cost savings, productivity improvements will increase customer directed marketing activity and increase revenue. In the worksheet the improvement in marketing productivity is assessed as a conservative increase of two campaigns at 50% volume or $429,950.

REDUCED RISK

The combined total so far relies heavily on the infrastructure to provide the ability to exploit more promotional opportunities. The opportunities created by enabling audience identification are provided by improved access to customer information. This same information provides marketers and management with more information on the connection between marketing activities and sales.

Improved information and access to that information provides a more certain planning environment. Information regarding pending successes as well as business challenges will be available earlier with more certainty and accuracy. This information will enable management to respond earlier and more effectively to changing business situations. The reduced uncertainty should be reflected in the P&L plan. As discussed earlier, this improvement in business information improves management's control of the business and reduces risk.

In this case the risk reduction is evaluated (guesstimated) as 1% of gross profit or $2.5million.

TOTAL IMPACT

The combined impact of these marketing-based improvements is summarized in Exhibit 8.2. Total impact derived from marketing automation capabilities is $19,297,025, equivalent to 7.7% of gross profit after costs of additional activities.

Almost half of the impact—43%—comes from the reduced circulation cost, attributed to the influence of modeling in reducing promotion volume; 16% comes from improved dialogue with customers; and 13% is attributed to risk reduction (Exhibit 8.2).

This is not a one-time, one-year impact, but an impact that is expected to be maintained year after year. In the same way that "holiday promotions" are repeated every year, the incremental campaigns created through improved infrastructure will become part of the annual marketing effort. Campaigns that demonstrate positive impact will be repeated, and those whose impact declines will be eliminated.

EXHIBIT 8.2   CUMULATIVE GAINS

Activity	Gain	Percent of Total
Analytics		
Reduced Circulation Cost	$8,267,500	43%
Additional Opportunities	$859,900	4%
Campaign Mgt		
Personalization/Channel	$2,149,750	11%
Lifetime Value Impact	$3,141,750	16%
Automated Delivery	$859,900	4%
Followup Response	$644,925	3%
Increased Frequency	$429,950	2%
Productivity		
Additional Campaign	$429,950	2%
Reduced Risk	$2,513,400	13%
Total Gain	$19,297,025	

In fact, as the infrastructure components—reporting, testing, and campaign management—become increasingly integrated into daily activity, further increases in communication volume with customers would be expected. In this example, the total increase in "new" campaigns is only 15 against a current volume of 200, a 7.5% increase, and a good portion of the 15 new campaigns are based on "response" promotions, follow-up to existing communications. Over 90% of existing campaigns still do not have any follow-up such as cross-sell and upsell promotions.

The limiting factor for improving communication with customers will be the volume of information available on customers. Identifying significant groups of customers for specific promotions is wholly reliant on the information available. The same is true of modeling: Without information on which to base analysis, modeling cannot be effective.

However, there is one source of information that should not be limited, particularly if marketing is successful. Customer purchase activity will be a continued source of relevant marketing information: the products purchased, the timing of purchases, the *market basket* content of purchases, recent purchase volume compared to prior purchase volume, as well as response or lack of response to prior promotions. This information comes under the general category of customer recency, frequency, and monetary value information (RFM). Improving customer information from more effective promotion and purchase tracking is and will be a valuable source of information for improving the effectiveness of modeling and audience selection.

ROI for Marketing Investment

The final step in the marketing investment proposal is to incorporate the incremental profit gains into an ROI profile that demonstrates the return on the investment.

Using the annualized gain on gross profit as a stream of income, the cost of the investment will be added to the initial year or years, and the ROI calculated as shown in the earlier examples. A fixed gain per year will be assumed, based on the values in the marketing financials spreadsheet.

The cost of the investment will consist of hardware, software, implementation costs, and maintenance. Maintenance may include software and hardware maintenance fees paid annually, and software costs may include operating system maintenance and support costs, which can be quite nominal. Costs are also likely to include chargeback costs from the IT department or data center.

There may also be a cost for additional headcount associated with keeping the project moving forward. The additional resource(s) may be folded back through the IT chargeback fees or could be absorbed directly by the project. IT chargeback expense will cover the cost of database maintenance, system backups, failover maintenance support, and security, as well as electricity and physical data center–related costs.

Considering the variety of costs involved in the project and the possible implementation scenarios available, it is nearly impossible to make reliable projections consistent with the marketing worksheet. Therefore the cost presentation here must be considered as a format to be followed for analysis, rather than a substantive example. The projected benefits taken from the marketing worksheet so far outpace the potential costs, the lack of specific cost factors in the example should not detract from its value. Exhibit 8.3 is a very simple ROI example based on a $5,000,000 investment in the first year.

The income flow in the exhibit includes 50% of the gain from the marketing worksheet in Year 1 and Year 2, the first two fully operational years, then 100% in years 3 and forward. The net gain discounted 10% is $81 million, and generates a 1,624% return on the investment of $5,000,000. On an IRR basis the discount rate is 213%. The project clearly pays for itself almost twice over in the first year of operation. And just as clearly the potential gains outlined in the marketing worksheet are enormous compared to the cost.

If the costs were to be separately estimated, they would appear something like Exhibit 8.4, in the context of the ROI analysis format. These figures are purely hypothetical but serve as an adequate example to outline the proposal format.

Hardware costs can involve an upfront purchase cost plus annual maintenance and failover protection,[1] plus the annual operating system

---

[1]Computer systems include various options for maintaining performance in the event of individual component failure. It would be typical for a large system to include two power supplies, for example. High-performance, high-availability systems could include *mirrored disc drives*, where all information is on redundant discs. Vendors can further provide ongoing monitoring of the system, heading off impending failures before the system itself fails.

EXHIBIT 8.3   PRESENT VALUE ANALYSIS OF MARKETING INVESTMENT

	Investment			Profit from Investment					
	Year 1	Year 2	Year 3	Year 4	Year 5	Year 6	Year 7	Year 8	Year 9
Profit Forecast $	(5,000,000)	9,648,513	9,648,513	19,297,025	19,297,025	19,297,025	19,297,025	19,297,025	19,297,025
Discounted at 10%	(5,000,000)	8,771,375	7,973,977	14,498,140	13,180,128	11,981,934	10,892,668	9,902,425	9,002,205

Total Value, 8 Years, 81,202,852   Discounted at 10%
1624% Return
IRR   213%

EXHIBIT 8.4   PRESENT VALUE INVESTMENT DETAIL

	Investment								
	Year 1	Year 2	Year 3	Year 4	Year 5	Year 6	Year 7	Year 8	Year 9
Investment Cost									
Hardware	500,000	25,000	25,000	25,000	25,000	25,000	25,000	25,000	25,000
Software	1,000,000	500,000	500,000	500,000	500,000	500,000	500,000	500,000	500,000
Implementation	300,000	300,000							
Data Center Costs	10,000	5,000	5,000	5,000	5,000	5,000	5,000	5,000	5,000
Headcount	120,000	120,000	120,000	120,000	120,000	120,000	120,000	120,000	120,000
Total Cost	1,930,000	950,000	650,000	650,000	650,000	650,000	650,000	650,000	650,000

maintenance and support expense. Specific costs are available from specific vendors.

Software costs will involve a first-year or multiyear purchase expense plus ongoing maintenance, which entitles the owner to upgrades and may include support. Ongoing support is highly recommended but may or may not involve an incremental cost.

Implementation expense can be a combination of costs from the hardware and software vendors, and it can be incorporated in a package provided by a consulting firm. The firm may also provide ongoing support for a fee.

Data center chargeback costs are included in the next line of the example. The expense for an additional person (headcount) has been included here to support ongoing maintenance of the system. This just as easily could have been incorporated into the data center chargeback costs to be negotiated.

The cost of the investment can be extremely variable. It is nonetheless easy to quantify based on discussion with the company's IT management as well as hardware and software vendors. Multiple scenarios can be generated on paper to scope the range of possibilities, providing further support for the proposal.

A combined cost-and-profit schedule could appear as shown in Exhibit 8.5. In this example, the total cost is cumulated on a single line, the profit forecast follows on its own line, and the combination of the cost and profit are noted on the line "ROI Cash Flow." This line is used for the calculation of the IRR, which in this case is 184%. The net return discounted 10%, the PV analysis method, is $42,902,077. The total return—profit divided by total expense—is 909%. In this example, the investment is spread over two years, Year 1 and Year 2, and the annual expected marketing gain is $9,648,513, with 25% achieved in the first year, 75% in the second year, and 100% thereafter. The investment generates positive cash flow beginning the second year, meaning it pays for itself in the second year. As shown in the worksheet, the return on marketing investment is sufficient to justify a sizable investment to bring these capabilities online.

* * * *

This concludes the discussion of marketing financials. A relationship between gross profit and marketing expense has been shown to facilitate analysis of marketing activities, to the point where ineffective marketing

EXHIBIT 8.5   PRESENT VALUE DETAIL (EXPANDED)

	Investment	Profit from Investment							
	Year 1	Year 2	Year 3	Year 4	Year 5	Year 6	Year 7	Year 8	Year 9
Investment Cost									
Hardware	500,000	25,000	25,000	25,000	25,000	25,000	25,000	25,000	25,000
Software	1,000,000	500,000	500,000	500,000	500,000	500,000	500,000	500,000	500,000
Implementation	300,000	300,000							
Data Center Costs	10,000	5,000	5,000	5,000	5,000	5,000	5,000	5,000	5,000
Headcount	120,000	120,000	120,000	120,000	120,000	120,000	120,000	120,000	120,000
Total Cost	1,930,000	950,000	650,000	650,000	650,000	650,000	650,000	650,000	650,000
Profit Forecast $	–	2,412,128	7,236,384	9,648,513	9,648,513	9,648,513	9,648,513	9,648,513	9,648,513
ROI Cash Flow	(1,930,000)	1,462,128	6,586,384	8,998,513	8,998,513	8,998,513	8,998,513	8,998,513	8,998,513
Discounted at 10%	–	2,192,844	5,980,483	7,249,070	6,590,064	5,990,967	5,446,334	4,951,213	4,501,102

Total Value, 8 Years,	**Discounted at 10%**
42,902,077	**909% Return**
IRR	**184%**

Marketing Financial Analysis Spreadsheet
(figures Based on Annual Estimates)

		Company specific figures entered in
		All other figures are derived/calculated

		Direct Mail	Telemarketing	Email	Direct Sales
Gross Profit	250,000,000				
Customers	20,000,000				
Marketing Budget	165,350,000				
Marketing Channels					
Number of Channels	4	1	1	1	1
Campaigns Per Channel		54	28	94	24
Circulation per Campaign		800,000	150,000	500,000	100,000
Total Circulation	96,800,000	43,200,000	4,200,000	47,000,000	2,400,000
		44.6%	4.3%	48.6%	2.5%
Cost Per Contact		1.25	2.40	0.01	42.00
Total Cost (Mktg Budget)	165,350,000	54,000,000	10,080,000	470,000	100,800,000
Response Rate		2.0%	5.0%	3.0%	40.0%
Total Response	3,444,000	864,000	210,000	1,410,000	960,000
Response Per Customer	0.17				
Value of Response (Profit)		35	45	65	125
Total Value (Profit)	251,340,000	30,240,000	9,450,000	91,650,000	120,000,000
(Ties to Gross Profit)					
Avg Annual Contacts	4.8				
Total Unique Campaigns	200				

Per Campaign Averages
Circ Per Campaign	484,000
Cost Per Contact	1.71
Response Per Campaign	17,220
Value Per Response	73
Response Rate	3.56%

Net Profit Per Campaign $ 429,950   **RMI**   52.0%

Analytics
Reduced Circulation Cos	8,267,500	Campaign Vol	50 Reduction	20%
Additional Opportunities $	859,900	Addt'l Campaign	4 Effectiveness	50%

Campaign Mgt
Personalization/Channel	2,149,750	Campaign Vol	100 Increase	5%
Lifetime Value Impact	3,141,750	Customers	25% Increase	5%
		Years	4 Purchase Value	73
Automated Delivery $	859,900	Addt'l Campaign	4 Effectiveness	50%
Followup Response $	644,925	Addt'l Campaign	3 Effectiveness	50%
Increased Frequency $	429,950	Addt'l Campaign	2 Effectiveness	50%

Productivity
Additional Campaign $	429,950	Addt'l Campaign	2 Effectiveness	50%

Reduced Risk
Reduced Risk	2,513,025	% of Gross Prof	1%

TOTAL BENEFIT   19,297,025   **NET ANNUAL Contribution to Overhead**
Percent of Gross Profit   7.7%   **Percent Increase in Gross Profit**

EXHIBIT 8.6   **Marketing Financials Worksheet**

investments can be identified and eliminated in favor of a more efficient allocation of the marketing budget. Analysis of customer information has been shown to facilitate identifying nonresponsive customers, as well as opening a door to modeling customer behavior in order to improve response to marketing promotions. Modeling has been shown to enable identification of small customer groups receptive to specific promotions, smaller but still-profitable promotional opportunities that cannot be exploited without an infrastructure to support identification and campaign execution.

The benefits provided by increased communication to smaller groups have been cumulated in a marketing financials spreadsheet (Exhibit 8.6), which in turn has been incorporated into an ROI proposal that demonstrates a very substantial return on investment based on conservative projections.

Marketing Automation

The application of marketing automation seeks to create a platform to drive more effective marketing, which will drive growth for a business. This is accomplished through analysis of the marketing investment in great detail, to highlight successful and unsuccessful efforts and support reallocation of funds to the best opportunities. Through the application of analytics, nonresponsive groups within the audience for existing marketing communications can be discovered and removed, providing a significant cost savings. The application of analytics will also facilitate the identification of smaller audiences for additional communications: repeatable opportunities such as cross-sell and upsell promotions, as well as unique, ad-hoc opportunities. Finally, the improvement in productivity provided by marketing automation will enable marketers to identify and exploit unique opportunities for new and existing customers.

All of these activities rely heavily on *marketing and customer information* that is accurate, consistent, timely, and easy to access. The following discussion addresses this fundamental component of marketing automation. The challenge for a marketing automation system is to store and manage a significant volume of source information on an ongoing basis, to make the information both accessible and easy to use, and to empower users to identify and act on relevant, actionable information.

CHAPTER 9

Relevant Marketing Automation Information

While the storage and maintenance of relevant information is a primary challenge, in fact it can be more difficult to complete the initial collection of relevant marketing information. This is because the information that marketing needs does not exist in the financial system alone, or in one database. Some of the information needs to be collected from the financial system, such as standard costs, other information needs to come from detailed customer records, and still other information needs to come from financial subsystems such as accounts payable. No single system will include all the information marketing needs, in the form and format that marketing requires.

FINANCIAL PROFIT AND LOSS INFORMATION

Recall the profit and loss (P&L) components from Part One: Revenue, Manufacturing Cost, Product Gross Margin, Marketing Expense, Overhead, and Profit. Recall, too, that the information had a time dimension consisting of Year and Month, and a Plan/Forecast/Actual dimension (which might be called "version"). Based on the value of information contributed by analysis of product cost information, a "product" dimension for the P&L would be a positive addition. As a "dimension" it can provide an incremental view for other dimensions (e.g., each product P&L could be viewed by month and year, current and prior years could be compared, and comparisons could be done similarly against Plan, Forecast and Actual).[1]

The information comprising the P&L is readily available to some level of detail. In fact it has to be—it is fundamental to the monthly business presentations that underlie the management of the business. An adaptable financial reporting system in fact can automate the generation of this content during the *closing period*[2] and free up financial analysts for the necessary analysis of the content, such as performance analysis to identify and explain variances to plan and forecast in sales and cost of sales. All of the earlier financial reports that were shown for OurCompany can be generated from such a financial reporting system.

Unfortunately, the same cannot be said for the level of reporting necessary to manage marketing expense. Existing financial systems are based on a dimension of "year and month." As noted in the footnote, the "monthly closing" literally closes the books on a month-by-month basis. Marketing investments—promotions—consistently span months, and year-end promotions will have an impact into the following fiscal year. The financial system can be used to identify sales by product—by month—and marketing expenses—by month—but the two will not necessarily relate to each other.

---

[1] The allocation of overhead by product can be both difficult and arbitrary, making the contributed value of the information less than the trouble and time spent in preparation. A more appropriate analysis of overhead is also a simpler one: Does the business generate sufficient total sales and gross profit to support the overhead expense? A reasonable target figure for overhead as a percent of net revenue could be 25%. The business will need to generate a proportional level of sales to cover, say, 50% manufacturing cost, 15% marketing, and 25% overhead, leaving 10% for profit: 100% Net Sales − 50% Manufacturing Cost − 15% Marketing − 25% Overhead = 10%.

[2] The closing period refers to the last few days of a fiscal period, typically a month or year, and the next several days to two weeks during which the financial figures relevant to the fiscal period are reviewed, revised, and finalized. "Closing" is a reference to "closing the books" for the period, meaning the figures are final, although revisions are still possible through "restatement." In times past, hardcopy ledgers would be produced on a daily or even twice-daily basis during the closing period, and relevant figures entered manually to Lotus and Excel spreadsheets by financial analysts for reporting results. Analysts frequently spent more time entering data than analyzing the import of the figures.

In other words, the marketing expense recorded in June will not relate to the sales generated in June. Marketing expense recorded in June may not realize a financial impact—sales—for one or more months following recognition in the financial system.

MARKETING INFORMATION GAPS

There are two areas where the financial reporting system can fail to have relevant marketing information available: marketing *project* cost and *sales attributable to a marketing investment*. The absence of this information must be resolved, as this information is necessary to manage marketing investment effectively.

ACCOUNTING SYSTEM GAP

A typical financial system will be organized by accounting entry: Sales, Cost of Sales, Cost of Sales by Product, and which fiscal period the value applies to. All accounting entries have a *timing* component. Other financial systems may include additional information, such as vendor information from the accounts payable system, and material cost from the inventory system. These costs will be recorded when the bills are presented by vendors, for example;[3] however, these costs will *not* necessarily relate to the marketing event itself, in either the timing or allocation.

Similarly, product shipments are recorded according to the timing of the shipment. Again, other accounting systems may contain incremental information—accounts receivable, for example, will record customer

---

[3]The cost will initially be recorded as a *liability* on the Balance Sheet; it represents money that is owed by the company to someone else, and is called a *payable*. Other liabilities include bank loans, mortgages, accrued salaries and bonus, and taxes. Accounting entries will be made to recognize the anticipated payment of the bill as an expense to ensure that the *timing of the event and the expense is consistent*. This does not imply the costs are recorded when the bill is paid. The bill requires approval for payment, and depending on the size of the bill several people including management may need to approve the payment. When the payment is actually made, the payable amount is eliminated, and the liability amount is reduced as well (the bill is paid; the company no longer owes the money).

information—but none of these systems will typically identify the marketing activity associated with the shipment.

Recorded Cost Timing Inconsistency

From a timing perspective, the recorded cost of marketing related activities will correspond to the vendor billing for delivery and receipt of the material or service. This may not be consistent with *when marketing delivers the final communication to a customer.* Worse, the recorded cost may not be recorded with sufficient information to relate the cost to a specific marketing event (e.g., a specific mailed promotion). The cost may represent *several* marketing activities or may not represent a complete marketing activity. Without sufficient cost detail recorded for marketing activities, specific marketing investments cannot be quantified. Without an agreed-upon value for the investment, the return cannot be measured based on the sales generated by subsequent customer purchases.

Marketing Expenses Lost in Overhead

Creative and marketing activities undertaken within the company are generally allocated and recorded as *overhead* expense, and will usually be found in the Departmental Expense detail. The cost will not be recorded based on what marketing projects creative and marketing people worked on in a given time period, such as specific promotions that may vary in complexity or amount of rework. Their "cost" (time) is recorded based simply on what department they are in. Since most are in the same department, and are in the same department during the course of the fiscal year, all of their costs—labor as well as materials—are lumped together, with no detail on the projects executed in the course of the year. As a result, internal creative design and development can be difficult or impossible to track as a nonrecurring development cost on a per-campaign and promotion basis.

It is at least conceivable for accounting to implement a project cost recording system that would enable project costs contained in overhead to be completely broken out according to the degree of attention individuals put into recording their costs consistently and accurately. The expected gain from this attention to detail has to be measured against the level of effort necessary to record the cost details and integrate the information into the financial system. A simple allocation of effort, an estimate of time and materials, may suffice for creating a reasonable picture of internal nonrecurring costs on a per-project basis.

VENDOR SERVICES LOST IN PAYABLES

Similarly, for vendor-related costs such as printing, letter-shop insertion, and postage expense for a direct mail campaign, these costs will be recorded by *vendor* in the accounts payable system and recorded as a marketing expense in the month the bill is presented, but details as to what campaign or promotion the expense was for will not be available or recorded. The specifics for the activity performed may also not be available, the bill being presented as a total. The nonrecurring and recurring cost components will then not be available for analysis, nor even the marketing activity behind the costs themselves. The bill may in fact collect costs for multiple projects, burying the detail that marketing needs.

ATTRIBUTING SALES AND REVENUE TO MARKETING ACTIVITIES

The same can be said for sales: The product sold will be recorded when it is shipped, but insufficient information will be available to identify what marketing vehicle may have prompted the purchase.

To make matters worse, the accounting system records sales by fiscal period: a month, a year. It does not recognize the almost arbitrary calendar timing of marketing expense and corresponding revenue. Campaign expenses billed in April will be expensed in April, while the revenue generated by the campaign may not appear in the financial system for a month or longer, and could continue to be recognized for several months after.

Just as problematic is the allocation of a "sale" to a marketing activity. In a typically broad marketing environment, how is a sale to be allocated for television, radio, newspaper, and similar nondirect promotions? How is the "sale credit" to be shared between the sales department, which may close the deal, and the marketing department, which created the product information and "presence" in the market? Both of these issues go to the core of investment return and how to justify the budget allocation or justify a change in the budget allocation.

To attribute revenue to marketing events will require a *separate* calculation of revenue based on *customer purchases and timing*. This will entail summarizing customer purchases based on which customers received what promotions over the period when the customer can be considered to be reasonably responding to a marketing promotion. The accounting system is not likely to provide this information.

In addition, because a separate effort will be required to calculate these sales, a reconciliation of the values must be made against the same values recorded in the accounting system, to ensure the marketing figures are consistent. Lost values and double-counted values must be prevented, and the best way to ensure all values are recognized is based on an effective reconciliation.

RETURN ON MARKETING INVESTMENT: TIMING OF CAMPAIGN EXECUTION COMPARED TO ACCOUNTING COST

The challenges for collecting marketing-relevant information on product sales and marketing expenses attributable to marketing activities must be overcome if the business is to achieve control over marketing activities and improve their effectiveness. Marketing expenses as well as revenue must be recorded in a financially accountable system that connects the expenses to the marketing-driven revenue. Expenses and revenue must continue to be related and recorded regardless of the length of time and fiscal period surrounding the marketing event. As seen in Exhibit 9.1, determination of the *return on marketing investment* (RMI) is based on a comparison of the costs and revenue for each marketing event (a campaign, an individual communication, a promotional event or activity), in order to generate the RMI figure. The RMI communicates the success or failure of the effort and demonstrates its value to the business. It bears no relation to accounting fiscal period.

RMI Calculation Example

A simple example will clarify how the RMI calculation depends on the ability to recognize the revenue and marketing costs from each campaign. Exhibit 9.1 shows how the expenses might be summarized from the financial

EXHIBIT 9.1   TIMING OF SALES AND COST OF SALES FOR RMI CALCULATION

Month	Cost		April	May				June				Total
Week				1	2	3	4	5	6	7	8	
							Revenue And Gross Profit					
Revenue												
Campaign 1				20	20	40	60	80	40	20		**280**
Campaign 2						40	60	100	80	20		**300**
Cumulative Sales				20	40	120	**240**	180	300	340		
Manufacturing Cost (50%)							**120**				**340** / **170**	
Gross Profit							**120**				**170**	
Marketing Cost												
Campaign 1	(24)	(32)										
Campaign 2	(31)	(37)										
Cumulative Total		(124)										

RMI Campaign 1 = (Total Revenue − Mfg Cost − Mktg Cost)/Mktg cost

RMI Campaign 1 = (280 −140 −56)/56:   150%

RMI Campaign 1 = (300 −150 −68)/68:   121%

system, by month and week within the month. Marketing costs for two campaigns are incurred in the final two weeks of April and noted in the lower-left columns. Revenue from these campaigns accrues over the next eight weeks, in May and June. Total revenue for Campaign 1 is 280; for Campaign 2 it is 300. For simplicity, manufacturing cost is 50% of revenue.

RMI is calculated as (Revenue − Cost)/Marketing Cost, where cost includes manufacturing and marketing components. For *Campaign 1,* this is (280 − 140 − 56)/56 or 150%. For *Campaign 2,* RMI is 121% ((300 − 150 − 68)/68). Both campaigns provide a positive and significant RMI.

However, from an accounting standpoint this assessment would be very difficult, if not impossible. To start with, the costs for marketing campaigns 1 and 2 are received in accounts payable in April and recorded as an expense in the accounting system for that month. The campaigns are initiated in May and revenues accumulate through June. Total revenue for Campaign 1 is 280 and for Campaign 2 is 300; however, the accounting system records total revenue for May of 240 and June of 340. *No relevant marketing expenses are recorded for either May or June.*

The accounting system has recognized the *relevant* marketing costs in the month of April, and recorded the total revenue in May and June as 240 and 340, respectively. Manufacturing cost here is 50% of revenue, so gross profit in May and June is 120 and 170. It is clear that the accounting system figures cannot be used at all to measure the RMI because of the timing difference in the recording of expense and revenue. It should also be clear that without a clear method to attribute RMI, the RMI calculation cannot be properly executed.

Hence it is vitally important to manage the P&L information in such a way that revenue can be attributed to marketing investments, and costs for marketing investments are retrievable in detail at the level of the marketing investment itself.

PROJECT-LEVEL COST IN ACCOUNTING

Collecting cost figures for marketing investments will require the cost accounting system to include a project-level cost collection ability or at least a project cost code. Government-funded projects traditionally have very detailed information available at the project level because the accounting system required for government projects is project cost based, to support cost and schedule monitoring of the use of government funds. Every direct hour and every dollar of materials is recorded using a "project–department–task" identification system. This is not necessarily the case for consumer and commercial company financial systems, particularly for internal project activities. These are frequently monitored using ad-hoc spreadsheets managed on personal computer workstations.

Payables Adaptation More Reliable than Spreadsheets

Collecting costs within the accounting system, such as through accounts payable, is much preferred over manual entry in personal spreadsheets. The costs are available by vendor and can be collected and summarized systematically and automatically, which reduces manual effort and improves accuracy, consistency, and availability throughout the company, particularly when compared with internal personal spreadsheets. The accounts payable system can be adapted to this purpose by introducing a project cost code to represent each marketing activity, and by asking vendors to submit all billings using the same cost code and to include costs at the component cost level, to ensure materials and outside service fees also respect the allocation of cost by project cost code. Relevant cost detail includes the separation of recurring costs from nonrecurring costs. Nonrecurring costs are one-time costs associated with the project, and not the cost of time and materials associated with each delivered promotion. Recurring costs are associated with media-based promotions, such as direct mail or email, and would include the cost for paper and postage on a per-promotion basis.

Marketing Cost Codes

The *marketing cost code* will become the cornerstone from which the collection of costs will be cumulated into a marketing cost allocation system. This code must identify the marketing project—a campaign, communication, activity—and the code must match sufficient descriptive information to identify what the activity was, what its goals were, the attributes of the audience, and the date of delivery.

Any cost that is available in the financial system that has this code attached to it will be available for a marketing RMI reporting system. This will not necessarily change the financial accounting system; it will simply enable marketing reports to be generated that summarize all related costs. These summaries can then be loaded into the marketing datamart, to facilitate the concentration of marketing-relevant information for online access as well as reporting.

REVENUE CODES FOR MARKETING

Similarly on the revenue side, marketing communications can be earmarked with a promotional code. Catalog marketers place these codes on the mailing label, and the code is requested and recorded when orders are made. The promotional code can clearly identify what marketing activity a customer is responding to. The promotional code is entered at the same time as the sale is recorded. The promotional code can then be mapped to the marketing cost code to accomplish the necessary mating of marketing revenue with marketing cost.

REVENUE ATTRIBUTION BASED ON TIMING OF SALE

Assuming a direct revenue tracking method is not available, the customer purchase activity can be summarized over the period a promotion can be considered active. The marketing cost code can be used to capture the sales summary by customer for direct relation to the marketing costs.

REVENUE ATTRIBUTION AND CONTACT HISTORY

In either circumstance, through the promotion code or attribution based on timing, the recipients of the communication or marketing activity must be recorded. Part of the marketing information to be collected and managed is the *contact history*, the record of which customers received what communications and when the promotion was delivered. This information will be used to facilitate the attribution of sales in specific time periods to specific activities, as well as for follow-up marketing communications. It also provides an important record of customer contacts over time.

Contact history will also be used to improve customer contact strategy by enabling management of customer contact activities. For example, audience selection can be influenced by desired contact frequency and contact channel. Competing offers to the same people can be eliminated by filtering mutually exclusive offers recorded in customer contact history. Communication redundancy and conflicting offers can be eliminated as well. Audiences for specific and targeted follow-up communications can be easily selected based on the record of prior communications. Response information can also be mated with contact history to provide response modeling information.

The collection of contact history over time (years) can create a massive volume of information. Large volumes of information can be difficult and time consuming to access, consume large online resources and time for storage as well as continual backup, and may contain a significant volume of irrelevant information. It is therefore important to understand what amount of information is relevant, what information can be summarized to be more useful, and how the remaining information can be archived to be retrievable (but not necessarily immediately).

Current information is relevant for collection and attribution of sales, analysis of response information, and avoidance of competing or conflicting offers. "Current" may apply to the previous six months or a year for these purposes. After a year, useful analysis can be done to determine the analytically relevant period for maintaining detailed contact information. For example, it may be demonstrated that a year of contact history is relevant for managing contact strategy and collecting sales information, while analysis of contacts and response demonstrates only the prior six months are relevant. This suggests that online maintenance of contact history could be limited to the prior 12 months. Every business will be different; some businesses may have much longer periods between purchases, in which case a year is too short a period.

The essential information for contact history includes:

- Recipient identification code (unique identifier for recipient)
- Promotion code (unique promotion identifier)
- Promotion wave code (for multiwave promotions)
- Promotion recurrence indicator (for recurring or repeated promotions)
- List pull date (when the list was generated)

The promotion code will enable identification of the recipient and the promotion. The promotion code will "map" to the table that maintains the promotion details. Promotion details are not appropriate to the contact history table[4]; this information would be the same for each recipient. A *relational database* excels at maintaining the relation between a table such as "Contact History," and the promotion details in a table such as "Promotion Information." This arrangement of information avoids the resource cost of having promotion information stored on every contact record in contact history. This approach also enables more detail to be maintained for each promotion, in a smaller and more easily maintained table.

Promotion information would include:

- Promotion purpose
- Promotion target audience size
- Actual audience size (the former is the expected or requested size)
- Audience description, required attributes
- Audience suppression attributes (attributes used to filter—reduce—the audience)
- Delivery date (when the list is due the vendor)
- List pull date (when the list is needed)
- Responsible marketing manager
- Media of delivery
- Description of offer or offers
- Description and sample (image) of media
- Expected nonrecurring cost
- Expected recurring cost
- Actual nonrecurring cost
- Actual recurring cost (with component details, such as paper, postage, insertion, delivery)

---

[4]There is an exception to this. Promotions that carry recipient-specific offers, for example, a mortgage rate calculated based on recipient-specific information, would require this promotion-specific information to be maintained. Contact history may be an appropriate place for recipient-specific offer information.

- Vendor and production information
- Test information

Promotions often will have multiple *groups* within the same promotion, for multiple offers or multiple test offers. In this case it may be appropriate to expand the promotion table to include a supplemental table of "Promotion Offers," which can include details for the individual offers or test offers. Alternatively, the promotion table could include a higher-level reference, such as "Campaign," with lower-level "Promotion" details:

CAMPAIGN	PROMOTION	OFFER	AUDIENCE	MEDIA	CREATIVE
Campaign 001	Promotion A		10% Off 10,000	Direct mail	AXYZ001
Campaign 001	Promotion B		15% Off 10,000	Direct mail	AXYZ002

Promotion information can be expanded further to contain summary response results, which could facilitate reporting, having all of the information in the same table, for example. However, it may be easier to evolve the promotion information if the table that contains it does not serve all purposes; it would be easier to maintain and easier to modify. The tables, it must be remembered, simply store the information. Reports are written to present the information, and reports can draw their data from multiple tables easily. How the data is stored is more a question for update, maintenance, and ease of modification.

PROMOTION RESPONSE INFORMATION

Response information is very important for managing analysis of customer response to contacts and initiating response-based promotions. Response information includes both direct and attributed response. Customers may respond directly or may be contacted directly, through telemarketing or customer service. Email response can be directly recorded through "open" and click-thru activity. Attribution of response may be appropriate and recorded through analysis of purchases. The essential information for response history includes the same information as contact history, in order to map back to the promotion that elicited the response, a response date, and a response code describing the type of response. Ideally it could include:

- Recipient identification code (unique identifier for recipient)
- Promotion code (unique promotion identifier)
- Promotion wave code (for multiwave promotions)
- Promotion recurrence indicator (for recurring, or repeated promotions)
- Response code (type of response)
- Response date
- Response value

The response information is recorded only for actual responses; an entry in the "Promotions" table with no corresponding entry in the "Response" table is the same as "no response."

The response code references the many types of response possible: For direct mail, "Purchase," "Cancellation" may be appropriate; for telemarketing, it might be "No Answer," "Bad Number," "Recipient Not Available," "Do-Not-Call Request," "Purchase." To expand on "Purchase," a *purchase code* could be added for additional clarity. The corresponding "Purchase Code" table would contain the descriptive information appropriate to the purchase code.

Adding "response value" to the table is problematic for maintenance. The customer may make an initial purchase, which is duly recorded in "Response History," and then subsequently return the purchase. "Purchase value" may describe more than one item, which means more than one sales transaction will need to be addressed in maintaining the "real value" of the field.

This issue is also at the root of the sales attribution process. Tracking the sales for multiple, overlapping promotions could make use of additional sales entry information, differentiating "telemarketing sales" from "customer service sales" or "direct sales." The marketing attribution code can be recorded with each sales entry to further aid in differentiating response.

The preceding discussion still leaves the maintenance issue for response history open. Promotions that are well received, generating high sales, would expect to be repeated in the future, but not if returns or customer cancellation rates are much greater than average. To prevent this, and to learn more about the true effectiveness of marketing communications, requires a realistic record of response. To facilitate maintenance, additional fields can be added for updating results and the updates can be performed weekly. Instead of recording just "response code" and "response date," additional fields can be added:

- Follow-up response value
- Follow-up date
- Return flag
- Cancellation flag

In this way the initial response is captured and a record of "actual" or "follow-up response" is established. If maintained through weekly updates, the system overhead for updates is minimized. The use of a *return flag* makes reporting easier, and "initial response" can be compared with "follow-up response" to ensure the response is not overstated.

MARKETING RMI DETAILED REPORT

Having separate contact and response history managed at the customer level, combined with detailed cost information, will facilitate summarization of marketing activities and analysis of the effectiveness of each marketing activity.

For example, as seen in Exhibit 9.2 from the customer sales detail, a summary is done using the promotion codes, and a similar summary is done for marketing costs. These summary values can now combine into the marketing RMI report.

The second column, labeled "CommID," contains the marketing *communication code*, in this case "Comm001," a very simple example. This marketing code is used to relate the cost and sales information for this communication. The marketing promotion information relevant to Comm001 will include a *name*, which in this example is called "Communication A," and additional descriptive information discussed in "Additional Marketing Information" (below).

The details included in this report are campaign volume (number of people promoted), the nonrecurring and recurring costs, recurring cost details for media, postage, and insertion, the volume of orders and sales, average order

EXHIBIT 9.2   DETAILED RMI REPORT FIELDS

Communication	CommID	Volume	Offer	Non Recurring Act/CPM	Media Act/CPM	Postage Act/CPM	Insertion Act/CPM	Total Campaign Cost/CPM	Orders / OPM	Sales/ SPM	Avg Order	Net Profit / PPM	RMI
Communication A	Comm001	1,234,000	OfferA	9,519	185,100	283,820	86,380	564,819	61,700	1,727,600	28	271,339	48%
				7.71	150.00	230.00	70.00	458	50	1,400		220	

EXHIBIT 9.3   COMPARING RMI FOR MULTIPLE COMMUNICATIONS

Communication	CommID	Volume	Offer	Non Recurring Act/CPM	Media Act/CPM	Postage Act/CPM	Insertion Act/CPM	Total Campaign Cost/CPM	Orders / OPM	Sales/ SPM	Avg Order	Net Profit / PPM	RMI
Communication A	Comm001	1,234,000	OfferA	9,519	185,100	283,820	86,380	564,819	61,700	1,727,600	28	271,339	48%
				7.71	150.00	230.00	70.00	458	50	1,400		220	
Communication B	Comm002	2,045,000	OfferA	13,958	251,535	470,350	143,150	878,993	75,665	2,042,955	27	109,798	12%
				6.83	123.00	230.00	70.00	430	37	999		54	
Communication C	Comm003	462,000	OfferA	12,417	169,554	900,900	97,020	1,179,891	55,440	1995,840	36	(213,904)	−18%
				26.88	367.00	1950.00	210.00	2,554	120	4,320		(463)	
Communication D	Comm004	873,004	OfferA	8,656	272,376	960,300	157,140	1,398,472	279,360	8,939,520	32	2,928,256	209%
				9.91	312.00	1100.00	180.00	1,602	320	10,240		3,354	
Total Direct Mail		**4,614,000**		44,549	878,565	2,615,370	483,690	4,022,174	472,165	14,705,915	31	3,095,489	**77%**
				9.66	312.00	566.83	104.83	**872**	102	3,187		**671**	

size, net profit, and RMI. Most of the figures are also re-presented in "per thousand" (CPM) terms. Nonrecurring costs, for example, are $7.71 per thousand, and total campaign costs are $458.00 per thousand. The promotion generated sales per thousand of 1,400, and a net profit of $220 per thousand (after marketing costs). The RMI is 48%.

This information is collected and managed for each marketing communication, and would continue to be managed for at least several years. Historical information can be used for prior-year comparisons of large individual promotions, channel performance, allocation of marketing expense by channel (channel usage), customer response, and RMI trends. A fundamental question would be, Does it cost more every year to generate the same response?

The cost-per-thousand figures become appropriately relevant when these comparisons are made between channels, years, and promotions. Individual communications can be both summarized and compared (see Exhibit 9.3).

In this example, 4.6 million pieces were mailed; in total, the sales per thousand was $3,187, and overall RMI was 77%. Behind the very reasonable *total* RMI, there is a big winner and a big loser: Comm004's return was a substantial 209%, driven by a very high $10,240 sales per thousand, while Comm003 generated a loss, in part due to the *total cost* (CPM) of $2,554, nearly double that of Comm004. Revenue was also not very high for Comm003; it generated only $4,320 per thousand. Assuming 50% gross margin, it is easy to calculate that this campaign in fact lost money:

$$\$4,320 \text{ Revenue} \times 50\% \text{ Margin} = \$2,160 \text{ Gross Profit} - \$2,554$$
$$\text{Campaign Cost} = -\$394 \text{ Net Profit}$$

[−$394 PPM is an acceptable *estimate*, a good practice to confirm the magnitude of reported figures is correct. The figure in the report, −$463 PPM, differs from the estimate, based on a calculation for returns (12%) and a 45% manufacturing cost.]

The addition of the "media type" to the information collected by promotion enables a view of performance by media type and a hierarchical presentation of all marketing activity. This hierarchical approach to cost and revenue collection enables direct comparisons among media-based promotions (Exhibit 9.4).

EXHIBIT 9.4   SUMMARIZING RMI RESULTS BY CHANNEL

$000	Marketing Cost	Contacts	Response Rate	Units	Sales	Profit	Price	Margin/ Order	Cost/ Contact	Profit Contact
Direct Mail	250	250	10%	100	2,000	50	20.00	32.00	1.00	0.20
Telemarketing	250	150	20%	80	2,000	50	25.00	25.33	1.67	0.33

COMPARISON TO DIFFERENT TIME PERIODS: PRIOR YEAR, SAME TIME

The marketing activity code can be further related to a hierarchical system, which in turn can support high levels of summarization to better manage the business. For example, the time element from the code can be used to summarize month-to-month activity such as June campaigns and April email communications. Year-over-year comparisons can be generated, such as March new-product showcase compared to March prior year or even March of the year prior to that. These reports and comparisons can and should include all relevant statistics, including cost, revenue, CPM, and PPM as well as RMI.

HIERARCHICAL ANALYSIS YEAR OVER YEAR

The hierarchical reporting will facilitate very useful analysis based on year-over-year activity and provide management with real and actionable information. The summary provided by the hierarchical organization supports both the knowledge derived from the summary content as well as the detail necessary to initiate action.

DETAIL IS CHALLENGING

As noted at the outset of this chapter, creating this level of detail at the marketing communication level can be very challenging. The systems themselves are not challenged by the volume of the information; in fact the volume for even a large marketing effort in a large organization is trivial compared to the volume of information to be maintained on a customer basis (thousands or tens of thousands of records compared to tens of millions for customer information). The challenge is finding the best source of the information, allocating the information to a marketing activity through application of a marketing cost or project code, and automating the retrieval into the marketing financial reporting system.

Adding the dimension of Plan and Forecast for the same information at nearly the same level of detail is similarly challenging, with the added factor that this information represents individual commitments for the current or upcoming year. Such commitments are fixed through estimates exchanged by emails and based on informal, albeit sometimes elaborate spreadsheets. Incorporating this haphazard collection of information into a database for ongoing reporting requires time, persistence, and organization.

One of the advantages provided by an effective collection of "actual" marketing financial information is the ability to then apply this information in developing the Plan or Forecast for the upcoming year *at the same level of detail*. The ability to summarize the actual information on different dimensions can be directly applied to the planning process. Prior-year information can be summarized at the channel level and used as the basis for deciding on the allocation of expenses by channel in the following year's plan. An assessment of "major" and "minor" marketing activities can be selected, summarized, and find use as a template for planning the following year. The "actual" information will be complete to the cost and response information. These factors can be *generalized* for the upcoming year, to establish expectations, or modified consistent with changing expectations: Costs may be higher or lower, revenue goals may be higher or lower, and response higher or lower. The prior-year information provides a firm foundation for expectations and a ready-made reporting framework for moving forward.

Increasing the level of detail for Plan and Forecast down to the *individual campaign* can be time consuming to develop and not necessarily effective relative to the time required to develop it. Plan and Forecast information can be used to establish targets at higher levels in the hierarchy. These generalized targets become the basis for comparison of individual marketing activities, instead of a Plan and Forecast for each individual marketing activity. Individual marketing opportunities can then be represented in the plan or forecast at a proxy or summary level, and summary values can be used to estimate costs by channel.

When establishing actual campaign implementation details, marketing allocates a budget and records expectations for response and revenue consistent with the proxy figures used in the plan. These values will in turn be merged with the Forecast to enable a summary from the bottom up. The additional information is collected through the marketing automation system when the marketing activities are planned and available for comparison following execution. This ensures that individual promotion performance is compared consistent with expectations established and formalized in the Plan or Forecast.

SCENARIO DEVELOPMENT WITH STANDARD COSTS

A second layer of detail could be considered that would further analysis and management understanding of the effects of changing business conditions. This layer of detail involves the ability to implement different cost or pricing profiles as plan assumptions. By changing the profile and recalculating the cumulative plan for expense, revenue, and profit, the effect of these changes in assumptions is immediately visible and its impact can be assessed.

This is not "sensitivity analysis" (e.g., "What happens to demand if I increase prices 10%?"); this is only to assess the financial impact of a 10% increase in prices or a 10% decline in demand. An interesting comparison is a current plan cast in prior-year-cost terms. Such a comparison identifies the proportional variance contributed by changes in plan costs over the prior year, the cumulative effect on profit of a change in costs alone. If the marketing management system is designed in a way that facilitates separation of unit volume, cost, and price information into a managed profile, values can be substituted for each in order to build Forecast and Plan scenarios based on different cost and pricing assumptions.

Initially, Plan and Forecast include actuals or assumptions for cost and pricing that obviously influence the results. The addition of cost and pricing assumptions based on Current Year and Prior Year Actual, Plan, and Forecast would enable comparisons such as Current Actuals using Prior Year Cost assumptions, or Current Year Actuals using Plan Cost assumptions, and the reverse, Current Year Plan using Actual Cost assumptions. The latter is usually fundamental to an effective forecast. A system that can support the interchange of cost as well as pricing assumptions can provide management further understanding of the changes in business conditions that are influencing business results as well as the impact of business condition *assumptions* that are influencing *expectations* for results.

Why Information Is Important

While the collection and management of this information is time consuming and challenging, it is nonetheless important to the effective management of the business. The goal is to improve the ability of marketers to understand variances in the response to marketing promotions on a per-campaign basis, over the life of the campaign. Visibility is extended to the impact of these variances on the business in the context of an annual plan. The goal is to motivate a reaction to changes and trends that offer new opportunities and challenges in managing marketing activities toward *achieving the business plan*.

Changes and trends are recognized by comparison of *actual* activity—Response, Revenue, and Costs—to expectations, and expectations are captured in the Plan and Forecast. To align expectations close to reality, the marketing financial information should be used to build a better business plan and forecast.

Comparing prior year with current actual performance also may highlight trends in costs or revenue. The earlier question, Does it cost more to generate the same response this year? can be asked and answered on a monthly basis, which improves management's knowledge of business conditions and the relative effectiveness of each marketing dollar investment in generating customer knowledge and response. It may not be individual sales and costs that challenge the business, but the cumulative and combined effect of changes in volume, prices, and cost components over time relative to expectations.

Additional Marketing Information

To review, the additional marketing information to be captured through the marketing automation system, outside of the financial system information, includes:

- Responsible people: marketing manager, creative manager, primary vendors
- Marketing cost codes: the codes required for collection of costs and revenue
- Promotion codes: the codes to be used in a promotional vehicle for response tracking

- Pricing and volume discounts: description of offers to be made that affect the price level
- Start and end date for audience selection: the period when the recipients for the activity will be selected
- Start and end date for sales activity: the period when sales are expected and attributed to the promotion
- Media: the promotional media used
- Creative copy: reference to the creative used in the marketing presentation (PDF copies)
- Audience selection criteria: who should be selected
- Audience suppression criteria: who should be rejected from selection
- Expected recipients: the total audience
- Expected nonrecurring cost, including list cost
- Expected net percentage (if using outside lists)
- Expected recurring costs and their components
- Expected purchase response: the volume of responders
- Expected order size: the number of units and value, or units and total value, based on average price
- Expected attrition response
- Expected response based on media specifics: email open rates, telemarketing bad-number rates
- Expected response in terms of number of responders, or a percentage
- Expected value of response
- Expectations for negative responses: cancellations, returns, opt-out requests

Much of this information is known and often exchanged in meetings and through email, as well as embedded in spreadsheets and marketing documents. This creates opportunity for multiple values for the same promotion, for more than one "version of the truth." Marketing automation can facilitate the systematic collection by providing a shared system-based focal point for entry when the marketing activity is defined. All contributors can record relevant information individually in the same place, and all contributors can look in one place to find out who the participants are and who is responsible for what information. Information collected through a marketing automation system can be extracted and embedded in reports for distribution, discussion, and agreement. Discussion will be able to focus on results rather than which number is the correct one.

At the same time, marketing automation provides the vehicle for generating the audience itself based on the definition of the selection attributes, to be discussed in Chapter 16. One system and one location can be used for defining the relevant information for the marketing audience and the expected results for the marketing campaign. Reports can be developed to surface this information in detail and summary form, forming the basis for near-term expectations. As actual information materializes, the same reports can be supplemented to demonstrate how the actual activity met with expectations.

CHAPTER 10

Financial and Marketing Information Integration

So far, the discussion has begun with the financial P&L, a collection of monthly and yearly financial performance information, and continued with an identification of the gaps in financial data and the corresponding need for a marketing financial information system, as well as the ability of such a system to support marketing planning moving forward, using as a basis the actual cost and revenue information collected and summarized from the financial system and copied to the marketing system.

This comes full circle: There is now a need to incorporate the marketing financial planning information into the *official* financial Business Plan, which is cast in a rigid monthly timeline. The P&L is based on fiscal periods (months, quarters, and years), while marketing activities exist over periods specific to campaigns, which will cross months as well as years, with the same assumption included in the *marketing financial plan*. This makes direct integration of marketing financials with the financial system challenging.

For marketing cost information, financial managers can pick up the actual monthly costs and massage these values into a Plan or Forecast. As noted, much of the nonrecurring internal marketing costs are captured in the departmental expenses. Use of outside services is similarly captured in the actual costs attributed to the marketing department or marketing activities.

The greater challenge is recognizing the timing effect on revenue attributed to marketing activities, and incorporating the revenue impact of promotional activities in the proper months. This will also involve allocating a suitable amount from the prior year to the current year, for marketing activities crossing from prior to current year, and the same for promotions that generate some revenue in the current year and the balance in the following year.

The allocation is based on an understanding of how customers react to promotions, and how their responses take place over time. A November campaign initiated early in the month and generating revenue for eight weeks might be expected to net the bulk of the gain in the fiscal year ending in December. The same campaign initiated in December might see 50% of the revenue in the current fiscal year, and 50% in the following fiscal year.

Depending on the variance in campaign revenue timing, it may also be reasonable to apply a revenue curve: Some campaigns may not generate constant revenue over their life. It may be more reasonable to expect revenue accumulation to be skewed earlier in the campaign cycle. It would be less reasonable to expect a constant flow of units every week for 9 weeks, for example (see Exhibit 10.1).

By comparison, the following result might be more consistent with expectations (see Exhibit 10.2). Unit sales begin at a fairly low level, 1,000 units in the first observation period, then 2,000 and 4,000, reaching a maximum of 11,000 units after 2.5 weeks, and falling gradually to little or no sales at all after 9 weeks.

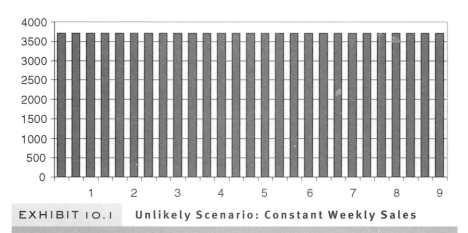

Sales Units Per Week

EXHIBIT 10.1   Unlikely Scenario: Constant Weekly Sales

Sales Units Per Week

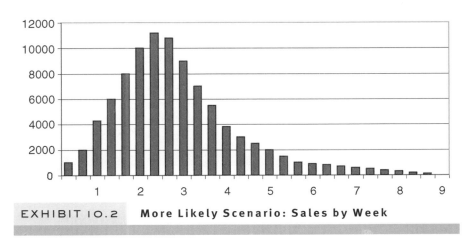

EXHIBIT 10.2   More Likely Scenario: Sales by Week

Daily units sold can be transformed to cumulative units for the promotion by week (see Exhibit 10.3).

In Exhibit 10.4, you can see that this can be easily translated to a percent complete by week.

Of significance for planning purposes, nearly 70% of the promotion sales have been recognized by the third week of the promotion, and over 90% by the fifth week. In this case, similar campaigns for OurCompany initiated in

Cumulative Sales Units Per Week

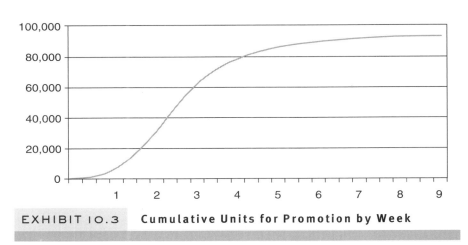

EXHIBIT 10.3   Cumulative Units for Promotion by Week

Promotion Percent Complete By Week

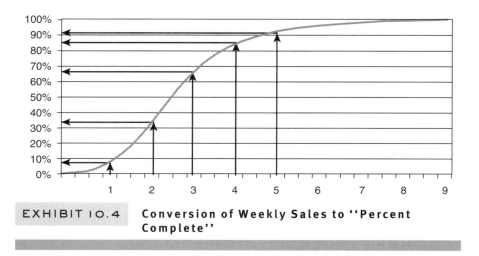

EXHIBIT 10.4   **Conversion of Weekly Sales to "Percent Complete"**

the final month of the fiscal year would prudently recognize 70% of the expected sales (or a more conservative 60%) in the fiscal year plan and the balance in the following year, to avoid overstating the plan in the final month of the year.

BENEFITS OF INTEGRATION

The creation of detailed and hierarchical marketing information for campaign results suggests useful application to financial planning. Year-over-year comparison of campaign results may point to changes in the effectiveness of the marketing mix. Year-over-year comparison may facilitate analysis of substantial changes to the mix and their potential impact on customer response. Two obvious examples are the legislation introduced to restrict telemarketing and the introduction of Internet marketing.

Knowing the budget allocation and results for telemarketing provides a direct planning assessment of the impact of new limits imposed on telemarketing. Similarly the allocation of budget and analysis of results of Internet marketing provide a real and tangible measure of this channel's revenue contribution to the Plan.

If the timing of response and revenue by campaign is known, then the assessment of year-end impact for Plan can be more precisely determined. If a late-year campaign is known to generate 60% of sales in the first 30 days, then the P&L plan can be adjusted accordingly, to reflect an expected 60% increase for the year or month of execution, while managing the impact of the remaining 40% to the following month, a new financial year.

Taking this point further, when the timing of results by week is known for the duration of the campaign, the impact of changes in the timing of execution can be assessed compared to expectations based on Plan. As shown in Exhibit 10.4, a one-week delay in execution could cut revenue results by a substantial amount in a current month or year. A business plan that assumes three weeks' revenue from a late-year campaign, or 65% of total sales, will lose nearly half that amount based on a one-week delay and only two weeks of sales. Although sales may just move to the next time period and not literally be lost, recall that financial results respect rigid calendar boundaries, and management is rewarded based on achieving these timebound goals. Knowing the timing of marketing-driven sales also highlights the positive benefit of delivering the campaign early instead of late.

Having Options

A marketer who knows how customers respond to different types of marketing promotions delivered through different channels is able to assess alternative actions when events conspire to challenge achievement of the financial plan. If a year-end campaign is unavoidably delayed, and the delay is known far enough in advance, the pending financial impact can be assessed and alternative one-time promotions inserted to make up the difference. Knowing the cost and benefits of alternatives based on recent actual experience reduces the uncertainty surrounding potential alternative marketing actions and improves management's ability to achieve results consistent with the Plan or Forecast goals.

Knowledge of the timing of marketing activities can also be used to address fluctuations in monthly activity. Analysis of the product mix behind the July P&L for OurCompany (Chapter 3) highlighted the shortfall in sales attributed to Product B, which largely explained the sales revenue and profit shortfall for the month. In the same way, knowledge of the timing of sales response to individual marketing activities provides visibility into sales fluctuations between months, as shown in the next example.

IMPACT OF MARKETING TIMING AND REVENUE VARIANCE

Marketing mix and timing can be analyzed to further an understanding of revenue fluctuations month to month. Take, for example, the sales by week generated by two marketing campaigns shown in Exhibit 10.5. Total sales for May are $240 and for June are $340. Both campaigns generate revenue in both months.

Assume Campaign 2 moves out a week due to a delay in executing the campaign. Campaign 2 has sales of $60 for the last week of May. If this campaign moves out a week, sales for May will decline by $60 or 25%, while sales for June will increase by $60 or almost 18% (17.65%). If this change were compounded by late timing in execution of Campaign 1 the effect would be even more negative for May's results: The decline would total $120, 50% of the total for May, as shown in Exhibit 10.6.

The analysis of campaign results extends to understanding variance in results by campaign. Assume a third campaign has unexpectedly good results in June, a campaign that parallels Campaign 2 due to a production timing issue in execution (see Exhibit 10.7). The *expected* results for Campaign 2

Month		May				June			Total
Week	1	2	3	4	5	6	7	8	
Campaign 1	20	20	40	60	80	40	20		280
Campaign 2	0	0	40	60	100	80	20		300
Total Sales	20	20	80	120	180	120	40	0	
Cumulative Sales May	20	40	120	240					
Cumulative Sales June					180	300	340	340	

EXHIBIT 10.5   Campaign Comparison for Revenue Timing

Month		May				June			Total
Week	1	2	3	4	5	6	7	8	
Campaign 1 (late 1 week)	0	20	20	80	60	80	40	20	260
Campaign 2 (late 1 week)			0	40	60	100	80	20	300
Total Sales	0	20	20	80	120	180	80	20	
Cumulative Sales May	0	40	40	120					
Cumulative Sales June					180	260	100	320	

EXHIBIT 10.6   Campaign Comparison for Revenue Timing: Offsetting results between Campaigns

Month	May				June				Total
Week	1	2	3	4	5	6	7	8	
Campaign 1	0	20	20	40	60	80	40		260
Campaign 2			0	40	40	60	20	0	160
Campaign 3				20	40	60	50	20	190
Total Sales	0	20	20	100	140	200	110	20	
Cumulative Sales May	0	20	40	140					
Cumulative Sales June					140	340	450	470	

EXHIBIT 10.7   **Campaign Comparison for Revenue Timing: Inter-Campaign Cannibalization**

were $200 in June. The one-week delay in execution raised expectations to $260 for June. June results for Campaign 2 are now $120, while Campaign 3 generated $170 in revenue (June). Why did revenue for Campaign 2 fall so far from expectations?

Campaign 3 suppressed or *cannibalized* sales for Campaign 2, causing the decline from an expected $260 to $120. The gain of $170 for Campaign 3 therefore nets to $30 when adjusted for the cannibalization of sales for Campaign 2. Campaign 1 is not affected because its presence was established far enough in advance of Campaign 3.

The ability to analyze campaign performance in the context of month-to-month financial results provides a valuable contribution to management's ability to understand business results and take appropriate action. In the example of Exhibit 10.7, improving adherence to campaign timetables can prevent avoidable sales cannibalization between parallel marketing actions.

CHAPTER 11

Marketing Customer Information

Exploiting customer information for marketing is vitally important but involves significant resources and management challenges in its collection, maintenance, security, and access for marketers. Even moderately sized businesses addressing 5 to 10 million customers can find the maintenance and security responsibility to be expensive if not overwhelming. As a result, the information can be difficult to access or simply unavailable for marketing.

Previously, acquiring and maintaining useful customer information may have been the greatest challenge; today the greatest challenge may be security of the information. Online hacking of customer databases has been publicized for some time. Recent news has highlighted exceptional security lapses at various companies and the U.S. government, including cases where customer lists have found their way to laptops, which in turn are stolen. At least one case has been prosecuted involving the deliberate and illegal acquisition of millions of customer names and addresses.[1]

These challenges must be addressed and overcome, as customer information plays the key role in developing successful analytically based marketing. At one time this would involve a six- or seven-figure investment in internal hardware and information support infrastructure,[2] but hardware resource costs have

---

[1] An online advertiser was charged on July 23, 2004 in the theft of "billions of records" from Acxiom. He was convicted and sentenced to eight years in prison on February 22, 2006. See article (July 24, 2004) in *Computerworld*.

[2] A data warehouse project in the early 1990s involved an investment of several million dollars. A second project, in 1998, included $300,000 in hardware and $150,000 in software, in the first year. Subsequent investments over the next several years included additional disk space and controllers, and over $100,000 in ongoing investment in software development for additional functionality.

declined dramatically in the past five to ten years. During this time there has also been an increase in the availability of hosting services, companies that manage customer information on a fee basis using their hardware and information technology (IT) infrastructure. Hence the cost of at least some of the resources required for storage and retrieval has declined significantly.

Customer information will include current as well as past customers, their contact information (name and address, phone number, email address), their transaction and payment history, their customer support contact information, their willingness to receive marketing communications (opt in and opt out), estimates for response and purchase likelihood (model scores), credit rating and credit history, and their acquisition source (how they became customers, the marketing acquisition communication code), as well as distinctly marketing information such as geographic segment, demographic segment, and marketing segment.

Customer information will also include *contact history*, a record of what communications or marketing activities have been delivered, including the date, the vehicle, the communications code that identifies the specific communication itself, and the response. This type of information will accumulate over time, becoming increasingly difficult to manage as well as apply. Some research[3] has demonstrated that older contact and response information loses relevance over time to present marketing activities. Therefore customer contact information can in fact become more manageable with repeated archiving or purging activities.

Finally, some of the more relevant information will involve *postprocessing* purchase activity, summarizing historical purchase activity by product, timing (recency and frequency), purchase size, and "market basket," the identification of products purchased as a group. This type of information is periodically updated and expanded over time, providing valuable source information for modeling response and developing "likelihood to respond" scores. As noted in Chapter 8, this information comes under the general reference of customer purchase *recency, frequency and monetary value* (RFM) information.

Summarizing this information improves the accessibility, by enabling query activity to ignore millions of sales transactions or millions of

---

[3]A research case on contact history data demonstrated that the prior nine contacts and responses were relevant for analytical modeling of customer response.

communication codes in contact history and response history, in favor of summarized measures of purchases, contacts, and responses. The summary information then becomes part of the customer information.

Further detail on specific customer information dimensions follows. In some cases, existing customer information and its physical representation (in a database) are simply extended by incremental or derived attributes, such as "Total Purchases." In other cases, information such as contact history can be maintained with the addition of one or more database tables. In the case of test information and analytical information particularly, the incremental tables containing the test and analytical customer information may be contained in separate databases known as *datamarts*.

SUMMARIZING CUSTOMER INFORMATION, RESPONSE, AND CONTACT HISTORY

To improve the utility of customer information, contact, response, and purchase information can be summarized in different ways. For example, the following measures improve access to relevant information for current and future marketing activities:

- Cumulative purchases, returns, and payments since acquisition, the customer's first purchase
- Purchases, returns, and payments in the last 30, 60, 90, 180, 360 days[4]
- Total contacts in the last 30, 60, 90, 180, 360 days

---

[4]The "day durations" specified here are common and recognizable given no other information to determine a more relevant window. Additional time durations can be derived from analysis of purchase activity. For example, some customers may show weaker response activity when their inactivity extends beyond "211 days" (an equally arbitrary time frame, but one chosen by analysis). An appropriate indicator—an attribute of customer information—for marketing use would then be a positive flag (database field or column) for "No Purchase in 211 Days." By managing this summary field in a database, marketers can quickly access these customers for special promotion: "Select all customers where 'No Purchase in 211 Days' = 1." The customer list can be selected quickly without having to repeatedly analyze sales transactions to determine who meets this attribute.

- Total contacts by email, mail, telemarketing, or sales in the last 30, 60, 90, 180, 360 days
- Total responses in the last 30, 60, 90, 180, 360 days
- Total responses by email, mail, telemarketing, or sales in the last 30, 60, 90, 180, 360 days
- Individual contacts in the past 30, 60, 90, 180 days, as well as contact by channel
- Individual responses in the past 30, 60, 90, 180 days
- Cumulative market mix indicators (variety of products purchased)
- Market mix indicators in the past 30, 60, 90, 180, 360 days, for specific or cumulative orders in the same period
- Customer ranking relative to other customers (top 3%, 5%, 10%; bottom 30%, 20%, 10%)
- Customer ranking relative to other customers with the same or similar demographic profile (urban top 3%, 5%, 10%; bottom 30%, 20%, 10%)

Summary measures such as these can be developed specific to the business and maintained as incremental customer attributes. The list can be expanded based on the relevance to ongoing marketing activities.

The process of acquiring and massaging customer information is an ongoing one, and some of the information may not demonstrate immediate relevance for action for some or even many customers. Further analysis or refinement may be required to generate relevant uses for marketing, and, as marketing expands the effort to generate incremental sales, new ways to entice response from customers will be accompanied by opportunities to generate new information about customers. As progress is made in the analytical information area, new indicators, field combinations, and scores will evolve. As always, the cost of *not* having the information available is an opportunity cost for ongoing incremental sales.

ANALYSIS OF CUSTOMER INFORMATION

Compiling summary measures of customer information and relating these to sales by customer segment can be very useful in determining some of the obvious and significant marketing goals:

- Pareto principle: What proportion of my customers contributes 80% of sales?

- Best customers: What proportion of sales is generated by the top 5% customers?

- Worst customers: What proportion of customers contributes less than 5% of sales?

Sales and response figures by such customer segment can be used to analyze trends in response over time. Declining response by specific segments may underlie declining sales over time, and may also signal declining marketing effectiveness to these segments. Early identification of declining sales by segment suggests marketing opportunities for tangible remedial action: new promotions to reactivate newly inactive customers.

Identification of the segments relevant and important to the business provides another financial view of marketing effectiveness. The performance of these segments can be monitored, relative to their corresponding share of the marketing investment as well as their share of the business revenue.

INTEGRATION OF CUSTOMER INFORMATION WITH MARKETING AND FINANCIAL INFORMATION

The composition of sales by customer and customer attributes such as segments provides an important view of sales from a customer standpoint. In the same way that sales attributed to marketing activities can be measured, sales attributed to customers and customer segments can be measured and applied to analysis of sales variance as well as planning. Customer information provides another dimension to sales activity. A sales decline attributed to product A may have less to do with product A's attributes and more to do with the customers no longer purchasing product A. A customer segment may be declining in volume, reduced by competition or attrition, both of which could be attributed to ineffective marketing.

TEST INFORMATION

When a business is in a position to track results to marketing activities at the customer level, it is in a position to test marketing ideas against smaller populations and identify both strong and weak opportunities at nominal risk and investment. Within the organization of campaign marketing information, test promotions should appear similar to any other marketing activity so that comparisons can be made between promotions.

The test populations themselves will need to be uniquely identifiable to prevent contamination from opposing or complementary and parallel (simultaneous) promotions. For a test to be successful, the populations in the test groups must be similarly chosen and the test itself consistently presented. A test population that does not receive consistent marketing communications will be contaminated and results will be inconsistent if not unusable.

Further detail for testing is included in the discussion on *test design* in Chapter 17. For now it must be recognized that a method for identifying test recipients must be defined. The method chosen must adapt to both one-time test promotions and long-term test promotions. A customer life-cycle test could attempt to evaluate the effectiveness of a specific sequence of promotions over a three-month, six-month, or even year-long period of time. During that time, the populations under test must be identifiable and excluded from competing—contaminating—promotions.

Since customers and customer information evolve over time, and summary measures are updated, a method of capturing a snapshot of customer state and status at the initiation of the test must be developed. Analysis of results for future application will entail determination of the characteristics of responders that are unique (different from those of nonresponders). Characteristics that can change over time will need to be captured as a snapshot and maintained for the duration of the test period, until analysis is complete. As a note of caution, the maintenance period—the time for holding the snapshot information—could be longer in order to support repeated analysis for contested or difficult-to-understand results. Some results may be immediately obvious; some results may require repeated attempts at analysis to make them meaningful.

ANALYTICAL CUSTOMER INFORMATION

The term *analytics* in marketing automation properly refers to the software functions associated with statistical analysis of customer response. This analysis is done in the process of developing models of customer response, likelihood to attrite, product preferences, contact preferences, and similar predictive attributes. The models are expected to improve response rates by identifying customers more likely to respond to classes of promotions or channels more likely to generate a response. Improving response rates means higher profits through more targeted communications.

In that sense, analytics is fundamental to marketing automation. A successful analytical effort can be the driver behind a successful marketing automation investment. The application of analytics depends on having useful differentiating attributes by customer, attributes that are also associated with response and nonresponse to marketing promotions. These differentiating attributes may or may not be associated with causation; they may or may not explain *why* some people responded to a promotion while others did not. For example, gender-specific marketing intuitively *should* elicit a different response level from men compared to women, even though the products themselves may appeal equally to both. However, for modeling purposes, the connection to causation is largely irrelevant. It would be nice if analytical variables associated with higher and lower customer response had meaning for marketing, if they would shed light on why a particular promotion was more or less successful. But it is not necessary for the development of the model or the application of the model results (the score).

Some analytical information can be derived from existing customer attributes, as well as combined attributes. Some models involve extraordinary manipulation of these basic attributes as well as the recombined attributes. The manipulation is referred to as *transformation*. Some basic transformations can involve a *standardization* calculation, designed to improve the utility of the attribute in modeling. That means model results are better—the score is more predictive—when the standardized value is used, rather than with the nonstandard, actual value.

Some attributes may not initially lend themselves to the application of analytics. In these cases, the attribute measures can be transformed to improve the strength of association to better predict responders from nonresponders. For example, customers can be grouped into categories such as High, Medium, and Low based on a cumulative sales measure. Analytics can be used to determine the breakpoints between groups, the level of sales where a person is moved to the High group from the Medium group.

Analytics can also be used to determine better breakpoints between groups where distributions are uneven. A marketing test could be

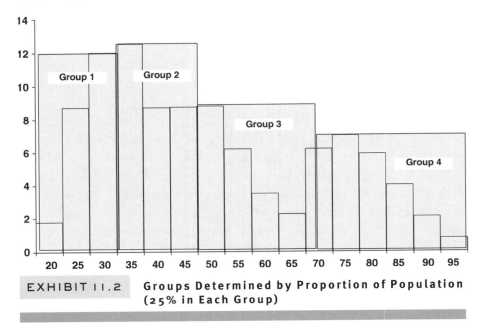

EXHIBIT 11.2   Groups Determined by Proportion of Population (25% in Each Group)

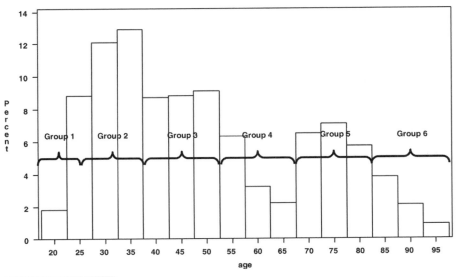

EXHIBIT 11.3   Groups Determined Manually by Observation of the Shape of Distribution

based on four to six groups whose determination is more or less arbitrary. For example, if customer age is distributed from 18 to 95, four groups could be derived by an even distribution by age, based on the calculation: (95–18)/4 = 19.25 increments: 18–37, 38–57, 58–77, and 78–95 (see Exhibit 11.1).

Groups can also be based on an even distribution by proportion of population, in this case 25% in each group, as shown in Exhibit 11.2.

In both of these cases, the actual attributes of the distribution are completely ignored, which could cloud or distort test results and lead to less effective marketing. From observation of the distribution, it seems there could be at least six distinct groups, as shown in Exhibit 11.3.

Observation-based discrimination of the groups is based on intuitive assessment of central features. Most obvious is the largest group, shown as Group 2 in Exhibit 11.3. On the other side of the spectrum are the smallest groups, Groups 1 and 6, and possibly Group 4. Group 5 stands out between Groups 4 and 6.

This type of grouping is known as *banding*, and can be generated automatically by statistical techniques. It is a less arbitrary approach to grouping customers for analysis, but its effectiveness must be measured

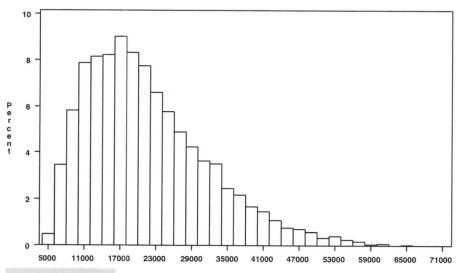

EXHIBIT 11.4   Customer Income Distribution

nonetheless. The importance of taking a more refined approach to grouping customers, in this case by age, is to highlight distinctive behavior. The distinctive behavior of smaller groups will be overwhelmed by larger groups, if the first or second approach is taken. Further refinement based on a technique such as cluster analysis may further highlight and demonstrate attributes important to marketing based on analysis of response.

Analytical information can also be created to measure likelihood of response using models. These created values are generally called *scores*. The models used to create scores will in turn rely on primary measures such as age, income, or recency of purchase. Models can also be based on transformations of primary measures, as well as combinations of primary measures, to improve the model's ability to predict response.

A simple example will help clarify this point, and its relevance will be clear shortly. In this case a business has numeric information on its customers (income). The distribution of income—the number of people earning $0 to $10,000; the number earning $10,000 to $20,000—is shown in Exhibit 11.4.

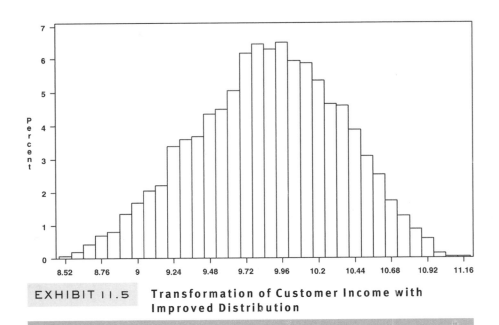

EXHIBIT 11.5   **Transformation of Customer Income with Improved Distribution**

Notice how the total number of customers earning less than approximately $25,000 seems to be much larger in volume than those earning more, and there are far fewer customers having much larger income levels. This weighting on the left side of the graph is referred to as a *skew* in the data distribution. This left-skewed distribution provides a weaker contribution to a model. Modeling works more effectively when the data is more evenly distributed.

Manipulating the data values, in this case income, can improve the model results. This manipulation is referred to as *transforming the original data*. There are numbers of common transformations—inverse, square, and log, for example. In this example, applying a log transformation will "spread the data out" and improve model results. This spreading-out effect is evident in Exhibit 11.5, which shows the same data transformed as log(income). The relationship between response and income is no longer simply "Response = 0.5 × Income," but "Response = 0.5 × log(Income)."

Such transformations are common, and have become standard in analytically derived model equations. To avoid having to repeat the calculations, and to provide a more stable environment for testing and expanding application of similar transformations, a separate database will commonly be created for analytical purposes. The marketer has limited use of "log(income)" so there is no reason to include this field in the marketing datamart. Log(income) will be captured in the score "Response X" on the marketing database. The modelers will maintain log(income) on the analytical datamart.

CHAPTER 12

Data Acquisition, Storage, and Retrieval

While exploitation of a marketing automation system will evolve with the acquired experience of the users, successful marketing automation efforts will rely heavily on availability of information, and information is derived from data. As noted earlier, there will be considerable data required for marketing and customer information. The preceding discussion identified some of the information useful to marketers, analysts, as well as modelers.

The volume of data will be expected to require an investment in data storage and retrieval technology: networked computer systems, computer disc storage, data storage and retrieval software, and data maintenance software for archiving, backup, and restore security. While some of the information already exists within the company data center, this information is not generally stored on broadly accessible platforms, nor is it easily expanded to include the incremental and relevant information just discussed. Frequently, the existing operational storage platforms are sized for operations use, with scheduled jobs filling the available resource window. A new platform tailored to marketing requirements is necessary to provide the incremental storage capacity, flexibility, and response capacity. Therefore a plan for *marketing* data acquisition, storage, and retrieval must be developed. These are the resources that were listed as "hardware" in the marketing investment return on investment (ROI) proposal.

INITIAL PROJECT IMPLEMENTATION GOALS

Before discussing the general platform requirements it is appropriate to view the project in the context of the original financial goals: return on investment. The marketing financial worksheet developed in Chapter 8 (Exhibit 8.6) demonstrated substantial potential gains. Chapters 9 and 11 outlined the information necessary to support marketing in improving promotional effectiveness. Part of making a marketing automation project successful is defining the information needed and where it will come from.

The scope of the project begins with the definition of the information and how it will be used. At this early stage, it is easy to overextend the information acquisition effort. Overextension is seductively easy: Specific information is identified as necessary for marketing and the source of this specific information is identified. Let us say 4 fields are needed for customer purchase activity and the information is contained in a database that has five tables and *40* fields. Because the emphasis in the marketing project is ease of access and broad utility, business purposes for the *additional* tables and fields can be all too easy to identify, and *a decision is made to add all five tables to the project*. A corollary decision follows to add an additional analysis project and corresponding reports based on the information in these incremental fields and tables.

The business benefit cannot be disagreed with and it may be very valuable. However, this is a simple example of *project scope creep*. Scope creep will cause the project to expand, the complexity to increase, and the implementation timelines to stretch out. Early payback supporting the project ROI *depends on* effective and timely *implementation* of the hardware, software, and data. The implementation plan should focus on a set of simple and achievable goals consistent with equally simple and achievable marketing goals for improving the return on the marketing investment. The emphasis is twofold: simple and achievable goals, and an *implementation plan* to support them.

If the project is allowed to move forward with an expanding scope and increasingly complex goals, even if accompanied by equally expansive and complex potential gains, an additional penalty will be paid: More time will be invested in the project definition and implementation by marketing and information technology (IT) participants. Worse, the risk of failure will increase with the added scope and complexity, and the cost of failure will be higher. Remember that "expected value" is defined as the likelihood (probability) of an event multiplied times the invested value: As complexity increases, the likelihood of failure goes up as well as the cost. The cost of failure increases in parallel.

If scope creep is allowed at the outset of the project plan it will likely delay achievement of the initial deployment goal, as more time is expended on revising the resource requirements to meet the new demands. If additional demands are added in the middle of the deployment of the project, the project may fail to meet the initial goals that justified the project to begin with.

Therefore the first step in developing a marketing automation implementation is the development of a plan for implementation of information acquisition, storage, and retrieval. This will entail identifying the information needed for marketing, the sources of data that can be used to create that information, and an acquisition process for accessing the primary sources of data for populating the data warehouse. The data warehouse design will include a plan for storage and retrieval of marketing campaign data, the data to be used in managing the marketing investment (campaign and response information), as well as customer data in its several forms: the data used for analyzing and selecting customers for marketing communications and promotions, contact and promotion history, and the analytical data mart.

As a further caveat to preventing scope creep, the plan should anticipate considerable change in the information maintained in the warehouse during the first two years of use, as users exploit what may be newly available information and develop new techniques in improving the effectiveness of marketing. Therefore the storage and retrieval design should be flexible and provide significant room for growth.

This need for flexibility in the implementation period deserves further emphasis. Flexibility strongly suggests a need to consider the data warehouse and datamarts as separate from the operational systems required to manufacture and ship products and receive and process payments as well as maintain the accounting systems. The data warehouse should be considered a repository of management information, with due attention to consistency, reliability, and accuracy of the information.

While some of the information in the data warehouse/datamarts will be unique to these environments, the source data will be largely derived from existing operational systems. The conclusion is the information is redundant; it is stored in two locations and requires duplicate maintenance effort. This is true, the data will by definition be redundant. This redundancy will afford the maximum level of flexibility in the design and maintenance of the data warehouse for maximizing *marketing utility* with a corresponding minimal impact on the operational systems.

Three Areas of Information

There are effectively three distinct data acquisition efforts required for marketing automation—profit and loss (P&L), marketing, and customer information—which include test and analytical information. It should be expected that each acquisition effort will encounter relevant information from different sources, including different *relational database management systems* (RDBMSs). Reconciliation of the different sources must be anticipated as a result. The development of the data warehouse from multiple sources of operational information is viewed in the customer relationship management (CRM) literature as developing a single view of the customer. It should also be considered a single view of the marketing investment.

Profit and Loss Data

Earlier it was said that the P&L information is (or should be) readily available from the accounting system, either directly or from tables extracted from the accounting system and made available expressly to support management reporting, including marketing management. The volume of information may be complex, involving detailed cost and sales information on many products as well as many marketing investments. Costs may be available from accounting vendor payables statements, requiring identification of the expense with products and marketing activities. This may require vendors to process orders and remit billings identifying the specific product or marketing activity associated with the order and billing statement.

Product sales data from the P&L is unlikely to contain either marketing or customer-related information. In this case other data sources will be required to associate sales activity with both the customer and the marketing investment. In the former case, customer transaction records may be required to associate customers placing orders with customers receiving specific marketing communications. Customer transaction records may include a marketing code that explicitly defines the promotion a customer has responded to. In the absence of a direct association such as a promotion code, the timing of the customer order will be used to associate the customer purchase with a marketing communication. Testing will confirm the strength of the association.

Using the customer sales transactions to record sales in a period for management review will necessitate reconciliation with the accounting sales system. The reconciliation process will ensure that sales transactions are treated by both systems consistently, and ensure that either the two systems report the same figures for sales, or differences are communicated using a reconciliation note.

Similarly, a source must be identified for *marketing expenses* and a reconciliation done to ensure the marketing and accounting systems report consistent figures. Assigning a coding scheme for tracking marketing expenses and ensuring that the coding scheme is used consistently both internally and by external vendors is mandatory.

Overhead expenses such as marketing salaries, rent allocations, and office expenses may be, from an ideal sense, relevant to associate with marketing investments. The creative effort associated with developing marketing communications may involve significant internal resources as well as external resources.

However, the accounting system may not be able to manage project-based cost accounting for departmental expenses. In this case, an independent project management approach could be tried internally to manage the allocation of creative time and resources by marketing project. Alternatively, an assumption can be used for cost recognition. Internally developed projects can be noted as "Internal" using the marketing promotion information system (see below) and the marketing cost simply assigned based on the *internal* flag. The goal is to represent the marketing investment fairly and accurately to establish an honest return on marketing investment. The goal is not to allocate marketing expenses for the sake of justifying the resources, which is a separate exercise.

MARKETING INVESTMENT DATA

Each marketing investment will entail development and delivery expenses. Many of these are discussed in Chapter 2, "Profit and Loss Component

Details," Additional marketing investment data is noted in the *marketing financials example* of Chapters 6 and 8, where the sales and profit are reported and a *return on marketing investment* (RMI) calculation is made. Marketing investment data includes all of these parameters, cost and profit as well as various measures of response.

These are summary measures based on the marketing activity as the lowest unit of measure. Considerable computing resources will be involved in summarizing sales at this level. Some organizations may recognize a business need for daily summarization of customer response; others may find that a weekly summary is sufficient to provide management visibility to performance, in time for action on poorer-performing as well as better-performing promotions.

Updates including summarization may be based on a smaller volume of more specific marketing activities. Email response measurement may benefit from daily summarization, in which case the sales activity for a small group of people may be summarized with less impact on computing resources.

The importance of recognizing the demand on computing resources is the fact that computing on many millions of records takes time, and the demand for information by marketers will revolve around a fairly predictable time window of Monday 8 A.M. to Friday 5 P.M. Summarizations preceding the update of the marketing investment data must anticipate availability on Monday, or daily, at 8 A.M. in the morning. Computing resources must be provided to accomplish this with time to spare. Demand for information will only increase over time as the benefits of marketing automation are recognized, and the demands on computing resources will grow accordingly.

Marketing investment data will encompass *acquisition investment, ongoing investment,* and *testing.* The time over which the data will be updated and maintained will vary. The longer the data is maintained as active, the more information will accumulate over time, and demand on computing resources used in maintenance will increase proportional to the volume of information.

Acquisition investment data could be maintained for three years, five years, or longer; its relevance should be measured according to the utility gained and the level of acquisition investment. A very expensive acquisition effort would merit a longer analytical period for analysis of return on the investment.

There are two beneficial views for ongoing marketing investments: the view of immediate-term return on the investment, and the utility provided by comparing current return with return from similar or dissimilar investments in prior years. The number of prior years to maintain will determine the volume of information required and the corresponding demand on resources. Retaining and maintaining prior-year information supports comparisons such as June direct mail with June of prior year, for example. Channel effectiveness can be measured year over year, providing analysis of both the cost per channel as well as channel mix year over year. These year-over-year views provide management with a measure of the effectiveness of the marketing investment allocation under changing conditions year over year.

An additional factor to consider is the opportunity to generate views of current and prior-year activity based on different assumptions. While P&L information is expected to be taken directly from the accounting system with minimal modification, the marketing investment information is more flexible. Instead of recording the absolute manufacturing cost as a total value, the cost per unit can be recorded, and the unit volume sold, which enables the total cost to be calculated based on *units* times *cost per unit*. In establishing this process in advance, analysis using *alternative cost per unit* can be initiated. As discussed earlier, current profit can be estimated using prior-year cost assumptions.

This approach, using estimated or standard unit costs, facilitates implementation of the reporting process. Focus is on the marketing return calculation, and not on the reconciliation of costs between the marketing and financial systems. Provided that the standard cost values are reasonably close to the financial system, the RMI results themselves will be reasonable.

Unlike acquisition investment tracking, which will involve continual update activity for most records, ongoing activities will be updated primarily for the window of response time. A direct mail promotion may elicit response for 90 days or so, and marginal increases may be noted for an incremental 90 days. The marginal additional value will lose relevance and maintenance could arbitrarily end at that point. However, ignoring the incremental sales, however small, introduces a reconciliation problem with the accounting sales system, which will recognize all sales over time. Adding another maintenance period of 90 days or so may minimize the relevance of the reconciliation difference. Analysis of specific investment response may provide more clear direction for determining how long the maintenance period should be for individual businesses and types of marketing promotions.

Marketing test data will be very similar to standard marketing investment data, with the addition of more information on the test itself and the audience selection basis. Providing this information in the same storage context as the marketing cost and response information can be beneficial for long-term security; however, most test definitions take the form of text documents and spreadsheets, which can present a challenge for storage and retrieval using a database. At a minimum, description for each test cell—a unique marketing investment—should be maintained with the goal of providing information for a predefined test report that can be generated on an automated basis. (See "Recommended Test Information" section of Chapter 17, "Response Testing".) A key support capability for marketing automation is the ability to create and manage many more marketing test promotions and activities. The ability to generate response analysis on test activities on an automated basis will ensure the test results will be reflected in improvement of ongoing marketing activities, and not simply more data buried in the marketing database. Marketing tests are expensive, both in setup time and actual cost. The investment will be wasted if the information cannot be published for review in time to act on the results.

Testing activities will also entail maintenance of snapshots of customer data taken at the outset of each test. The snapshot will contain static values of customer information; therefore updates will not be required. It may be worth capturing customer sales transactions relevant to the test period in addition to the snapshot. This redundant information can simplify ongoing analysis of the results, and is recommended. Test results can sometimes be difficult to interpret, and the marketing analysts' ability to interpret results should improve over time. This introduces the possibility that prior results will be revisited at a later date for improved analysis. Therefore, the test information should be expected to be maintained as active for as long as a year beyond the test completion date. Capturing the relevant sales information can simplify the analysis in such cases considerably, obviating the need to scan possibly hundreds of millions of sales records in order to retrieve the few thousand transactions appropriate to the test results.

Customer Data

Marketing information focuses on the information required to calculate the return on the marketing investment and identify good versus bad investments. Improving marketing investment results requires information on customer activity, from demographics to transactions. A bad marketing investment could easily be a good investment if the right people were targeted. Distinguishing likely responders from nonresponders will depend on the ability to access relevant customer data easily and quickly.

The type of customer data to be maintained has been addressed in earlier chapters, and the role of customer information cannot be over-emphasized in refining audiences to improve results. The information management system must support the selection process and anticipate evolution of the customer data: More customer information, such as that associated with *recency, frequency, and monetary value* (RFM) analysis will be added over time. Customer data will not be limited to name and demo-graphics. RFM indicators, segmentation, and modeling information will be generated to augment basic customer information. Storage capacity and retrieval performance must be sized with an expectation for expansion of volume over time.

Data Quality

People with experience in direct mail are familiar with the numerous responders named "Mickey Mouse" periodically recorded in database updates. Early in Part One, reference was made to the common concern over presenting wrong information in operational presentations. A single incorrect value can implicate the accuracy of the remaining content.

Cleaning data and enforcing data quality is the topic of a number of books and there are several software applications available that manage both functions. A brief review of data quality features is nonetheless appropriate.

One of the more common data quality issues is multiple records of the same customer with relatively minor differences in address or spelling of the first or last name. Multiple mailings to the same person mute the message, cause annoyance, and cost money over time. A common cleaning feature for data quality software is the ability to group similar records that might refer to the same "person" and suggest a standard update for records within each group. The data table is reprocessed to eliminate the duplicates, and the standardization algorithm is added to the filtering processes on the front end, as the data enters the system, so future similar errors will not be repeated.

To eliminate values that are out of range, such as Age equal to a negative number or an arbitrarily large and unlikely value (120), the applications provide range filters, and highlight values out of range. These values can be eliminated as part of the cleaning process.

Enforcing Data Quality

Within the database, the data can be regarded with a certain level of confidence if the processes have been initially validated correctly and no changes have been made in either the representation of the data, the storage environment, or the processes themselves.

One technique of enforcing ongoing values to stay within a legitimate range is specifying valid values and letting the database do the work. Any record that includes a data value out of range will be rejected in an update or insert. The value can be corrected and the record reinserted or submitted for update. This process is known as *maintaining referential integrity*, by reference to tables containing valid values. This can be a time-consuming process affecting updates and new data inserts.

Any changes to upstream data processes should be viewed with skepticism until the data has been thoroughly reviewed from beginning to end. Small process changes that might seem innocuous in the context of 100 or so new data entries can show surprising volatility in the context of millions of new records. Take the example of a direct mail company that installed new scanning software and discovered that a small proportion of mail pieces were being misprocessed and discarded in the process. The amount was small, less than 1%. Unfortunately, the pieces being discarded were orders; the proportion of orders was approximately 10% of the total mail volume, hence fully 10% of the orders were being discarded. The missing orders were not obvious in the reporting process, being attributed to a minor slowdown in sales. The error was not identified for two weeks. Another week was required to correct it. Unfortunately, 10% of sales for a two-week period were necessarily processed in a single day, affecting all systems and reports downstream, as well as in future reports.

Resources for Storing Customer Data

The investment in resources required to access and manage customer data will parallel the volume of customers. Managing information on 100 million customers will necessarily be more involved and expensive than 10 million, although the relationship may not be linear, meaning it may not be 10 times more involved or more expensive.

Customer data available in the organization may be quite detailed for operational purposes, and not all of the information may be relevant to meet the near-term goals following implementation of marketing automation. Considerable useful information at the customer level will be based on summarizations of more detailed information, and the detail will be less relevant than the summarized information.

As a result, the relative volume of immediately useful data will be substantially less that of the available data, and implementation of a datamart for immediately relevant and actionable customer information may be very useful, in addition to the implementation of a customer data warehouse to house the available detailed information.

Datamart and Warehouse

Using both a warehouse and a datamart has significant utility for improving flexibility, access, and performance. The content of the data warehouse will be larger, perhaps significantly larger, and subject to operational update considerations, limiting the ability to make even small changes. The larger volume will affect speed of access. Providing database-oriented improvements to improve response performance, such as indexes, will increase the space demands on these resources. The need to retain some level of correspondence with the expected finer detail of the operational record definitions will place a higher demand on the knowledge of the users to create useful information from the operationally defined detail: Sometimes several fields from the operational data will be required to create a single field of relevance for marketing. All of these considerations support the use of a datamart for direct use by marketers in the context of marketing automation.

Using a datamart in conjunction with a data warehouse also separates the two challenges of acquisition and access. In the first case, acquiring data from primary sources will entail ETL (extract, transform and load) processes that place demands on both primary source systems and the data warehouse. It is often simpler, faster, and cheaper to acquire the detail information for the data warehouse than to determine the necessary filters and transformation processes necessary to convert the detailed data to useful marketing information in line with extraction from the primary sources. This is true particularly in the context of the evolution of the ability of people involved in marketing to exploit the available information. Continually revising the extract processes for marketing transformations to support expanding marketing capabilities places continual demands on operational IT resources. Evolving extract requirements may encounter delays and bottlenecks at multiple points in this evolution, which will affect the ability to meet the marketing objectives. Evolving extract requirements will risk creating an impression of "marketing aimlessness" in operational IT circles, voiced as "marketing can't decide what information they need."

The most significant drawbacks are the delays that will be encountered when additional information is identified as necessary to complete analysis but not available, and the situation that follows where the demands of ongoing events take precedence over incomplete analysis of events in the past. It should be understood and accepted that as marketing analysts pursue deeper segmentation of customers and analyze more operationally derived information, their experience will increase and their ability to manage and exploit sometimes complex operational information will also increase. Having to delay or forgo opportunities to exploit additional information, while operational IT issues are resolved to make the additional information available and corresponding extract processes are modified to support these new opportunities, will be a source of frustration for both marketers and operational IT managers.

Therefore, it is strongly recommended that data associated with primary sources identified as supporting marketing activities be acquired and updated on an ongoing basis with as much detail as possible at the outset of the project, to ensure that when information is needed by marketers and analysts it will be available and not still buried in the operational systems.

Sampling Customer Data

In many circumstances it will be very useful to have available a sample of the customer data in its entirety. The purpose of the sample will be to provide very rapid access to a meaningful subset of the customer data. Queries against very large databases may conceivably take 20 minutes, an hour, or several hours to complete. The results may not match expectations: The query may be incorrectly formed, the data may not be distributed as expected, the complexity of the target information may require several query formulation attempts, and the results may raise more questions requiring answers and refined queries before the final query can be said to provide the results desired.

Revision and reexecution of the query or queries takes time, particularly if the entire customer data of millions of records is repeatedly accessed. Using a sample of the customer data, where response will be in seconds or minutes and not longer, will enable the users to achieve their goals of a correct query with expected results much more quickly. Faster response also minimizes demands on the resources used to access the complete customer database, which will improve response times for all users and processes accessing the complete database.

There are limitations to using samples that will affect the reliability of figures obtained using the sample data. Even if the sample is taken randomly, it will be possible to miss some values completely if those values are sufficiently small. Extrapolating sample counts to the full population is problematic due to sampling error. Therefore, using sample data has inherent limitations for effectiveness. The following example should make this clear.

In this example, marketing wants to know quickly what the initial results for a new product test are indicating. Their initial concern is that sales of Product Z promoted in the test are being recognized. The test is three weeks old; the expected sales at this point are 1,200 units. A decision is made to use the sample data for preliminary results *now*, and query the full customer database during the evening for confirmation. The sample data is a 5% sample of the complete customer transactions database, which includes 300,000,000 records. Marketing is therefore expecting to find 5% of the expected 1,200 transactions in a sample of 15,000,000 records.[1]

Since there is a completely random expectation for the distribution of the records in the sample, the probability that there are some product sales records of interest in the sample of 15,000,000 can be calculated. Marketing is primarily interested that *any* sales of the new product have been recorded, and, if sales are similar to expectations, the likelihood of finding at least one such

---

[1] It must be noted that the sample of transactions themselves will not be random, but be based on all transactions belonging to a 5% random sample of *customers*.

transaction is very high. The sample size could be as small as 250,000 to create a strong likelihood of at least one "Product Z" transaction in the sample.

Unfortunately, this is true "on average," across many samples. The number of "Product Z" transactions in any single sample can vary, and will vary, from as few as 20 (small likelihood) to as many as 110 (similarly small likelihood). It is only true that on average the 5% sample will contain 60 "Product Z" transactions (5% of 1,200). Any single sample will differ, sometimes by a broad range.

As a result, predicting "Product Z" test results based on the records found in the sample, compared to the expectation of 1,200 units, can only be accurate for a fairly broad range, a range too broad to be a reliable indication of the success in marketing Product Z.

This discussion can be extended to demonstrate that the likelihood of finding specific volumes in a sample must be restricted to volumes that are at least X in relation to the sample proportion. Trying to find smaller values is too prone to sampling error to draw a reliable conclusion. This means that finding no values in the sample is not a reliable indication that in fact there are none. In these cases the primary transaction tables must be used to determine a reliable answer.

Alternatively, if the answer to such questions is frequently sought, and important enough, the sample size itself can be increased. The drawback to increasing the sample size is the impact to performance: Queries will take longer and data storage and maintenance will increase. What appears to be a small increase of 1% on a sample size of 3% is in fact a 33% increase in the sample size, and a corresponding impact on storage resources and the time for query response.

If there is a repeated need to assess similar information such as small quantities that are not reliably determined from the sample, alternative techniques are also available. Transaction flags could be set when specific transactions occur in the operational environment. Counters can be established to track specific product sales activity, similarly driven by operational processes or implemented as part of the marketing data load process, to provide deeper visibility into customer transactions.

ACQUISITION, STORAGE, AND RETRIEVAL

By establishing a data warehousing plan in combination with a datamart, the data acquisition process can be empowered to maximize the acquisition of data, while the datamart can be developed in parallel on an incremental basis, focusing on what information can be acted on in the immediate term. The datamart will be expected to grow over time as people in the organization gain experience integrating information with marketing activities. As marketing activities expand, additional information can be extracted from the data warehouse and added to the datamart.

The focus on a near-term set of marketing goals is expected to support near-term incremental revenue, improving the payback period for the investment in marketing automation.

DATA WAREHOUSE SIZING

A primary concern in designing a data warehouse is sizing for available information and performance. Performance includes the ability to load, update, back up, and restore the warehouse from primary operational sources while maximizing the availability of the information for users. The loading of the warehouse includes any postprocessing activities required on the new or newly updated data, such as customer segmentation, weekly and monthly sales summaries by product and region, as well as execution of the load processes that update the datamart.

Sizing the warehouse and the supporting infrastructure supporting the load process is based on the available window for update processes. This window could be a weekend, for example. The "weekend update window" might be considered to begin as early as midnight Friday night, following completion of necessary operational update processes, and continue to Monday morning 8 a.m. Some processes could conceivably continue through noon on Monday or later, depending on the type of information needed and when it is needed. Some information will be of significant interest first thing Monday morning, such as sales results for new marketing promotions, introduction of new channels, and new product introductions, or to support analysis of disruptive sales trends. Other information may be needed to support reports of more casual interest later in the week.

INFORMATION DELIVERY TIMING
FOR THE WAREHOUSE

Because of the number of activities to be executed with sequential dependencies (e.g., a backup cannot begin until the data is loaded; reports cannot be generated until the data is finalized), a timeline-based plan is appropriate to analyze requirements and estimate performance brackets for specific activities associated with updating the warehouse. Even a primitive schedule such as the one shown in Exhibit 12.1 can be sufficient to size the hardware and support infrastructure. The timeline both highlights all processes and their dependencies and surfaces performance bottlenecks. Who, for example, might have expected that indexing the data would require five hours? The plan highlights the end-to-end requirements, including weekly report updates.

Another valuable feature of the plan in Exhibit 12.1 is the last item, Reserve Time. This emphasizes the cushion available to absorb risks such as a late start, a failure in the middle of the process, or delayed availability of source files, delayed due to unrelated but dependent production activities.

This schedule highlights the fundamental warehousing activities:

- Data load (read/convert/write datasets)
- Indexing
- Ancillary table creation (e.g., weekly and monthly sales summaries)
- Backup
- Reporting
- Report distribution (e.g., updating the internal web site or email distribution)
- Reserve time, in this case almost 30% (9 hours in a 32-hour window

Over time the schedule can be continuously validated through production reports that document the activities. The times in the preproduction schedule should be validated through testing with actual data, based on large samples if unavoidable, but preferably actual data at full scale. This is critical at the outset of the project. Hardware and software vendors should be encouraged to participate in test deployment to develop these validation times, to ensure against such an easily avoidable failure as a poorly sized system. An undersized system dooms the project to a short lifetime and incremental investment, or worse, early failure.

At the same time, users' professed needs for fresh information must be measured against the cost to provide that information. Marketers may need to demonstrate the monetary gains—or opportunity costs—provided by

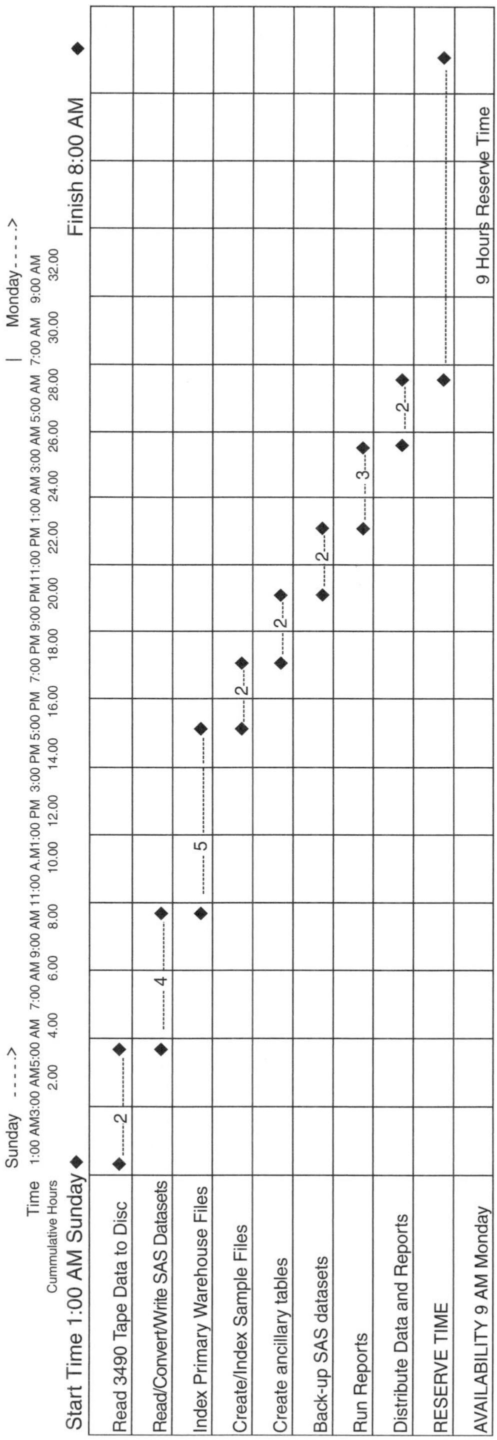

EXHIBIT 12.1   Data Warehouse Weekend Operational Update Schedule

daily updates as compared with weekly or even monthly updates. It should be expected that daily updates are more costly in terms of hardware and maintenance, although this may not always be the case.

Furthermore, it is easy and tempting to look at the schedule in Exhibit 12.1 and try to find more data to fill the nine-hour reserve time, conveniently overlooking the earlier goal of having a reserve time to meet unforeseen delays in the update process.

Warehouse Update Alternatives to Improve Timing

If a need is demonstrated for daily updates, analysis may suggest alternative means to access sufficient information without requiring a full system update every evening. Sample data may satisfy information requirements, for example. Ancillary tables might be generated to capture necessary daily sales information, to exist in parallel with the weekly or monthly full system updates. The ancillary tables could be quite small and easily added to the data warehouse, providing valuable and timely information at small cost.

This issue also highlights another opportunity to forestall the risk of scope creep. Adding daily updates to a project that started out with a weekly warehouse update is a good example. The data warehouse can be particularly subject to scope creep: As the project progresses and more people become familiar with the broad potential for easy available information, there's an implicit tendency to add more data and accelerate the update process.

Datamart

A datamart can be used to provide most of the information needed to meet day-to-day marketing information requirements. It is smaller in size than the data warehouse and can be organized to provide rapid access to the most often used information. Some of the information will be redundant, being "copied" directly from the data warehouse, and some of the information will be derived from the data warehouse, measures such as summary sales information. The existence of *data redundancy* appears inconsistent with good resource management philosophy and the importance of conserving data storage space. However, the paramount importance for any organization of the data for marketing use is *rapid information access* for marketers. A datamart can improve access to information; therefore data redundancy is merited. As noted, the datamart will include summarized and derived information, which will be unique to the datamart. Information retrieval performance and ease of access will maximize people's efforts in determining the direction for the company's marketing activities.

The datamart will include information such as the following contact, response, and recency, frequency, and monetary (RFM) information:

- Cumulative purchases, returns, and payments since acquisition, the customer's first purchase
- Purchases, returns, and payments in the last 30, 60, 90, 180, 360 days[2]
- Total contacts in the last 30, 60, 90, 180, 360 days
- Total contacts by email, mail, telemarketing, or sales in the last 30, 60, 90, 180, 360 days
- Total responses in the last 30, 60, 90, 180, 360 days
- Total response by email, mail, telemarketing, or sales in the last 30, 60, 90, 180, 360 days
- Individual contacts in the past 30, 60, 90, 180 days, as well as contact by channel
- Individual responses in the past 30, 60, 90, 180 days
- Cumulative market mix indicators (variety of products purchased)
- Market mix indicators in the past 30, 60, 90, 180, 360 days, for specific or cumulative orders in the same period
- Customer ranking relative to other customers (top 3%, 5%, 10%; bottom 30%, 20% 10%)

---

[2]The "day durations" specified here are common and recognizable given no other information to determine a more relevant window. Additional time durations can be derived from analysis of purchase activity. For example, some customers may show weaker response activity when their inactivity extends beyond "211 days" (an equally arbitrary time frame, but one chosen by analysis). An appropriate indicator—an attribute of customer information—for marketing use would then be a positive flag (database field or column) for "No Purchase in 211 Days." By managing this summary field in a database, marketers can quickly access these customers for special promotion: "Select all customers where 'No Purchase in 211 Days' = 1. The customer list can be selected quickly without having to repeatedly analyze sales transactions to determine who meets this attribute.

- Customer ranking relative to other customers with the same or similar demographic profile (Urban top 3%, 5%, 10%; bottom 30%, 20% 10%)

DATA TYPES, STORAGE, AND PERFORMANCE CONSIDERATIONS

An interesting and often not well considered area of the data warehouse is the selection of appropriate data types for the data. "Data type" refers initially to character compared to numeric information. In an RDBMS, an additional data type is "date."[3] While all three types of information occupy "bytes" of space in a computer system, an effective data design can minimize data storage and improve performance. The following details may be very granular relative to the bigger picture, but may nonetheless provide a benefit wherever many millions of rows of data are involved. As smaller size means lower storage, reduced maintenance cost, and faster response, it is very beneficial to understand the level of accuracy and scale required for each piece of customer information.

A byte is 8 bits of data; each bit can be "on" or "off." The information is a "1" if the bit is on and a "0" if it is off. That is the only information a single bit can carry: 1 or 0. Two such bits can carry 4 pieces of information: 00, 01, 10, and 11. This binary code represents the numbers 0 through 3 in decimal form, also known as base 10. Using binary arithmetic, 3 bits can hold 8 pieces of information, $2^3 = 8$. And if a byte is 8 such bits, a byte can hold 2^8 or 256 unique pieces of information.

Character data ("A," "B," "c") occupies bytes; "256" is more than enough range to manage the U.S. character set A–Z as well as a–z, 0–9, and many special characters besides, such as !, @, #, $, and %.

Numeric information is different: There are requirements to store very small numbers as well as very large numbers, and numbers of very high precision (many digits) and not very high precision. IBM's earnings in a recent year required 12 digits, being approximately $7,938,932,669.44, while most grocery bills contain 5 or fewer digits ($999.99), a much lower

---

[3] A "date" or "datetime" data type is a number representing seconds or days from a fixed point in the calendar, typically January 1, 1960. A negative number represents a date prior to that time, a positive number after. The database provides formatting options to present the information in a meaningful way.

level of precision. Many more bits are required to manage both the precision of IBM's financial system entries as well as their magnitude, than those required to manage weekly grocery bills.

If 8 bits will manage only 256 unique combinations, a single byte might store only a positive number from 1 through 256.[4] To include negative numbers would require an additional bit to identify the sign of the number. This would reduce the range of a byte to $\pm 2^7$, which is equal to 128. A single byte could therefore store a range from -128 to $+128$.

This is a very limited range; therefore, numbers are stored using multiple bytes and the bytes manage both precision (number of digits) and magnitude ("10" compared to "10,000") separately, based on a numeric representation known as *floating point*. Floating-point arithmetic, in which numbers are represented as a number and an exponent, has been implemented in most present-day computers using a separate processor, known as a *floating-point processor*, to improve calculation performance. The hardware takes care of the mathematical conversion requirements and performs calculations very quickly using exponential notation: The exponent can be added and subtracted for multiplication and division, while the mantissa can be handled as it would be normally.

Recognizing the different storage requirements for large and small numbers, a database provides more than one datatype for representing information. For information of high precision (many digits) there is single- and double-precision floating point. Double precision requires twice the storage space of single precision. For information of less precision there are integer and "small" integer types, and some databases continue to the byte level.

Choosing a datatype consistent with the scope of the information provides an opportunity to conserve disc space in the database. Marketing data that does not exceed "8,092" could be represented with 3 bytes instead of 8, a savings of 5 bytes. Two such values stored in 6 bytes instead of 16 is a savings of 10 bytes. In a customer data warehouse with hundreds of fields and millions of records, 10 bytes could represent a significant savings. This

---

[4]This discussion has been simplified to make the point. In fact the mantissa can be stored using a series of fractions based on the powers of 2, which increases the range of the mantissa, from 256, based on 2^8, to 0.996094, based on the sum of the series $\frac{1}{2} + \frac{1}{4} + 1/8 + \ldots 1/256$. The last figure is based on $\frac{1}{2}^8$.

savings translates primarily to better performance, and better performance means higher productivity. The storage issues associated with bytes in hardware (the size of the disc drives) is inconsequential in this context. Marketing productivity is paramount to hardware cost. All RDBMSs provide flexibility for specifying the appropriate data type for customer information. This flexibility should be taken advantage of to efficiently manage the allocation of physical space for data. "Efficient" means better performance (faster retrieval) and lower maintenance cost (smaller space).

Surprisingly, the default storage level commonly used is 8-byte floating point for all numeric, and a character column default can be surprisingly large, 200 bytes or more. Casual treatment of data types (accepting the defaults) can therefore result in unnecessarily high storage requirements, slower performance, and higher total cost of ownership. It is surprising because, relatively speaking, a binary value such as Gender could be represented by 1 bit—a 0 or a 1—and 8 bytes is 64 times larger. Amplified by tens of millions of records, this gives a good example of the scale of the potential savings.

This discussion may seem unnecessarily detailed, but the relevant issue continues to be marketing productivity in the context of the datamart, the retrieval and maintenance of many millions of records accessed multiple times per day by more than one person and the system itself in the execution of campaigns.

ETL Processes

ETL means *extract, transform and load* and refers to the process of loading and updating the data warehouse and datamart with updated data. The goal for the ETL processes is to complete the load process in time for availability to marketing as useful data and information. Utility will mean access for reporting as well as selecting audiences for marketing communications. It should be expected that a weekly load process will be used to generate information for reports to be available on Monday, or at the latest on Tuesday, in time for the information to be analyzed, assessed, and acted on during the remainder of the week.

The ETL process will represent a substantial load to the system resources. Meeting this demand successfully will require that the system have the processing and data throughput capacity necessary to accomplish the transmission of data—bytes—from disc to user or disc to disc, in the case of extract, transform, and load activities. This capacity will be determined by the number of central processing units (CPUs), gigabytes of memory, channel capacity of disc controllers, data read/write capacity of disc drives, and the arrangement of data on the discs (RAID configuration for mirroring, striping, and/or error correction).

Data warehouse technology has evolved to the point where reasonable estimates of system performance can be made, based on different system configurations. This is a complicated process; there are a host of variables involved, particularly the type of data, the type of RDBMS, as well as the arrangement of data on the discs. There are in fact several ways to arrange data on a disc or disc drives that has an impact on the performance. There is also the issue of "software" versus "hardware": Hardware vendors are not in control of the second most significant variable, the database, and how the database is configured to load data, as well as how the ETL processes themselves are structured to use the database software to load the data. The hardware performance of the individual components (i.e., CPU, memory, disc) is very well known, but the combined performance of software and hardware is not.

The marketer and particularly the database marketer can provide important information to aid in the process of assessing suitable system configurations. They know the types of queries that are generated, the type of information returned, and how frequently these queries are executed. This information provides the baseline for establishing system performance requirements. Further discussion can clarify how many users will be driving these types of queries, whether certain information is accessed more often than other information, and how much information is "written" compared to "read." This type of information is extremely useful in establishing how much shared disc space is necessary, for example, and the volume of "reads" generated against this shared information. Hardware *I/O subsystems* are very flexible, provided that these requirements can be surfaced and not left to assumptions.

To further assist in determining the correct system configuration, hardware and software vendors can be very cooperative in supporting customers and potential customers in testing and verifying data load processes and data access scenarios, as well as providing expert advice in how to improve existing load processes. Careful research on performance requirements can be followed by testing that will demonstrate and confirm the best configuration of hardware and software required to accomplish the combined goals of data ETL and data access by marketers.

Research and testing will also provide a significant reduction in the risk of the project, risk associated with loading and accessing the volumes of data necessary for the success of a marketing automation investment. Since this is a significant component of marketing automation, the reduction in risk from testing the configuration eliminates a substantial portion of the risk associated with a marketing automation project as a whole, and is highly recommended.

A significantly overlooked aspect of data warehouses is the backup-and-archive capability. Effort is focused on ETL process performance, the type of data needed by marketers, and how fast it can be accessed, but not necessarily on the ability to back up or restore the data in a reasonable period of time. Consider a 4-hour load period followed by a 12-hour backup period for the same data. If the data was expected to load overnight, it would, but the backup system would still be running in the morning. And just as obvious in this case is that it would be easier and faster to simply reload the data, rather than spend three times the effort to back it up. Clearly attention must be paid to ensure that the backup process performance is adequate.

Archiving information, as an ETL process, involves transfer of less-used data to slower media, from disc to tape, for example. Archived data may be permanently archived, to an offsite vault, for example, or archived with an eye toward faster retrievability than offsite, in a finite future. This can be done through an online archive utility that automatically provides constant archive-and-restore facility. Such a system can significantly improve long-term maintainability and maximize the utility—and payback—of online disc storage, by moving older and less frequently used content to tape, for example.

As the marketing automation system is exploited by marketers and analysts alike, and more campaigns are generated, the volume of information generated for contact history and response history, as well as expanded use of the analytical datamart, will combine to increase the use of online storage. An automated backup and retrieval system will ensure that these users will continue to have access to information on an ad-hoc basis, without consuming dynamic resources within the system itself. An automated archiving system provides this needed protection.

CHAPTER 13

Data Warehouse Hardware and Software Configuration

Larger scale software applications today distribute their functionality across multiple computer systems. The database/data warehouse will typically occupy a single system and provide shared access for DBAs, modelers, marketing database analysts, as well as software applications such as marketing automation. The marketing automation software itself may occupy one or more systems, depending on how it's designed. A client server based system will have multiple client applications distributed to user desktops and a server based component which provides specific functionality for the clients.

This distribution of the functionality among multiple systems provides long term flexibility and scalability for growth with the business. If the number of users and/or the volume of customers reach the capacity of the system, the hardware can be upgraded with additional CPUs, memory, disc drives, or simply replaced with a larger system. The software remains the same.

The flexibility of the hardware and the variety of marketing automation software deployment possibilities makes it difficult to provide specific statements or guidelines for system sizing, scalability, or configuration. A brief discussion on several topics relevant to the data warehouse, which is a core component of any marketing automation application, is relevant and appropriate, based on the author's prior experience with both a failed system and a very successful system.

HARDWARE CONFIGURATION

The available options for configuring hardware to support a data warehouse are:

- Number of CPUs: 1 to 64
- Memory: to 64 gigabytes or larger
- Disc controllers: Depends on level of redundancy for failover protection and number of channels relative to disc drive configurations
- Discs: Depends on data storage technique, mirroring, and number of discs per controller channel

For all but the largest data warehouse purposes, the number of discs and disc controllers will be dictated by the volume of information required for disc storage, the database requirements for overage and logging, the access rate required relative to CPU and memory throughput capacity, and the level of redundancy for failover protection.

Before discussing hardware and software configuration for performance, consideration for failover protection needs to be addressed. Failover protection typically involves hardware redundancy, with a corresponding impact on cost as well as the configuration of the data on the disc drives.

Reliability Protection (Failover)

Considerable reliability has been designed into hardware systems, recognizing their key role in maintaining day-to-day business operations. That being said, planning for reliability by assessing failover protection is an important part of planning the data warehousing processes that will support a marketing automation system. Failover protection is a difficult topic to address conclusively when it involves someone else's data; the tendency would be to recommend more rather than less. Loss of data usually means loss of revenue or worse, and to recommend no failover protection would be foolhardy. However, as the data warehouse design has been discussed in the context of a marketing information system, there is a stated redundancy in the available information. The primary data is available and maintained elsewhere in the operational systems. Assuming these systems have built-in redundancy for significant data protection, the failover considerations for the marketing customer database could be reduced.

One approach to failover protection could be placed in the following context: Marketing information consumed in the context of a marketing automation implementation is used to develop analysis for future marketing communications, as well as present communications. If most automated communications can be delayed by one day without a major impact, then hardware support must be available to meet a 24-hour response window.

In other words, if the marketing system is completely unavailable for one full day due to a hardware failure of some kind, any activity scheduled during that period must be safely recoverable in the following day without causing a domino effect that impacts later marketing activities and communications. Chapter 10 highlighted the response timing of campaigns and the impact on revenue: A week's delay in campaign execution could have extremely serious implications for revenue.

Assuming a level of failover protection sufficient to restore the system to full operation in 24 hours will have a significant effect on data organization possibilities and load and response performance. This approach must be considered carefully in discussion with prospective hardware vendors.

To further reduce the risk of such a consideration, redundancy can be added for hardware components, from redundant (more than one) system power supplies, to additional disc drives deployed in a "hot swappable" arrangement, to complete clustered systems. This does not suggest that power supplies, disc drives, or systems fail and disrupt system performance on a regular basis. In general systems are very reliable. In addition, some systems incorporate self-monitoring, for example IBM Predictive Failure Analysis (PFA), and signal potential failures in advance of their occurrence. Disc drives signaling impending failure can be swapped out prior to the next data load, and users and processes will not be impacted at all. In my personal experience, a 300-gigabyte (20 drives) data warehouse maintained in a standard data center experienced only two disc drive failures in three years, and the system had no downtime other than installation of an additional disc drawer for more storage capacity. The system capacity has since been increased to 1.2 terabytes and has been in active use for over seven years.

The following discussion of guidelines for central processing unit, memory, and disc requirements assumes a typical (vendor standard) configuration for failover redundancy.

CPU and Memory Requirements

Dual core processors and now quad core processors point to the importance of the central processing unit (CPU) in servicing system demands. "Multithreaded software" aims to take advantage of multiple CPUs for accomplishing more than one activity simultaneously. The number of CPUs will correlate to the expected ability to make use of parallel processes for transformations and summarization in the load process, as well as the use of parallel data structures for scanning large volumes of customer data. This means a query against 20 million customer records might be implemented as four queries against 5 million customer records each, with each query executing simultaneously. Response time could be 400% faster as a result. In real time, this could mean 4 minutes instead of 16 minutes. Transformations in the load process can be accomplished inline, meaning as the data is loaded, depending on the data storage software in use. Large-scale summarization of millions of customer transactions can be accomplished more quickly by running multiple parallel summaries executed on large subsets of the data. For example, customer transaction summaries could be executed on four CPUs using four subsets of the transaction data. These subsummaries can then be resummarized and the summary process will complete faster than if all transactions were summarized in one process.

Parallel processing in the data warehouse based on multiple CPUs has implications for the way customer data is stored. Database storage can be configured using partitions to take advantage of multiple CPUs supporting parallel query execution. The same query can be executed against four data partitions, for example, returning records effectively four times faster.

It goes without saying that system-driven parallel processes have their parallel in multiple simultaneous (or nearly so) user queries, which execute on an ad-hoc basis when users submit queries. Multiple CPUs will provide more rapid response to multiple user queries in most cases.

The amount of memory for the system depends on the number of CPUs, the number of users and applications, and the database. An assessment of these factors provides a starting point, after which system analysis can show the level of CPU usage in the course of the day. User feedback is also useful, but needs to be correlated to system activity. The penalty for less-than-optimal memory is usually slower performance. Memory is used to maintain and feed software instructions to the CPUs. When memory is low, the system must move current software out of memory to disc, and then back again based on demand. This constant swapping of instructions between memory and disc is very costly to performance, and can create a bottleneck impacting overall system capabilities. System performance depends on a balance of response from sufficient CPUs, memory, disc controllers, and disc drives.

Disc Drive Storage Requirements

The number of disc drives required is measured by the amount of data storage required, an allowance for growth, plus an allowance for dynamic sort and processing space. It should be recognized at the initial stage of planning that the least information is available to predict initial requirements, and the data warehouse is expected to be available and useful for some time; therefore the amount of disc space for growth need not be conservative. Similarly, the amount of free space to support disc-based processing should not be conservatively estimated early in the project. The flexibility provided by available, unused disc space in situations that may result in substantial marketing-generated revenue cannot be overemphasized. The cost of the additional space will be small relative to the overall cost of the system and the potential for supporting new revenue generating opportunities in a timely way.

A storage method for disc-based data known as striping can significantly improve data retrieval performance, with the caveat that loss of a single drive in some striped configurations could mandate reloading the entire striped segment of data. Additional striping configurations (RAID—redundant array of independent discs) can provide a measure of protection, along with higher read performance, at a cost in write performance. The data load process is frequently the most resource- and time-intensive process; therefore the added cost for striping with protection may not be affordable in the time available to accomplish the load process. If the time is available, the additional reliability can be worthwhile.

A storage configuration known as *mirroring* can provide substantial performance and failover protection. In mirroring, all (or a part) of the data will be mirrored on an additional disc drive. The mirrored drive will be just as available as the "primary" drive to service requests for data, and this provides a performance improvement where contention for data from the same disc creates a bottleneck. Mirroring will double the expense of the configuration; therefore the cost must be measured against the benefit of higher data availability, performance or failover redundancy protection needed. A heavily used system in a critical marketing role in a business may benefit from the additional cost of mirroring. That being said, mirroring of the operating system is very common and very inexpensive for the protection it provides in the event an operating system drive fails. In this case, the redundant disc will be online immediately to provide continued operation.

As stated at the outset of this chapter, the discussion of hardware configuration here is intended to expose the options that can be manipulated to improve performance and availability, so that the ETL processes required to make the data available as information to users of marketing automation will be able to achieve that goal in the limited time frame available for use. This part of the text also imparts in a small way my personal experience with a very successful data warehouse deployment. The success of that deployment was based largely on just the considerations for performance improvement brought out here.

Software Configuration

There is more than one database software vendor whose products can service small as well as very-large-scale data warehouse and datamart requirements. Database software is very sophisticated, and most vendors provide a host of configuration options for fulfilling a variety of data storage and retrieval goals. A discussion of these options as well as the long-term maintenance considerations for database systems is the topic of a number of books, publications, and courses provided by both vendors and independent experts. This book cannot delve into these topics with the same level of expertise or breadth of coverage, particularly in light of the strength and depth of the mainstream database products.

However, there are several considerations that are not vendor specific that are worth noting regarding the use of databases.

RDBMS Selection

Most databases make use of a storage technique that should improve retrieval response. This is done by colocating similar records in the same segment space.[1] To do this, space must be reserved for new data in the same segment. This will necessarily increase the amount of storage required to house data, such as customer data for the data warehouse. Increasing the storage for what is effectively empty space will affect the amount of discs required and the cost.

Databases also utilize a data security technique to prevent loss of information should an update fail, and prevent loss from overwriting good data with bad or simply adding bad data. The process is referred to as *logging*. Logging can be used to back out bad data, be it an overwrite of existing data or an append of new data.

Logging has two impacts: It significantly increases the amount of storage required because the data is redundant; and it will slow the update and insert process for writing new data, as two entries are written, one for the log and one for the database. Consideration must be made for the impact of logging

---

[1] *Segment space* is a database term referring to a section or segment of the space allocated for storing data. A database administrator, in building a database, will typically allocate a space called "tablespace" to the database that will approximate the amount of space required to house the data for a medium-term outlook. Additional tablespaces can be added over time as the data grows. The process of *defining* the tablespace is done by the database; the space will be broken up into equal-sized segments, and a record is kept as to what data is located in what segment and what free space exists in the segment for new data. This process of allocating data to segments of known location improves the ability of the database to retrieve the data quickly. Allocating new data to an appropriate segment (the segment that contains similar data) will further improve retrieval speed. Should the segment become full, then a new segment will be selected for additional data, but it will not be located close to the original segment; therefore retrieval of a complete range of similar data will take longer: The two segments will be far apart when viewed as part of the disc drive.

An active database, receiving constant inserts and deletes, will require periodic maintenance to maintain performance. The maintenance can involve rebuilding the tablespace, to colocate data in sequential segments, restore the availability of free space for new data, and reallocate deleted record space. This periodic maintenance activity is time consuming and must be considered in the overall configuration and deployment of the data warehouse.

on storage estimates and the impact on performance of logging. In many cases, a data warehouse log may not be necessary, which will improve write performance and minimize the additional storage space required. Logging for transaction-based updates, however, is generally recommended.

RDBMS Maintenance

Most databases will require ongoing maintenance by appropriately skilled people known as database administrators (DBAs). An expectation for IT management is to be able to spread the time of the DBAs across more than one database implementation to better manage maintenance costs. IT management will typically establish an RDBMS vendor preference to avoid a need to employ distinct DBAs responsible for each unique database software application. Therefore, IT management will look for any new large-scale deployment to make use of the IT RDBMS *standard*. This is good practice and will minimize the incremental cost of bringing up a new data warehouse for customer data.

While databases are primarily designed to manage small additions to the data, such as sales transactions, they also include software capability to enable a large-scale addition to a new table as well as additional data to the same table. The process is known as *bulk loading*. Bulk loading is typically very fast and the bulk load options are several and differ by database. Any consideration for using an RDBMS for the data warehouse must resolve the optimal bulk loading settings to ensure maximum throughput (loading speed) for the data. Some of these settings may involve use of partitions, turning off logging functionality, use of "append" hints, and similar tuning considerations to improve the ability to load large volumes of data to the database quickly.

Software configuration of the database must also take into account options specific to the hardware, such as the availability of multiple CPUs and the location of multiple controllers by disc drive. Data that is in high and constant demand may benefit from a location on disc with access to mirroring, redundant controllers, or both, to improve user access performance as demanded.

This discussion only touches on some of the considerations for tuning the performance of a database in achieving the best performance. As noted earlier, the ability of the data warehouse to load large amounts of data within the time frame available before marketing and management use will become a critical component to the success of a marketing automation implementation. Time and resources should be allocated for evaluating alternative database configurations, but also for testing the ability of the hardware and software in combination to achieve the desired throughput necessary to accomplish the data warehouse loading goals on an ongoing basis.

ANALYTICAL SUPPORT

It is not uncommon to allocate separate resources for supporting *analytics*, the development of predictive models for customer response, attrition, churn, and credit risk. Significant transformations are typically done as part of the model development process. These transformations can be extensive and demanding of system resources. To improve model performance as well as query response time, these transformations may become part of the *marketing customer datamart*, or a separate datamart known as an *analytical datamart*.

The resource requirements for analytics support will not entail complete redundancy of the data. The analytical datamart will include transformed warehouse variables (standardized and/or transformed), as well as many calculated summary variables, such as sales over different time periods (prior week, prior two weeks, prior three weeks), recent order value, and prior order value.

Modeling that surfaces successful scoring algorithms will often be updated to the customer datamart on a regular basis, a process known as *scoring* the customer. It is not unusual to have many scores available, for likelihood to purchase, likelihood to purchase a particular product or product family, credit scores, and attrition scores. The scoring equation and scoring process (transformations and data massaging) will become part of the ETL process used in updating the datamart. Therefore, the datamart ETL process must be flexible for modification and augmentation on demand.

CHAPTER 14

Making Information Useful: Access, Delivery, and Organization

At this point in the discussion, marketing uses for financial, marketing, and customer information have been identified; specific content has been described; and data storage considerations have been outlined. Management of the information on an ongoing basis was said to require the services of skilled database managers (DBAs).

Accessing the marketing information stored in relational database management systems (RDBMSs) normally involves a similarly skilled group of people referred to as *database analysts* or *database marketers*. A typical analyst has detailed knowledge of the database, the allocation of information to tables and fields, and particularly the query syntax necessary to extract specific information from the many tables and fields that contain the data itself.

Typically marketers must create information requests to be fulfilled by this group. These marketing requests may be the basis for a promotional campaign ("Select customers having X but not Y attributes, who have purchased Z products within the past N days") or information needed to plan a prospective campaign ("How many people have characteristics X and Y but not Z, and have opted in?"). A request can also contribute to developing a profile of specific customer groups ("What are the attributes of our top 5% customers?").

In fulfilling a request, the analyst may codify the request (create a *query*) and schedule it consistent with a campaign delivery date, or schedule the request as a recurring query and integrate the results into a new or existing customer information report. Some results may require further analysis or refinement to meet quantity goals, the initial group being too small or too large, or to further refine a previous query response to a marketing "customer question."

There are a finite number of analysts ("number" being small), and there are typically many marketers making many query requests. Database analysts usually don't knock out responses with a few keystrokes: A response will involve query construction, testing, scheduling, executing, and validating results, all of which take time (both execution time as well as the time of the analyst). As a result, information flow into the marketing organization is limited; the analysts and the process are a bottleneck.

A central objective of marketing automation is to facilitate this query process and improve the flow of information to marketers. It does this primarily by providing an easier method to access the information in the database. Making information easier to access increases the number of people who can participate in the process. Making the information easier to access also improves the productivity of database marketers and analysts. Increasing participation in the process is necessary, if not essential, to the challenge of planning more frequent campaigns targeting smaller groups of people. And as a side benefit, greater participation in the process of accessing company and customer information will increase general customer knowledge, with the presumption that better-informed marketers will generate more effective customer communications.

To do this, the marketing automation system must overcome two principal issues: The data in the data warehouse or datamart must be *recognizable* and obvious to marketers, and the query process must be *accessible* to marketers.

RDBMS Complexity as Barrier to Use

Relational database management systems (RDBMSs) are software systems that manage data, providing a storage and retrieval infrastructure that is generally flexible, easy to update, reliable, and—if properly configured,

			Columns contain attributes

CustomerID	FirstName	LastName	Gender	Age
123467681	Bob	Smith	M	37
123467682	Mary	Loren	F	45
123467683	Susan	Marks	F	67
123467684	Richard	Dreir	M	24
123467685	David	Barrow	M	32
123467686	Mark	Fontaine	M	29

Rows contain observations

EXHIBIT 14.1   Example Database Table: Customer Table

maintained, and deployed, very responsive to business demands for information.

The term *relational* refers to the ability of an RDBMS to combine data from multiple tables in response to a query. Data is stored in tables having multiple columns and rows. Each row is a *record*, a single observation. Each column is a *field* containing an attribute for that record. If each record is a customer, then the columns will contain customer attributes such as Gender, Age, and First Name (see Exhibit 14.1).

Having data in multiple tables saves space, provided that the information in the tables can be related from one to the other. For example, it is more efficient to have one table for *customer contact information*, and another table for *customer attributes*. There is both a space-saving aspect here as well as a relevance aspect: Marketers querying the database for likely responders are not often going to make use of the customer's name and street address in their quest for response information. If the marketer is looking at sales transactions, it is not necessary for the database to access the customer's name and address in a query for each sales transaction.

However, a marketer having found suitable responders for a cross-sell promotion based on prior purchase history will need the name and address information to address the mailing. To enable the information from the purchase history table to be used to pull the name and address from a customer contact information table requires a common field between the two tables. This field would normally be based on a contrived number uniquely identifying the customer, commonly called the "customer ID," "client ID," or "customer number." The RDBMS can interpret the following query request and return the correct customer address records by joining the two tables as instructed in the query. This query request clearly identifies what the marketer desires from the ContactInfo table for name and address fields, and how the database should select only those names and addresses that are also in the CrossSellList:

Select FirstName, LastName, StreetNum, StreetName, City, State,
Zip from
ContactInfoTable
Inner Join CrossSellList on ContactInfoTable.ClientID =
CrossSellList.ClientID;

Each record or line of data from ContactInfoTable will be *joined* with the corresponding customer record in the CrossSellList table. An RDBMS excels at this join operation. As an aside, this query is not syntactically correct, but it demonstrates how the RDBMS is instructed to use the common field ClientID in order to join information from two tables and select specific fields from one table that share ClientID in a second table, the CrossSellList.

The initial CrossSellList table is created dynamically; it would not normally be considered part of the standard database customer tables. It could have been created as follows:

Select ClientID from RecentPurchasesTable
where PurchaseItemType = "Camera" and PurchaseItemPrice > 500;

In a relational database system there is no reason these two queries could not be combined into one query, since ContactInfoTable and Recent-PurchasesTable both share the customer number field ClientID. This example captures the important contribution of relational data organization for marketers: It is possible to find customers (and their contact information) who exhibit behaviors that signal marketing opportunities, even when this information is contained in more than one table:

Select FirstName, LastName, StreetNum, StreetName, City, State,
Zip from
ContactInfoTable
Inner Join RecentPurchasesTable on ContactInfoTable.ClientID =
RecentPurchasesTable.ClientID
where PurchaseItemType = "Camera" and PurchaseItemPrice > 500;

Once again it is worth noting that the syntax of this query has been simplified for clarity of meaning.

A business will have many tables managed within a single RDBMS database. To extend the example, Bob purchases seven items in one transaction and uses a discount coupon received in a marketing mailing. The sales ticket shows a list of the items, the total, the tax, the time of the transaction, the form of payment, a transaction code to identify the discount coupon that has a marketing code included, and Bob's Best Customer account number. The business has a need to save this information for future use: to record revenue, to update inventory, to record Bob's response to the marketing promotion, and to record Bob's purchase points for addition to his Best Customer account.

The transaction information could be saved as a single record in a database, including Bob's Best Customer information and the transaction details. This would result in a collection of data that would be very challenging to integrate with other business systems, revenue, and inventory, as well as marketing's Best Customer records.

Therefore, the information is broken down and new information is added to facilitate integration. The sale value is given a sales account code so it can be updated to the correct financial revenue account; the tax value is given a tax account code so the appropriate financial system tax account can be updated; Bob's Best Customer account number is used to update a record in the Best Customer member table; and the SKU code for each purchase is used to update the inventory table. If a marketing database is being used, a summary of the transaction and the date could be added to the Recent Purchases fields of the Customer RecentPurchases table. All of these information transactions can rely on the queries and processes running on a relational database management system. (That being said, there are still many systems that rely instead on alternatives to an RDBMS—legacy COBOL-based business systems for, example.)

The query example included above carried the caveat that it was syntactically incorrect; it had been simplified for clarity. The correct syntax, known as Structured Query Language (SQL), provides an adept facility for accomplishing sometimes-intricate joins. For example, a marketer may need a list of customers who have at least one open account active in the prior 30 days but more than one closed account, where no closed account has an outstanding balance due greater than $100 or days delinquent greater than 45. Creating such a query requires facility with the join syntax to select customers and not just account numbers, to select customers with multiple accounts—but accounts that meet the specified criteria. Creating the query requires knowledge of the tables and the columns in the tables that contain the correct information, and knowledge of how the tables are joined and the field or fields used to define the join.

Facility with SQL and knowledge of the data, the tables, and the fields creates a barrier to broader participation in the process of acquiring and exploiting customer information. The barriers imposed by the RDBMSs that house the company and customer data as well as provide access to the data are significant challenges to increasing participation in the marketing process. Access barriers are not specific to any one database; in fact most database systems (Oracle, IBM DB2, Teradata, Microsoft SQL Server, to name the most prominent) are similar and share the fundamental query language known as SQL.

However, a relational database is not simply a collection of tables and fields. For example, taking an Oracle 9i Enterprise Management view of a database highlights several high-level database management functions.

Oracle's Enterprise Management view presents a hierarchical display of databases accessible *from the network*. Right away the presumption is that there is more than one database within the organization, running on more than one platform. The example in Exhibit 14.2 shows only one database, labeled *OCDWORA*.

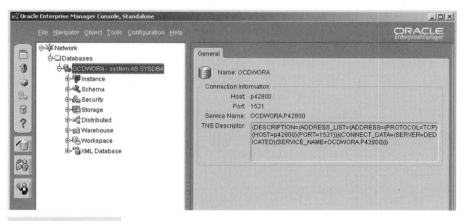

EXHIBIT 14.2   **High-Level View of Oracle Database from Oracle Enterprise Manager**

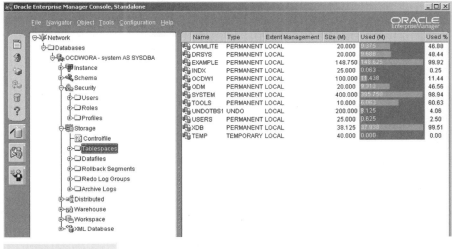

Name	Type	Extent Management	Size (M)	Used (M)		Used %
CWMLITE	PERMANENT LOCAL		20.000	9.375		46.88
DRSYS	PERMANENT LOCAL		20.000	9.688		48.44
EXAMPLE	PERMANENT LOCAL		148.750	148.625		99.92
INDX	PERMANENT LOCAL		25.000	0.063		0.25
OCDW1	PERMANENT LOCAL		100.000	11.438		11.44
ODM	PERMANENT LOCAL		20.000	9.313		46.56
SYSTEM	PERMANENT LOCAL		400.000	395.750		98.94
TOOLS	PERMANENT LOCAL		10.000	6.063		60.63
UNDOTBS1	UNDO	LOCAL	200.000	8.125		4.06
USERS	PERMANENT LOCAL		25.000	0.625		2.50
XDB	PERMANENT LOCAL		38.125	37.938		99.51
TEMP	TEMPORARY LOCAL		40.000	0.000		0.00

EXHIBIT 14.3   High-Level View of Oracle Database: Storage

Below the database identifier are the primary database management functions. *Instance* refers to the operational database and provides functions for starting, pausing, and stopping the database. If the database is stopped it will not respond to query attempts.

Schema refers to specific arrangements of tables and fields; each schema would contain a set of conceptually related tables, or sets of tables grouped by owner. *Security* provides access to functions that manage users, roles, and which schema, tables, and fields individual users or roles have access to.

Additional levels of complexity are exposed in viewing the *Storage* tab (Exhibit 14.3): The tables and fields associated with a Schema have a physical location in an area referred to as a *tablespace*. A database will allocate the physical space using *segments* and allow a certain amount of free space in each segment for additional records to be added in the future. New records will be added to a segment using the same index order sequence, in order to minimize disc-seek time when records are retrieved using queries. *Tablespaces* are finite but expandable. The storage section also highlights additional spaces alluded to earlier: *logging* space and *rollback segment* space.

Highlighting the *Schema* level in the hierarchy exposes the conceptual *schema* view of tables and fields (Exhibit 14.4). The schema labeled *OCDW* has been opened exposing the table-specific tab functions *Tables, Indexes*, and

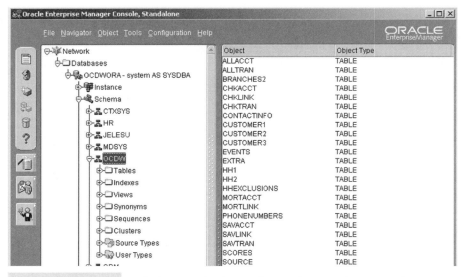

Object	Object Type
ALLACCT	TABLE
ALLTRAN	TABLE
BRANCHES2	TABLE
CHKACCT	TABLE
CHKLINK	TABLE
CHKTRAN	TABLE
CONTACTINFO	TABLE
CUSTOMER1	TABLE
CUSTOMER2	TABLE
CUSTOMER3	TABLE
EVENTS	TABLE
EXTRA	TABLE
HH1	TABLE
HH2	TABLE
HHEXCLUSIONS	TABLE
MORTACCT	TABLE
MORTLINK	TABLE
PHONENUMBERS	TABLE
SAVACCT	TABLE
SAVLINK	TABLE
SAVTRAN	TABLE
SCORES	TABLE
SOURCE	TABLE

EXHIBIT 14.4   High-Level View of Oracle Database: Schema

Views. Tables synonymous with data—information arranged in rows and columns; a table can be *indexed* so a specific record or ranges of records can be accessed more quickly,[1] similar to the page numbers of chapters listed in a table of contents.

Opening the Tables tab exposes a list of tables: *ALLACCT, ALLTRAN, BRANCHES2*, and so on. The fields of a table can be viewed just by highlighting the table name, as shown in Exhibit 14.5 for the table CONTACTINFO. This table contains (barely recognizable) fields such as *WorkPhone* ("*CWPH*"), *HomePhone* ("*CHPH*"), *Zip* ("*CZIP*"), and *City* ("*CCITY_T*").

The "field definition," which defines the data type,[2] includes *Datatype, Size,* and *Scale,* and whether Nulls are allowed. The data type *Varchar2* means character data.[3] *Size* means size in bytes. By examination the expected

---

[1]An *index* is a list of the unique values for a specific field, along with the value's record location, where the record is stored. The location is recorded by *segment location*, not the location on a physical disc.

[2]See discussion of data types in Chapter 12.

[3]The "2" in "varchar2" refers to double-byte storage for Unicode support.

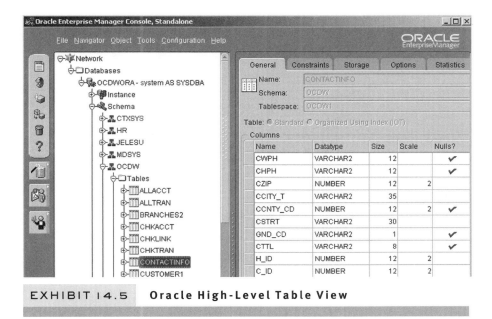

EXHIBIT 14.5   Oracle High-Level Table View

format for *WorkPhone,* which is 12 bytes in length, could be a North American–derived "999-999-9999," which encompasses 12 characters. The *Scale* column is used for numeric variables and refers to the number of decimal places. A checkmark in the "Nulls?" category means that null values (no value) are allowed. Some fields, such as *Customer Number ("C_ID"),* would not have a checkmark in the Nulls column; having no value in this field would prevent the database from being able to relate this record to customer records in other tables. Having the Nulls? field unchecked would cause the database to reject any record update that included null values for this field. The same is true of "CZIP" to improve addressability.

There are a number of additional functions that can be applied to tables, besides viewing the fields and their attributes: *Create* a new table, *Create* a new table *Like* the present table, *Create Index, Create Synonym, Grant Privileges On,* and *View/Edit Contents* (see Exhibit 14.6).

Using View/Edit Contents enables a view of the row-and-column data for this table (Exhibit 14.7).

Remaining database management functions (Exhibit 14.8) available from the Enterprise Management console view include functions more specific to RDBMS technology: the ability to define *Views,* create *Synonyms* and *Sequences,* and define *Clusters, Source Types,* and *User Types.*

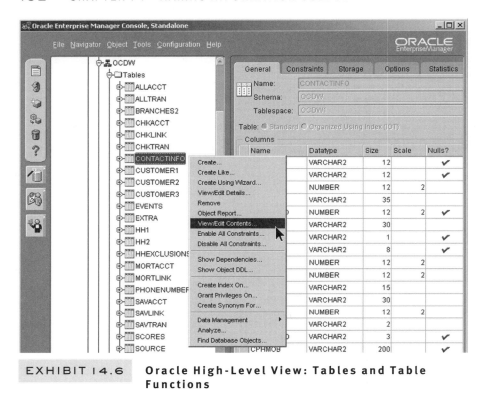

Oracle High-Level View: Tables and Table Functions

Data Columns and Variable Names

Data in the database is organized primarily by tables and fields (columns, variables) within tables. The table and field names are often confusing; the underlying content is not necessarily obvious from the name (as seen in the table example for customer contact information). For convenience a DBA will employ a short reference, known as a mnemonic, instead of a longer name. This makes it easier to write queries that include repeated references to table and field names. Customer information stored in a data warehouse or datamart will be derived from primary sources and may retain the primary source attributes, including the column name. Older systems housing legacy data may retain a column name that had significant length restrictions; for example, eight characters may have been the maximum allowed in the older system.

As an example, "Gender" might have a column name of GNDR or GENDER in a database; it is fairly short. "First Name" is not short and is

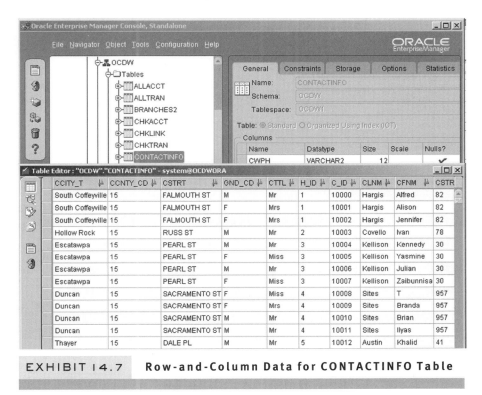

EXHIBIT 14.7   Row-and-Column Data for CONTACTINFO Table

EXHIBIT 14.7   Row-and-Column Data for CONTACTINFO Table

made up of two words; a shorthand mnemonic could be FNAME. A column representing "Occupation Code" could be mnemonically represented as OCCUP. Because occupation code is probably a number requiring a translation table, the DBA might standardize all numerically coded columns with the suffix "_CD." OCCUP becomes OCC_CD or OCCUP_CD. The only common denominator for column names within the database is usually the lack of spaces in the name, and the more obtuse the content, the more cryptic the name can become.

Legacy Definitions

Inherited legacy applications can further frustrate attempts to decipher information from the database. "Account Number," representing a client account, could be labeled ACCTNUM or ACCT or perhaps MACCR_CD, programmer shorthand for "master account reference code," a legacy from an earlier time when perhaps there *was* a master account reference code. It may be

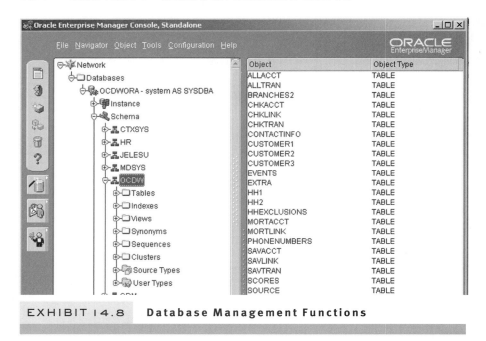

EXHIBIT 14.8   **Database Management Functions**

tempting to change these values to clarify their purpose; unfortunately these values can be inherited from legacy accounting and operations applications coded in COBOL. Making changes to internal software applications that have been in operation for many years is very expensive and can be very risky.

The data itself can be difficult to decipher without accompanying translations. Gender, for example, might be expected to be "Male" or "Female" in the database, but this is unlikely as there are too many characters: Several million records coded "Male" or "Female" will require much more space than a single character such as M or F or 0 or 1. A database that uses eight characters where one character will suffice will require eight times more disc storage. More storage space means higher purchase and maintenance costs as well as longer response times for update and retrieval. The DBA will therefore code Gender as M or F or 1 or 0,[4] to minimize space, reduce cost, and improve performance.

---

[4]"0" or "1" in this case refers to a single-byte character data type, not a numeric data type. If it were numeric, it would take up more physical space and contribute to higher storage costs and lower performance. Even the most likely minimum level of storage would be 24 bits, which can be recalled from the earlier discussion on digital information representation (Chapter 12).

Making information useful will also entail combinations of fields, as well as calculated fields. Many key pieces of information are derived in the database from several fields. Other information, such as summaries of sales over different periods, requires aggregate calculations (sum, average, count) on several fields. The individual purchase transactions are not necessarily as interesting as their frequency, count, average value, and summary value during the past 30, 60, or 90 days. Combining fields and calculating aggregates increases the complexity of the query.

The potential for obscurity and the corresponding translation challenge is increased by the necessary use of operational variables, which, though even more cryptically named, are often critical to marketing use. Confronting a hundred or so such obscure mnemonic representations over and above their sometimes equally obscure operational derivation is an even more significant barrier to the use of the information underlying these designations. While a database table view could be tailored to the individual information needs of each specific group of users (a view where only those fields relevant to that group are presented), this is very unusual in practice. Hence a database table view usually contains all fields in the table, with no indication of the relative value—for marketing—of each field. There can be thousands of fields spread across a hundred or more tables.

OPERATIONS-BASED SUPPRESSION CRITERIA

In addition, most businesses have standardized *suppression criteria* that sometimes involve sophisticated knowledge of the criteria as well as how the criteria—customer attributes—are coded or represented in the customer database. Suppression criteria include fields identifying opt-out customers, internal accounts held by employees, accounts whose mailing address is restricted, and accounts whose owners are deceased or no longer resident at the address. Operationally dictated customer attributes may not be represented in the database in a straightforward manner, and each campaign list of prospective recipients must use these criteria as filters to reduce the list according to the applicable suppression criteria.

Having selected and *cleaned* a list of prospective recipients, the final step is to merge in the contact information and format the resulting list according to the requirements of the fulfillment vendor, such as a call center or letter shop. Service agencies will expect specific fields (name, address, phone) in specific locations in the file, and the file to be in a particular format.

Viewing a table is not the same as extracting a list of prospective customers; tables can contain tens of millions of records. For example, a 20 million customer database could contain 50% (or more) additional customer records, representing previous and nonactive customers, for a total of 30 million rows. Assuming 1.5 customers per household, there would be an equivalent count of 20 million records in a *household*-level table. Contact information might include one or more prior addresses, for an additional 20 million or more records. Customers may have more than one account, active or otherwise, for possibly 2 × 30 million or 60 million account records. And finally, individual transactions should be accessible; assuming five purchases per customer (average, including returned purchases), a transaction table would comprise 150 million rows or more.

The mnemonics may be associated with a longer "name," called a *column descriptor,* to make the information clearer outside of the context of the database. This is not automatic or mandatory; it is up to the DBA creating the database to include this information. If it is included, it may not be intended for marketers' use and so provide limited clarification. Similarly, a *data dictionary* is not automatically part of the database documentation; it is produced and maintained by the DBA or data architect. The RDBMS will include system tables that do contain very detailed information on the *database-specific* aspects of the tables and columns, and these are not very helpful for a marketer trying to understand the business- or customer-relevant content of a table or column.

Marketers, in fact any non–DBA, will find the raw database environment so described to be very difficult to decipher. The prominent use of mnemonics, even those that are conventional, and a data dictionary targeting primarily other DBAs will employ an unnatural language and may reference other tables and fields with just as cryptic and hard-to-decipher language. This is not at all to cast aspersions on database architects and DBAs. By the very nature of data organization, its maintenance, security, and the need to produce desired results quickly and efficiently, the process of creating lists of customers targeted for marketing communications using a relational database can be very challenging and require appropriate relational database skills and experience.

STRUCTURED QUERY LANGUAGE

As a result of this challenge, individuals who know the business database and the query language of RDBMS systems are very useful for organizations in their ability to extract information from a data warehouse or mart for marketers' use. The organization of tables and fields has an inherent level of complexity, for example, the concepts of *relationship* and *cardinality*: A marketing campaign might require selection of *households* derived from *individuals* (one–to–many cardinality) who have purchased *two or more products* from a *particular product family* (a table relationship) in the *past 60 days,* who have a *response score of at least 0.45,* have not received an *alternative promotion* in the *past 30 days,* and are not on any of the *Do Not Mail* lists. Part of SQL covers *table join criteria,* which accounts for both cardinality and relationship.

Additional *suppressions* may be required as part of any production campaign, such as foreign mailing address, special arrangements, company employees, and prior testing audiences. Multiple queries (in SQL form) may be required to merge the initial list of selected customers with their call center or mailing information (name, address, phone number). The resulting list may need resorting based on the type of promotion or promotion group. Additional work may be required in setting up a back test to confirm response results, structuring the list as text for transmission to a letter shop or call center, and finally loading the list to an ftp directory for receipt by the letter shop, followed by a call to the letter shop to let them know the list is ready and to confirm successful receipt.

The process of building the list for campaign use is a lot of work, sometimes sophisticated work, and more so when there are problems, delays, or mistakes in the day–to–day process of creating the resources for a marketing campaign. And for the people who do the work there are more requests than time to fulfill them.

The language used to build the queries is known as Structured Query Language. The knowledge and experience required to use SQL effectively, to extract information for marketing requirements and audience selection, can be significant. Using SQL effectively means both designing a query that translates the marketing requirements correctly as well as building a query that uses machine resources efficiently. It is possible to create a query that extracts the correct information but takes hours to execute. Such queries impact other users, whose queries in turn take longer to execute, and so on down the line. A well-designed SQL query must respect marketing requirements as well as system resource requirements. Marketers typically do not have the knowledge or the time to develop the experience in order to use SQL with confidence.

Databases are designed to facilitate storage and extraction of information or data. That being said, *facilitate* is less "to make easy" than "to make possible" and "to make efficient." Response is in the form of a multiple of rows from tables that contain many millions of records. To extract information from a table or combination of tables, a query is necessary; the semantics for constructing the query are known as *Structured Query Language* (SQL). The Oracle tool for querying tables is called *SQL+*. Using SQL+, queries can be constructed to extract information (*Select column, column. . .*), create a new table (*Create table Example as. . .*), and count records (*Select Count(*). . .*). Selecting customers with specific attributes can be done using a *Where clause* in the query: *Where Gender='F' and Zip=26034.* (Quotes are used with character data, not numeric data.)

These same cases are demonstrated using an SQL+ session log in Exhibit 14.9. First the table Example is created, containing the fields Clientid, Firstname, Lastname, City, State, and Zip. The query must state from which table these fields are to be selected—*Select . . . From . . .* —which is Tdata.Contactinfo. Finally, the query requests only records that have an "F" in the column Gender, and 26034 in the column Zip, *Where Gender='F' and Zip=26034.* SQL+ responds "Table Created." The next query requests a count of all records in the newly created table: *Select count(*) from Example.* SQL+ responds with a column name, "COUNT(*)" and a count of 2. The final query from Exhibit 14.9 requests a display of the records in the table: *Select * from Example* (" *" means "Select all fields"). *Select count(*)* means count all records.

The database marketer knows the relationship between tables and the primary key and foreign key information that defines the relationship. The key values are critical to maintaining the integrity of the data. These key values must be unique, and the database can maintain the uniqueness of these key values whenever it is updated to ensure there are no ambiguous duplicate entries. A duplicate entry is ambiguous because there is no way to know

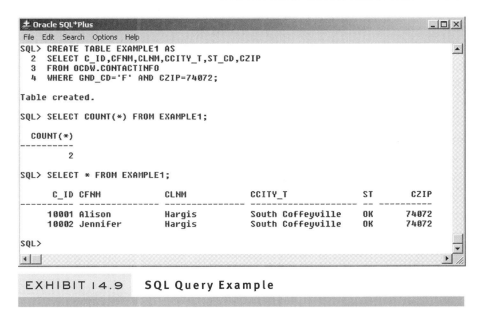

```
Oracle SQL*Plus                                                        _ □ ×
File  Edit  Search  Options  Help
SQL> CREATE TABLE EXAMPLE1 AS
  2   SELECT C_ID,CFNM,CLNM,CCITY_T,ST_CD,CZIP
  3   FROM OCDW.CONTACTINFO
  4   WHERE GND_CD='F' AND CZIP=74072;

Table created.

SQL> SELECT COUNT(*) FROM EXAMPLE1;

  COUNT(*)
----------
         2

SQL> SELECT * FROM EXAMPLE1;

    C_ID CFNM              CLNM              CCITY_T               ST    CZIP
-------- ----------------  ----------------  --------------------  --  --------
   10001 Alison            Hargis            South Coffeyville     OK     74072
   10002 Jennifer          Hargis            South Coffeyville     OK     74072

SQL>
```

EXHIBIT 14.9   SQL Query Example

which of two duplicate key records contains the correct or preferred values. For example, if the column C_ID is a primary key, which is the correct street address for C_ID = 1000 below?

C_ID	STREET NUMBER	STREET NAME	CITY	STATE	ZIP
1000	14	Main St.	Montague	Montana	23723
1000	21	Central St.	Montague	Montana	23723

As new data is added to an RDBMS, the records are typically checked for mutual exclusivity along primary key fields. Another RDBMS function can be used to ensure that the contents of other fields are checked to confirm their contents are consistent with defined values for these fields. The coding for Gender may be F or M, for example; the database can reject a record update where Gender = K instead of F or M. This process is known as *maintaining referential integrity*.

To construct queries that return the correct and expected information requires the ability to *select* specific fields from specific tables and to correctly *join* multiple tables as required. To do this well requires a thorough and intimate knowledge of the many tables and fields in the database, *even more so* than that of the DBA responsible for managing the environment. The DBA is primarily concerned with the health and integrity of the *framework,* the database that *contains* the tables, fields, and records. The database marketers merge their knowledge of the data with their knowledge of the business, to provide appropriate response to marketing information requests.

Database marketers are specialists, and their skills are applied to selecting audiences for marketing activities; summarizing and describing marketing segments, collecting, summarizing, and interpreting test results; puzzling through and validating ambiguous or incorrect marketing information reports, as well as pursuing operational problems due to their understanding of the business and how the business is represented by the operational data. While operational people do have access to the primary systems whose data is replicated in the data warehouse or datamart, the warehouse and datamart can include information from different operational systems and the ease and speed of access can contribute to resolution of operational problems, easier and faster than through operational systems.

As might be expected, the database marketers can become a significant bottleneck for marketers trying to develop more and more frequent promotions with increasingly targeted and filtered audiences. Not only is the flow of information impeded by such a bottleneck; in fact the operational execution of increasingly targeted communications is slowed by lack of resources required in selecting the audiences themselves. Even when some marketing analysts attempt to bridge the gap and participate in the process of audience selection and customer information–based activities, the information access barriers discussed throughout this chapter can result in incorrect results: The wrong audience is selected or no audience at all is selected. The first challenge for the SQL-initiate may be crafting the correct SQL syntax to generate a result; the next challenge, shared by novices and experts, is confirming that the results of the query are correct and consistent with the request.

The point should be clear now that the RDBMS provides a wealth of services associated with a framework for maintaining customer data and extracting customer information to form lists for marketing promotions. Databases are not simply a collection of tables and fields; there are a large number of support functions included. Maintenance includes table main-tenance as well as logging, rollback, physical table spaces, and user and resource security. Information is included in fields that are spread across multiple tables, joined by primary keys that are defined to ensure relational consistency and integrity; tables are indexed to speed query execution. Information is extracted using SQL, a powerful but complex language that appears to be necessarily complex because of the nature of relational information organization.

At the same time, the RDBMS raises a number of barriers to accessing information using the relational database management functions of the system. These barriers frustrate attempts to engage marketers more directly in the process of communicating with customers. To summarize, they are as follows:

- Breadth of tables and columns.
- Data organization is based on RDBMS requirements.
- Lack of marketing weight given to highlight relevant marketing information.
- Cryptic mnemonic representations of tables and columns as well as the underlying data.
- Multiple fields/columns are required to create information relevant to marketing.
- Calculated columns are required to create relevant customer indexes,
- Aggregate calculations are required to summarize customer information such as transactions.
- Specialized language (SQL) is required for accessing the database.
- Limited skilled resources are available to respond to marketing requests.
- Multiple views of customer data are required based on skill level and area of application.
- Standardized queries are required to manage common queries, such as suppression lists.
- Standardized "export formats" are required to meet individual vendor requirements, such as letter shop and call center.

Information Map as Facilitator

To overcome these barriers without sacrificing the utility of the RDBMS, an interface or a map between the data in the database and the marketer's use of customer information is necessary. In fact, if a marketer were to describe the information required to address marketing needs, and such a list were to be compared to the database, there would be obvious inconsistencies: The *data* is stored one way and the marketer views the *information* in another way.

The information map is not a replacement for the RDBMS, which continues to hold an essential position in the information management hierarchy. An RDBMS has a necessary level of complexity. A map between the database and the marketer's view of customer information would:

- Be organized according to the view of the user—the *marketer's* view.
- Provide better visibility to *marketing* information, and hide or obscure information of less relevance, if not exclude it altogether.
- Provide clear identification of the information in terms most *marketers* would recognize and understand.
- Provide preaggregations and calculations of necessary calculated fields, or at least provide the *syntax* for execution behind the scenes.
- Provide a more intuitive technique for creating the customer selection queries, one that does not require a knowledge of SQL.
- Augment the capabilities of the database marketers, and not provide a dumbed-down replacement for SQL.

The information map would provide better documentation; it would provide clarification of relevant and obscurely termed fields and keep the interference of irrelevant content out of the marketer's view, improving access by removing unnecessarily confusing content.

The information map would also not be subject to the "table–field" organization of information. While a skilled SQL practitioner must know which field is in which table as well as the fields needed to join tables in order to design the query correctly, using an information map should enable the table and table-join criteria to be defined—but defined *outside of* the marketer's view of the customer *information,* which is defined and presented according to how the *marketers* view customer information.

An information map is not just additional documentation for existing tables and fields, nor is it a one-for-one literal translation of tables and fields into "marketing-speak." For example, some marketers may view customer information in a single dimension; the information is collected/defined/

organized into a single conceptual view labeled "Customer Information." All relevant customer information can be saved in this conceptual view, even if the information comes from more than one table. For other marketers and companies, customers occupy households; there is often more than one customer per household, and information exists specific to a household that is not specific to a customer, and vice versa. Hence an additional view of *Household* can be appropriate. What is important is that the table/field designations do not exist as a restriction on the presentation of information in the information map.

The information map is another fundamental component of a marketing automation system. However, the information map provides a window or view of the data but it does not provide any other function. Audience lists based on information about customers must still be *selected, extracted,* and *counted* for marketing purposes, using a tool much like SQL+, preferably without the need to know Structured Query Language. Therefore, in addition to an information map, a marketing automation system must provide an alternative to SQL-based queries, and this functionality needs to encompass the ability to schedule and monitor execution of the queries that drive selection of customers for marketing communications. After execution of customer selections, the system must provide feedback to marketing on the results of the promotions, and the results must be incorporated into marketing management reports.

These necessary capabilities are interesting to discuss and elaborate from, but provide little tangible benefit in the clarification of what marketing automation can actually accomplish. Therefore, the discussion proceeds based on an actual marketing automation system. SAS Marketing Automation includes software applications that provide information map functionality, an intuitive query capability, and campaign management capabilities, and will be used to substantiate the tangible opportunities provided by a marketing automation system.

In the next chapter, the information map will be discussed based on the example of SAS Information Map Studio. Chapter 16 will discuss how queries can be constructed and scheduled for selecting marketing audiences without SQL+ based on the example of SAS Campaign Studio. These two software applications are examples of functional cornerstones in any marketing automation system.

CHAPTER 15

Information Map

Translating the variable names and data to terms meaningful for marketers is the first step in broadening participation in the marketing process and improving the effectiveness of the marketing team by improving accessibility to relevant information and removing bottlenecks imposed by knowledge resources such as database marketers. The translation is represented by an *information map*, a collection of information about the actual data stored in the RDBMS.

Any collection of data about data can be referred to as *metadata*. Assume that the customer data for OurCompany has been assembled in a data warehouse based in Oracle. The arrangement of the tables is referred to as the *physical data*. The RDBMS can be interrogated to acquire information about the tables and fields contained in the database. In turn this information can be used to advantage by other applications to facilitate the information mapping process.

To initiate the mapping process first requires identification of the RDBMS on the network and importing the database metadata, the information about the tables and fields, which is exemplified using Exhibits 15.1 and 15.2. The metadata about the database server and database is acquired once and stored in a metadata repository, literally a database containing information about other databases and their servers. Thereafter the datasource can be defined for other applications, which can interrogate the metadata repository for information required to make a connection to the database.

After the database and tables metadata has been acquired it can be shared by an information mapping application such as SAS Information Map Studio. The table information is implemented for the information

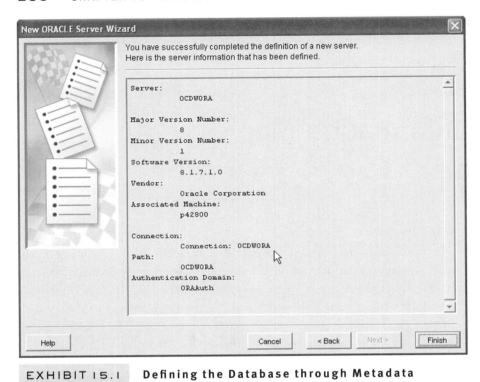

New ORACLE Server Wizard

You have successfully completed the definition of a new server.
Here is the server information that has been defined.

```
Server:
        OCDWORA

Major Version Number:
        8
Minor Version Number:
        1
Software Version:
        8.1.7.1.0
Vendor:
        Oracle Corporation
Associated Machine:
        p42800

Connection:
        Connection: OCDWORA
Path:
        OCDWORA
Authentication Domain:
        ORAAuth
```

| Help | | Cancel | < Back | Next > | Finish |

EXHIBIT 15.1　**Defining the Database through Metadata**

map by selecting specific tables from a list of available tables (Exhibit 15.1).[1] After adding the table and field information, the translation of the table and column information to marketing terms can begin.

The process of making the information map useful to a marketer is actually fairly simple. The initial information (metadata) about tables and columns needs to be augmented by some additional information such as primary keys and join criteria (see Exhibit 15.2). This information is added to the metadata about the tables and columns, stored in the same metadata repository, and used in the construction of queries—queries that are built by an application such as SAS Campaign Studio. The additional information needs to be specified only once; thereafter it is available for applications that need it.

---

[1]SAS can access most databases individually or in combination, and does not rely on a specific database.

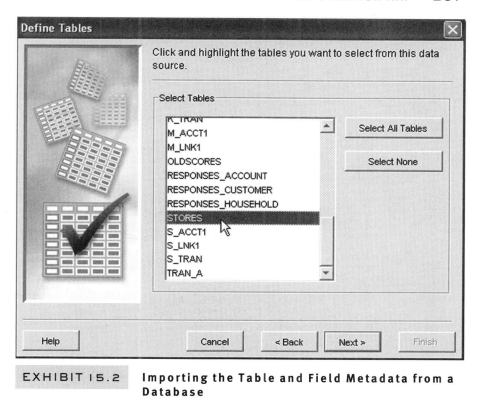

Define Tables

Click and highlight the tables you want to select from this data source.

Select Tables

| R_TRAN |
| M_ACCT1 |
| M_LNK1 |
| OLDSCORES |
| RESPONSES_ACCOUNT |
| RESPONSES_CUSTOMER |
| RESPONSES_HOUSEHOLD |
| STORES |
| S_ACCT1 |
| S_LNK1 |
| S_TRAN |
| TRAN_A |

Select All Tables

Select None

Help   Cancel   < Back   Next >   Finish

EXHIBIT 15.2   Importing the Table and Field Metadata from a Database

This *expansion* of the metadata beyond that provided by the RDBMS is needed to accommodate user-defined information. User-defined information includes marketer-specific content, such as data labels a marketer understands, and data-specific information needed to develop consistent queries on the database. Providing this information as metadata enables the query activity to take place without requiring the marketer's active knowledge of the RDBMS or the data organization of table names and column names. If the market needs to access data contained in two tables, the marketer need not even know there are two tables in the RDBMS, provided this information and the join criteria are contained *in the metadata*. By enabling applications to make use of augmented metadata, queries can be effectively constructed *on behalf of* marketing users, requiring only the marketers' understanding of the *customer information*, not its physical

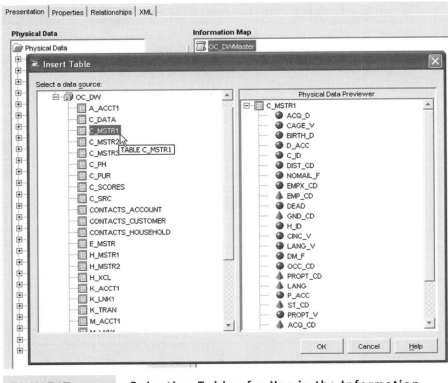

EXHIBIT 15.3   Selecting Tables for Use in the Information Map

implementation in the RDBMS. This will be demonstrated more clearly by the examples that follow.

For this example the physical tables in Exhibit 15.4 from the Oracle RDBMS have been identified to Information Map Studio using the "Insert Table" function shown in Exhibit 15.3. This is the *physical data* that will form the foundation of the information map.

There are 20 or so tables representing *customer information, customer contact information*, and *customer responses*. Customer data is located in three tables, here labeled C_Mstr1, C_Mstr2, and C_Mstr3. Two tables are used to hold household-specific information: H_MSTR1 and H_MSTR2. Another table contains customer account information: A_ACCT1. The table TRAN_A contains customer transactions. In addition, there is a table for

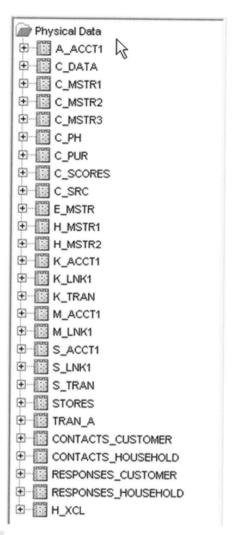

Physical Data
- A_ACCT1
- C_DATA
- C_MSTR1
- C_MSTR2
- C_MSTR3
- C_PH
- C_PUR
- C_SCORES
- C_SRC
- E_MSTR
- H_MSTR1
- H_MSTR2
- K_ACCT1
- K_LNK1
- K_TRAN
- M_ACCT1
- M_LNK1
- S_ACCT1
- S_LNK1
- S_TRAN
- STORES
- TRAN_A
- CONTACTS_CUSTOMER
- CONTACTS_HOUSEHOLD
- RESPONSES_CUSTOMER
- RESPONSES_HOUSEHOLD
- H_XCL

EXHIBIT 15.4   Database Physical Table View

events: E_MSTR. Events might be a large deposit or withdrawal in a bank, or a significant purchase or lack of purchase in a retail business. There is a table for scores, labeled C_SCORES.

Security is enhanced by separating customer contact information contained in the table C_DATA from the customer attributes: Access to the customer contact information table and its fields can be restricted to specific people or processes.

All customers for OurCompany have specific *client identification codes*, unique identification numbers that are called *Client IDs* and denoted in the database by the variable name C_ID. The C_ID is unique for each customer and the customer table does not have duplicate entries for C_ID. A unique identifier for each record in a table is also known as a *primary key* for a table.

The column C_ID is also present in the Customer Contact Information table; therefore customer information can be selected along with contact information by matching records in the two tables based on matching their respective C_ID fields. The matching process between tables is called *joining* the two tables. The join is done based on the specified field C_ID. The RDBMS manages the join process between tables, and is optimized to do this efficiently and quickly based on the DBA definition for the join criteria. Relational database systems derive their name from an emphasis on their ability to *relate* records from different tables.

The marketer will not need to know of the existence of the two tables or of the join criteria; this is one of the challenges overcome by an information map. The tables and join criteria for all of the tables are defined in the information map, in advance, through the application. The join is represented in Exhibit 15.5.

In this view, the Primary Table *C_MSTR1* key field *C_ID* is identified with the corresponding Related Table *C_DATA* and its key field, which is the field used to define an *inner join*.[2]

SAS Information Map Studio represents the marketer's perspective of the information using a second view labeled "Information Map" (see Exhibit 15.6). Exhibit 15.6 demonstrates an organization of information that is not based on physical tables at all; it is based on a marketer's perspective on customer information. A set of folders have been defined: "Customer," "Households," and "Contact Information." Within each folder data items will be added based on (or derived from, if multiple columns or calculations are required) physical columns. These column names will be elaborated in

---

[2]Inner and outer joins are easy to understand: An inner join will match rows from two tables and select only the matching rows between both tables. If the left table has additional rows (more than the right table) the nonmatching rows will be ignored. An outer join will include the rows from the left table that do not match any rows in the right table.

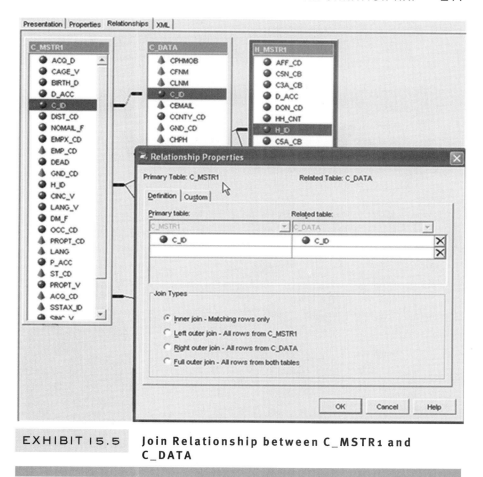

EXHIBIT 15.5   Join Relationship between C_MSTR1 and C_DATA

marketing terms to make their purpose clear (see Exhibit 15.7). Exhibit 15.7, for example, highlights the definition of "Occupation Code (Primary)," which corresponds to the physical column OCC_CD from table C_Mstr1.

The map uses the series of folders to group information. The information itself is referred to as a *data item*. The folders are based on the marketer's view of customer information. Exhibits 15.8 and 15.9 demonstrate the contents of two such folders, "Customer" and "Contact Information." Within the folders are the data items representing columns from the RDBMS. While this example displays specific columns from the database, such as "First Name" and "Last Name," a data item can also be based on combinations of columns or calculations based on columns. The data items in any one folder

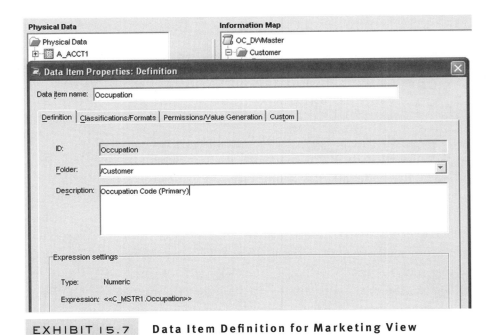

| Presentation | Properties | Relationships | XML |

Physical Data

- Physical Data
  - A_ACCT1
  - C_DATA
  - C_MSTR1
  - C_MSTR2
  - C_MSTR3
  - C_PH
  - C_PUR
  - C_SCORES
  - C_SRC
  - E_MSTR
  - H_MSTR1
  - H_MSTR2

Information Map

- OC_DWMaster
  - Customer
  - Contact Information
  - Households
  - Accounts
  - Events
  - Scores
  - Transactions
  - Contact History Customer
  - Response History Customer
  - Contact History Household
  - Response History Household

EXHIBIT 15.6 Marketer's ''Information Map'' View of Database

Physical Data

- Physical Data
  - A_ACCT1

Information Map

- OC_DWMaster
  - Customer

Data Item Properties: Definition

Data item name: Occupation

| Definition | Classifications/Formats | Permissions/Value Generation | Custom |

ID: Occupation

Folder: /Customer

Description: Occupation Code (Primary)

Expression settings

Type: Numeric

Expression: <<C_MSTR1.Occupation>>

EXHIBIT 15.7 Data Item Definition for Marketing View

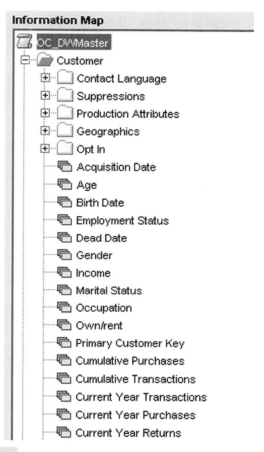

EXHIBIT 15.8   Information Map View of Customer Folder and Customer Data Items

can come from any table; the folders do not have to contain data items from any one table. This maintains the *marketer's view* of customer information in the information map.

Continuing the example, the columns representing customer contact information have been added to the information map. These data items are derived primarily from the columns in the *ContactInfo* table shown from Oracle Enterprise Manager in the previous chapter (Exhibit 15.5). Note that the previously cryptic column names are now very clear (Exhibit 15.9).

The folder is clearly labeled "Contact Information" and each field is readily identifiable, for example "First Name," "Last Name," and mailing

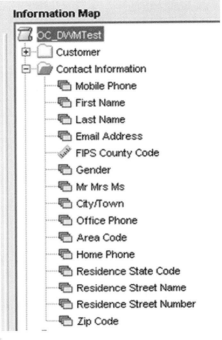

Information Map

- ▣ OC_DWMTest
  - ⊞ ☐ Customer
  - ⊟ 🗀 Contact Information
    - 🗐 Mobile Phone
    - 🗐 First Name
    - 🗐 Last Name
    - 🗐 Email Address
    - 🖉 FIPS County Code
    - 🗐 Gender
    - 🗐 Mr Mrs Ms
    - 🗐 City/Town
    - 🗐 Office Phone
    - 🗐 Area Code
    - 🗐 Home Phone
    - 🗐 Residence State Code
    - 🗐 Residence Street Name
    - 🗐 Residence Street Number
    - 🗐 Zip Code

EXHIBIT 15.9   Information Map View of Contact Information

address information. For contrast, the same information from the database is shown in Exhibit 15.10.

Several steps have been taken in the information map to simplify use of the information for marketing. Some steps are not immediately obvious, and some steps are even less obvious, those that extend the use of the information map to SAS's marketing automation application. Examining the steps in more detail will demonstrate the importance of the ability to represent the data using additional information—*metadata*—and *extend* the metadata for broader use by other applications.

Keep in mind that the information map is *data about data*; it is not the data itself, nor does it modify the data it is describing. It is purely a tool to facilitate *accessing* the data by describing it more fully through the additional information referred to as *metadata*.

Continuing the example above, and expanding the view to include the source data, it is clear the information from the database is also contained in

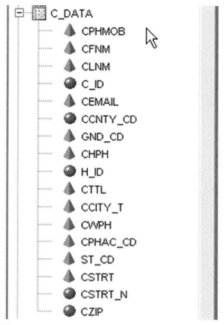

EXHIBIT 15.10   **Database Table and Fields for Customer Contact Information**

the information map so the derivation of the marketer's view from the physical content is clearly available (Exhibit 15.11). On the left side is the information taken directly from the source database, in this case an Oracle database. This is table names and column names. The customer contact information table is called C_DATA. The first field, CPHMOB, represents customer mobile phone, and the next two fields are first name, CFNM, and last name, CLNM. The fourth field is recognizable from previous examples: C_ID or Customer ID.

The information map has a distinct advantage—for marketers—over the organization of information in tables and columns in a database. Information in the information map is *not constrained* by the location of information by table or column. In fact, the flexibility of the information map means that the *marketer's view* of information about customers can dictate how the information map itself is designed. The view of the data presented to the marketers by an application using this information map will be consistent with how marketers view and use information about their customers.

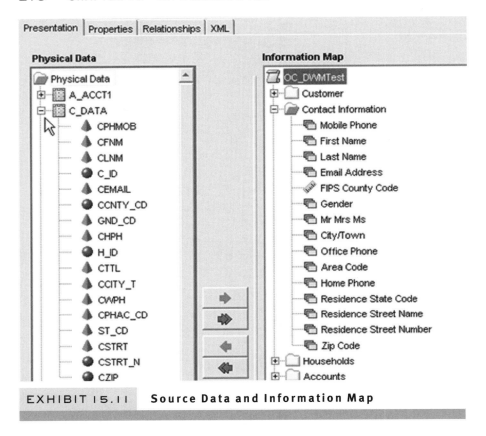

EXHIBIT 15.11   Source Data and Information Map

In fact, the organization of information in the information map can and should be dictated by marketers, making the customer information from the customer table—or any other relevant table—more obvious.

In the case of OurCompany, marketers view the information in Exhibit 15.12 as relevant for describing customers in the context of making selections for marketing purposes.

For OurCompany, information is organized by folders. Different folders have been established representing information about Customers, Households, Accounts, and Transactions. Additional folders were created to hold Model Scores and Events. Contact History and Response information were also given to separate folders, and the same for contact information. Expanding the Customer folder highlights additional levels through additional folders: *Contact Language*, *Suppressions*, *Production Attributes*, *Geographics*, and *Opt-In* customer attributes (Exhibit 15.13).

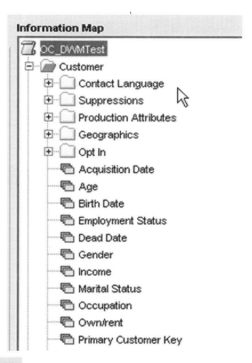

EXHIBIT 15.12   Information Map Folders and Customer View

EXHIBIT 15.13   Customer Folder Expansion

As described earlier, the individual data items within folders are not limited to database columns exclusively. Their flexibility is quite broad:

- Calculated columns, such as Monthly Average Purchases
- Binary filters (select only occupation codes 023, 024, and 025)
- Fact table selections (credit score based on score table where Score Code="21")
- Summary information (cumulative sales for current year)
- Range information (maximum purchase greater than $2,000)
- Count information (total purchases greater than 7)

While the marketer focuses on the data item itself, and in fact the data item is defined in marketing terms, how the data item is derived can be determined by opening the properties of a data item. For example, a calculated item is shown in Exhibit 15.14.

Score values are frequently maintained in a single table, to facilitate periodic update. These values can be specified in the information map based on a filter that selects the appropriate score values based on the score ID, an identifier similar to "Customer Number" (Exhibit 15.15 and 15.16). The marketer need not know the score ID, as it is implemented through the information map by reference to the name "Response Score," shown in Exhibit 15.16.

Earlier a reference to "additional information" (to be added to the metadata) was made. This additional information is added through *extended*

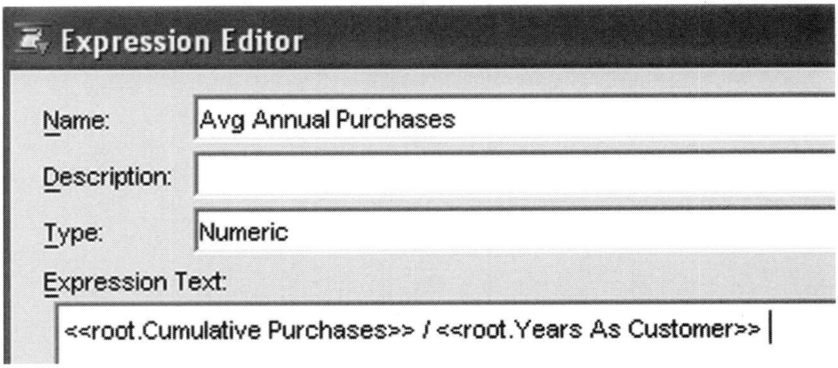

Expression Editor

Name: Avg Annual Purchases

Description:

Type: Numeric

Expression Text:

<<root.Cumulative Purchases>> / <<root.Years As Customer>>

EXHIBIT 15.14   Calculated Data Item Example

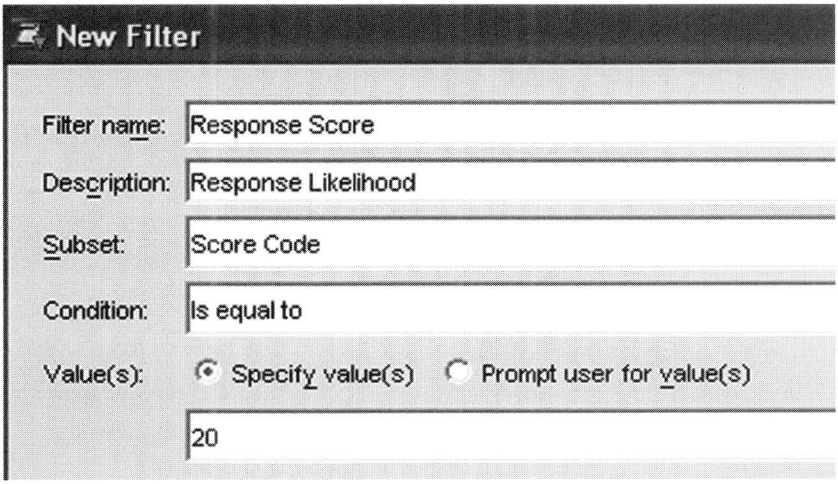

New Filter

Filter name: Response Score

Description: Response Likelihood

Subset: Score Code

Condition: Is equal to

Value(s): ⦿ Specify value(s)   ○ Prompt user for value(s)

20

EXHIBIT 15.15   Score Definition through Metadata

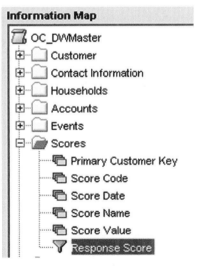

Information Map

📜 OC_DWMaster
  ⊞ ☐ Customer
  ⊞ ☐ Contact Information
  ⊞ ☐ Households
  ⊞ ☐ Accounts
  ⊞ ☐ Events
  ⊟ 📁 Scores
      🗂 Primary Customer Key
      🗂 Score Code
      🗂 Score Date
      🗂 Score Name
      🗂 Score Value
      🔻 Response Score

EXHIBIT 15.16   "Response Score" Available Directly from Information Map Scores Folder

Values:

Priority	Select	Value	Total		Selected	
			Count	Percent	Count	Percent
	☐	F	5,191	51		
	☐	M	4,963	49		

EXHIBIT 15.17   **Frequency Table for Gender**

attributes for the data item, an extension to the metadata available from the RDBMS. Extended attributes are used to define the data type so that appropriate summary views can be created. Summary information for each data item can be represented by a table or a histogram, or by statistical measures such as average. Histograms and summary statistics are based on numerical data, such as age.

Tables and histograms provide great value in helping marketers learn more about their customers (see Exhibits 15.17 and 15.18). How would an application that summarizes information know that Occupation Code, which is a numeric code, should have a table summary instead of a histogram summary? This information is added to the information map *metadata* about the data item. Table information is defined as "nominal," while a histogram view is dictated by the attribute "interval."

A frequency table would apply to variables such as Occupation Code and Gender: how many Males, how many Females in the customer table, how many Clerical workers, how many Electricians, how many Managers

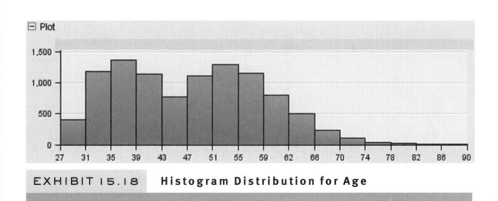

EXHIBIT 15.18   **Histogram Distribution for Age**

(Exhibits 15.17 [Gender] and 15.20 [Occupation Code with Description]). Table and histogram views expand the descriptive information available on customer attributes.

Exhibit 15.17 shows 51% of the customers are "F" or female.

The histogram in Exhibit 15.18 shows a little under 500 customers are between the ages of 27 and 31; almost 1,500 are between the ages of 35 and 39.

In Exhibit 15.17 for Gender, the meaning is reasonably clear from the data values: "M" is Male and "F" is Female. For Occupation Code the codes need to reference a descriptor; it is impossible to know what the specific numeric codes refer to, as shown in Exhibit 15.19.

As shown in Exhibit 15.20, it is clear that code "4" for Occupation (with a count of 722) refers to "Advertising, Promotions Managers," and code "7" (count 1,358) refers to "Administrative Services Managers." Using the expanded descriptive information accomplishes two things of significance for a marketer: The actual distribution of this type of coded information is immediately available, and when a marketer needs to select one or more of these categories, the actual code is no longer needed. If "Financial Managers" is to be selected, the box is checked; there is no need to find out what the code is for "Financial Managers" to be added to the query. The

Data Item: Occupation

Select Data Item...

Values:

Priority	Select	Value	Total		Selected	
			Count	Percent	Count	Percent
	☐	1	2	0		
	☐	2	46	0		
	☐	3	296	3		
	☐	4	722	7		
	☐	5	1,176	12		
	☐	6	1,393	14		
	☐	7	1,358	13		
	☐	8	1,289	13		
	☐	9	1,060	10		
	☐	10	825	8		
	☐	11	672	7		

EXHIBIT 15.19   Frequency Table for Occupation Code

Occupation Properties   ☒

Name: Occupation

Data Item: Occupation   Select Data Item...

Values:

Priority	Select	Value ▲	Total		Selec...	
			Count	Percent	...	...
	☐	Administrative Services Managers	1,358	13		
	☐	Advertising, Promotions Managers	722	7		
	☐	Chief Executives	2	0		
	☐	Computer, Information Systems Managers	1,289	13		
	☐	Construction Managers	4	0		
	☐	Education Administrators	3	0		
	☐	Engineering Managers	1	0		
	☐	Farm, Ranch, and Other Agricultural Manag...	15	0		
	☐	Farmers and Ranchers	11	0		
	☐	Financial Managers	416	4		
	☐	Food Service Managers	58	1		
	☐	Funeral Directors	36	0		
	☐	Gaming Managers	22	0		
	☐	General and Operations Managers	46	0		

Rule: Any ▼

☐ Exclude Customer that meet these criteria

Total Customer:

| Update Counts | Last run on: OK   Cancel   Help

EXHIBIT 15.20   **Frequency Table for Occupation, Sorted by Description**

information map will accomplish the necessary translation of description to underlying coded value.

A reasonable question can be raised as to why the metadata from the Oracle environment is not used to define the table and histogram designation. As shown in Exhibit 15.21, each variable data type is declared.

The "City" data type is *character*, similar to "Gender," and "County" is *number*. However, some numeric variables with a broad range, such as Occupation Code, County Code, and Zip Code, do not make sense to display as a histogram. The histogram displays the distribution of the customer values; it highlights the smallest and largest values, and the shape of the distribution, showing whether there is a broad, even distribution of

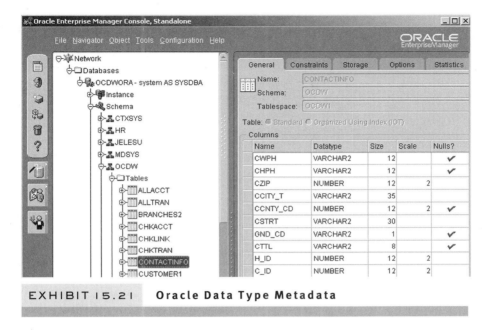

EXHIBIT 15.21   **Oracle Data Type Metadata**

values or a narrowly peaked distribution. From a narrowly peaked distribution it can be observed that a high proportion of the population has the same or very similar values.[3] Even though the table display may be quite large, the histogram display would not be useful. More clearly, such variables as "Opt Out" and "Do Not Mail" may be coded as 1 or 0, and similarly the histogram would not be as useful for displaying the distribution of these variables. Does a 1 mean "I wish to receive more marketing promotions" or "Please refrain from sending further promotions"?

There are some cases where neither a histogram nor a table display is useful; usually these variables have large tables and widely different values. Think of a table with nine-digit Zip codes, for example. The granularity is

---

[3]Or there is a problem in the data: One very extreme value could force the remaining population to appear very similar, even though they are very different. This issue is normally addressed through data quality filters, which highlight extreme values. Mistakes are usually corrected, while very extreme values, called *outliers*, can be filtered or ignored.

very small; there would likely be a lot of unique values for a geographically dispersed population. In these cases an additional metadata attribute can be applied to negate the creation of summary information.

The table and histogram displays are one example of how an application can make use of the additional information about the data (metadata) for a unique purpose, in choosing the correct display format for summary information. A marketing automation application can make use of additional metadata attributes in several ways, for example, in the selection of specific fields for internal reports, or for use in specialized analytical routines such as *cluster analysis*. In these two cases, not all customer fields would be desirable for either reporting or analytics. Metadata makes it possible to identify "options" such as "reporting" or "analytic" for specific fields. Other options may include the option to create table summaries of field values only, with no counts or no summarization at all (e.g., Zip code). Another option could be the ability to mask certain fields from view. If the extension of metadata is open ended, other applications can add metadata attributes specific to their requirements.

REPORTING

With the introduction of a data warehouse and augmentation by an information map, the process of creating and updating reports can achieve a higher level of detail and comprehension with even less involvement from the marketers and analysts previously engaged in producing periodic reports. The warehouse consolidates information from many sources; the corresponding Extract-Transform-Load (ETL) processes effectively eliminate most of the manual effort in collecting information from the different sources. The ETL processes are extended to create valuable summaries and previously difficult and ad-hoc manual steps are embedded in regular system reporting activities.

Best of all, the processes, being automated, can be continually augmented with new views of the business and the customers. Each new view and report is added to the automated processes already in place. With access to sales transactions linked to customers, the profit and loss (P&L) statement can be mirrored in customer terms and customer/product terms: who is buying what products. Customer purchase activity can then be integrated with marketing promotion activity to complete the picture: who is buying what products in response to what marketing activities.

PROFIT AND LOSS REPORTS

The monthly operational P&L can be augmented with the *customer P&L*. The business can be viewed in marketing and customer terms. This facilitates analysis of sales and profit, and illuminates opportunities for follow-up marketing activities such as cross-sell and upsell promotions. Customers who have purchased certain products can be selected for a follow-up promotion based on customers who have purchased the same and related products. Base product presentations can be tailored to anticipate the incremental opportunities to be offered. Customer contact information maintained in the data warehouse becomes the basis both for evaluating response as well as demonstrating the distribution of sales by marketing promotions.

MARKETING INVESTMENT REPORTS

P&L reports driven by the data warehouse content parallel and mimic the P&L: The time frame is monthly, similar to the P&L, and the structure is similar, the goal being to understand the business from the perspective of customer sales activity in addition to sales, profit, and product perspectives. The goal for marketing investment reports is demonstration of profitability from the perspective of the marketing investments. The time frame is relative to the effective time frame for marketing promotions. Response to an email promotion has a limited realistic time frame: Most sales should be garnered in the 5 to 10 days immediately following the promotion, for products with reasonably short sales cycles.[4] Phone sales, of course, are usually immediate, the effects visible with each sales update from the call center. Direct mail sales may occur over several weeks, hardcopy promotions being known to "stay

---

[4]The sales cycle assumed here is necessarily short: Marketing is trying to induce customers to come into the store or go to the web site and make a purchase. Other products can have much longer sales cycles, and for these items, individual promotions may simply contribute to the final sale, which could conceivably take several months. "Big-ticket items" such as automobiles, mortgages, consumer loans, possibly household appliances such as refrigerators and washers, and large entertainment items such as vacations or boats may require analysis of the cross-sell effect of multiple promotions. It is not any single marketing effort that closes the sale; it is the accumulation of marketing communications that leads to closing the deal.

on a kitchen counter" or in an in-box pending an opportunity for the recipient to make a decision.

As a result, the marketing investment reports identify the cost of the promotion at inception and track sales activity for the recipients over a relatively long period of time. In the meantime, customers may receive additional communications. The difficulty then becomes one of imputing the source of a sale. Various techniques such as promotion codes can be used to facilitate tracking of sales by promotion to improve recognition of the marketing effort that is linked to the sale. Improving the linkage is important to ongoing analysis of what activities—investments—are creating sales, and which ones need to be improved or eliminated.

A testing approach can further improve recognition of marketing-driven sales activity. A *holdout sample* is identified for each promotion audience—a group that will not receive the promotion at all or will receive the "standard" promotion. Their sales activity is cumulated along with the rest of the audience, and comparisons are made to identify the expected increase in sales from those who did receive the promotion. The expected increase is known as a *lift*. If sales from the promotion are 5% higher than the sample audience, the promotion is said to have achieved a lift of 5%. Positive, neutral, and negative lift are all possibilities.

TEST REPORTS

One of the major advantages of analyzing lift identified through marketing investment reports is the opportunity to test new promotions at dramatically lower cost than full-scale distributions. The relative setup cost factor will be higher, of course, as it is no longer spread across as many final recipients. This cost can be controlled by assuming a normal expected setup cost per recipient.

The data warehouse provides access on an ongoing basis to the sales activity for each customer. It also provides a flexible environment to create support for a testing datamart. The testing datamart includes tables of test attributes, and test codes to identify individual tests. These codes are mirrored in the customer records so every sale within the relative time frame can be rightfully assigned to the customer.

The data warehouse also provides the ability to control the test population. As noted earlier, a goal for marketing automation is to deliver more and more frequent communications to customers. There is every opportunity to overcommunicate, sending more promotions than appropriate to optimize sales. With testing, the risk is contamination of the test group from multiple promotions. It would be expected that not all customers will receive the same mix of communications: The mix will differ dramatically. In this case, the impact of the original promotion that is part of the test is muted, eliminated, or confused by the other promotional activities. A clear case of cannibalization was identified earlier; customers purchased from the higher discount offer and not from the promotion of the original test.

In such cases the test should be rerun, if still relevant.

Customer Segmentation Reports

Finally, the data warehouse provides a wonderful opportunity to simply learn more about customers through customer segmentation exercises. Demographic information is interesting and may suggest further marketing opportunities, but segmentation analysis may identify opportunities for new marketing activities, refinement of existing marketing audiences, and refinement of existing communications, as well as the possibility of different channels for marketing communications.

CHAPTER 16

Using Information

Considerable space has been allocated to discussing what information is needed for marketing purposes, how the information can be stored, retrieved, updated, and managed, and how an information map can facilitate access to information for applications as well as people who use the applications, particularly in reporting.

The most significant use of the information, beyond describing customers and reporting on the effectiveness of marketing activities, is the selection of incremental audiences for receiving new and continuing marketing communications.

As noted earlier, there is a significant barrier presented by Structured Query Language (SQL) and the cryptic, mnemonic language used by database administrators (DBAs) to define a database, its tables and columns, and the infrastructure that contains the customer information. The database contains the information that a marketer can use to select and refine an audience, but the marketer is not generally familiar with SQL. The information map can remove the language barrier, making customer information easily identifiable and accessible. The remaining barrier is an easy-to-use alternative to SQL.

A key component of a marketing automation system is the application that implements an alternative to SQL for selecting audiences as recipients of marketing activities. Such an application will use a visual palette and functional icons—the visual equivalent to a mnemonic—to invoke functions that have their equivalent in SQL, thereby sidestepping the syntactical complexity associated with SQL-based queries. These functions will implement the information map, so a marketer will quickly become attuned to the relationship between the function and the customer information available from the information map. As noted in the prior chapter, the information map contains all of the join criteria and cardinality designations required for producing the required SQL syntax. The SQL syntax is still used against the data warehouse or datamart, but it is captured and submitted behind the scenes when the campaign is submitted or counts requested. The marketer is almost free to *symbolically* use natural language to select an audience.

SELECTING AN AUDIENCE

The basic functions required in selecting a target audience using a marketing automation application can be derived from some of the basic campaigns that OurCompany currently uses. But before addressing such a campaign as an example, an introduction to the symbolic query language is appropriate, using SAS Campaign Studio.[1]

The earlier graphical examples of tables and histograms were taken from the SAS Campaign Studio Selection feature. Most audience selection begins with several initial attributes, such as gender, age, and income. These attributes are selected from a table of available customer attributes, the table being presented directly from the information map that frames the data itself. Exhibits 16.1 and 16.2 are snapshots of the Customer folder of the information map, compared with the same information viewed from within SAS Campaign Studio.

The views are nearly identical. The SAS Campaign Studio view includes additional information: attribute description, data item type, and level. (Recall the discussion of *level*: *nominal* indicates a tabular view, such as Gender, and *interval* indicates a histogram view of a numeric data item.)

In the upper-left corner of the screen a small rectangular icon represents the *select* function. Initially the marketer can choose a data item and view the distribution, using Age (see Exhibit 16.3).

A variety of choices are available for selecting the age range for the audience, including more than one range (see Exhibit 16.4).

The selection is done using the mouse to drag and drop the bars.

---

[1] As noted at the outset, there are a number of campaign management and marketing automation software applications available.

There are various reasons for selecting multiple bands. In this example, the purpose is to refine the audience selection based on income, using a split function (Exhibits 16.5, 16.6, and 16.7). First the Split icon is dragged onto the palette and connected with the Select icon.

Then the split attribute is selected to create four audiences based on the ranges selected; the option is "Split Using Values from a Previous Node" (Exhibit 16.6). Its effect can be seen in Exhibits 16.7 and 16.8.

Within the diagram, there are now four cells representing the results of the split, and each can be further refined based on additional criteria. In this example, different income ranges are used (Exhibit 16.8).

As shown in Exhibit 16.9, the additional income selection criteria have been added. One concern at this point would be the size of the audience: A minimum audience may be appropriate and a simple check can be done to determine the present distribution, using the *update counts* function available from the tool bar after selecting the cells using the mouse (Exhibit 16.10).

Each cell is updated with its specific count (Exhibit 16.11).

Inline counts can be very advantageous for a marketer developing a new campaign using suggested—but not proven—criteria. In this case, the income floor criterion results in a significant reduction for the older customers; less than 5% of the older group remains after applying an income floor filter of $62,000. The results may suggest refinement of the criteria, or revisiting the relevance of the criteria altogether, when such a significant impact is noted. This initial count may also bring to light new information about customers. Previous information regarding income distribution may not have existed for specific age groups; the company may not have used these attributes in combination before.

This is another example to stress the benefit of engaging marketers in the marketing process using an application such as marketing automation: The marketer is able to find this information in line with the activity of planning a campaign, without having to engage a database marketer, and without having to distribute a campaign and view results after the fact. The results may be surprising given the impact of the income filtering: too few customers in the campaign to generate a material result.

To reinforce the benefit of a drag-and-drop user interface for generating SQL, the following is the SQL syntax generated to create the counts in the 8 cells shown in Exhibit 16.11 on page 228.

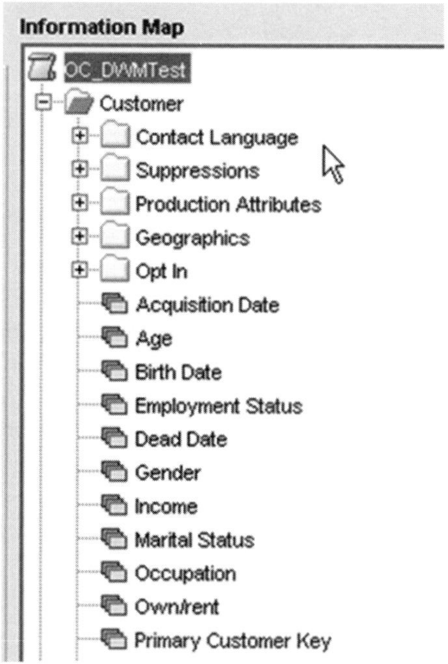

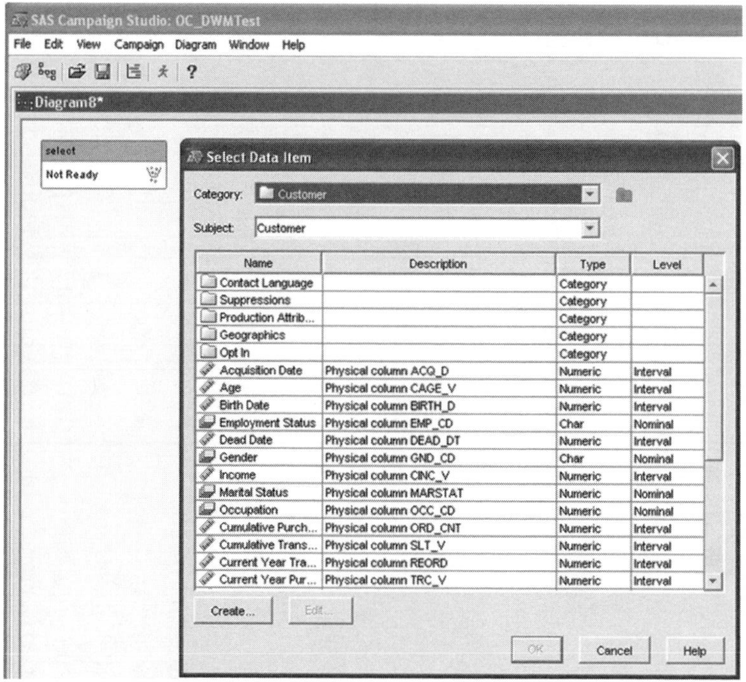

EXHIBIT 16.2   SAS Campaign Studio View of Customer

EXHIBIT 16.1   Information Map View of Customer

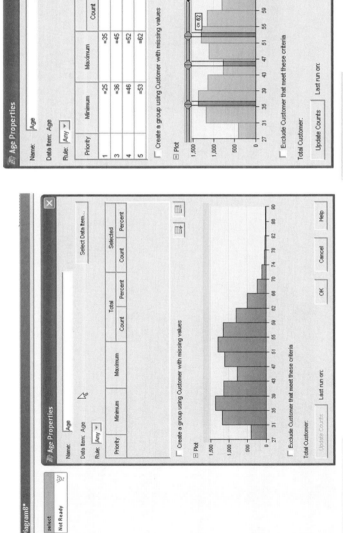

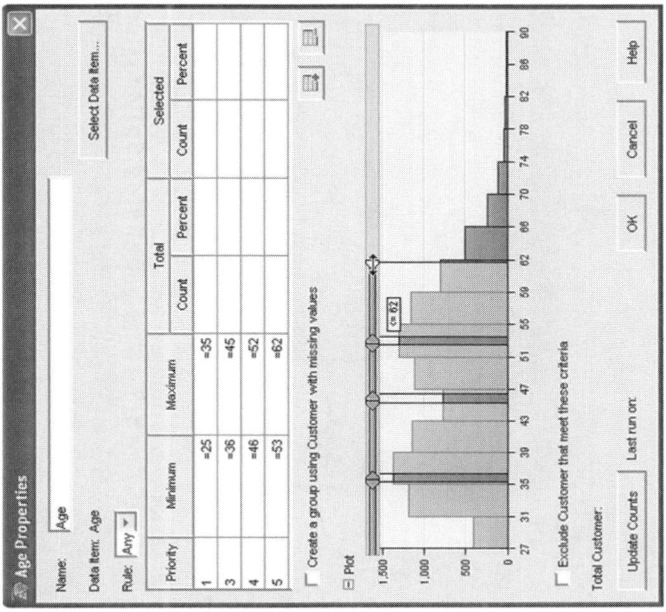

EXHIBIT 16.4   Selecting Multiple Age Ranges

EXHIBIT 16.3   Age Selection with Histogram

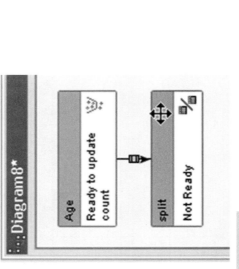

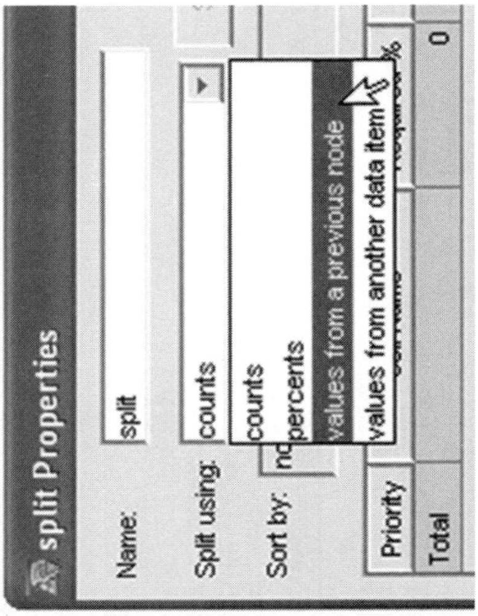

EXHIBIT 16.6   Defining Split Criteria

EXHIBIT 16.5   Implementing the Split Icon

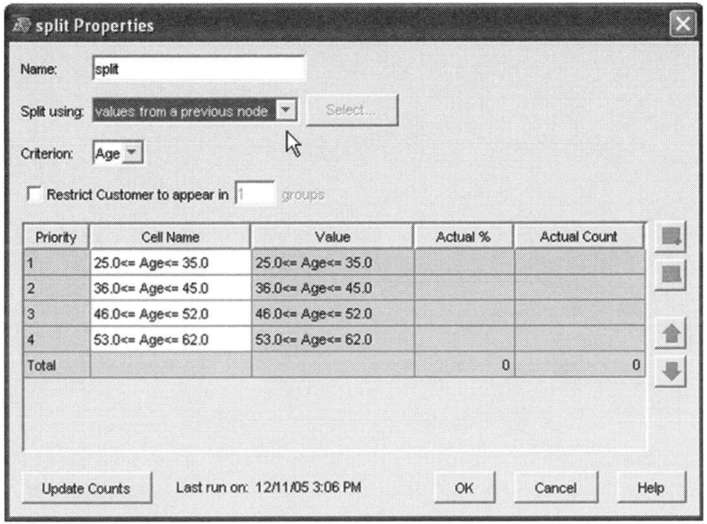

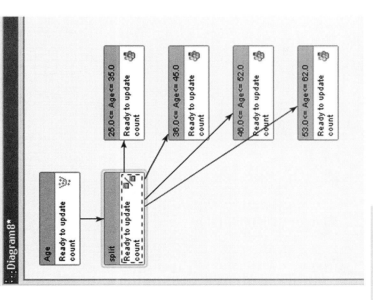

EXHIBIT 16.8   Split Using Age Bands Creates New Cells

EXHIBIT 16.7   Split Using Age Bands

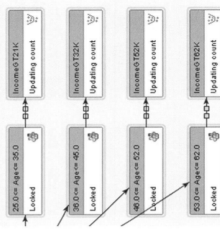

EXHIBIT 16.10 Creating a Count for Each Cell

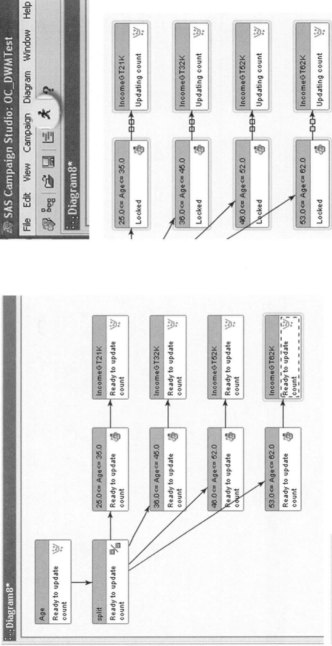

EXHIBIT 16.9 Age Refined with Income Floor for Each Group

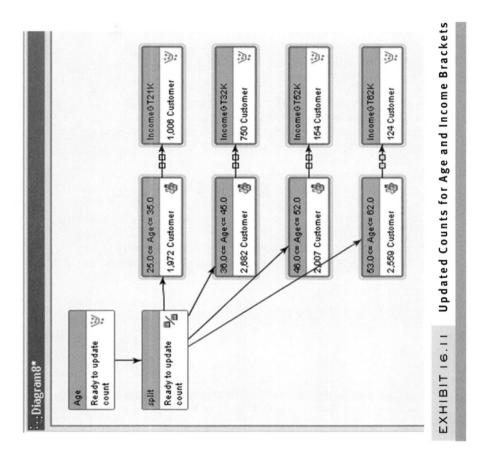

EXHIBIT 16.11 Updated Counts for Age and Income Brackets

```
CREATE TABLE MATables.TACSWGOBW4JWLAAAPSASWebAdminis AS
SELECT DISTINCT
        table0.CAGE_V AS CAGE_V LABEL='Age',
        table0.C_ID AS C_ID LABEL='Primary Customer Key'
FROM
        OC_DW.C_MSTR1 table0
WHERE
        (((((table0.CAGE_V >= 25.0 AND table0.CAGE_V <= 35.0)
        OR (table0.CAGE_V >= 36.0 AND table0.CAGE_V <= 45.0))
        OR (table0.CAGE_V >= 46.0 AND table0.CAGE_V <= 52.0))
        OR (table0.CAGE_V >= 53.0 AND table0.CAGE_V <= 62.0));
CREATE TABLE WORK.null11 AS
SELECT (count(*)) AS DII_1 LABEL="
FROM    (
        SELECT DISTINCT table1.C_ID AS C_ID LABEL='Primary Customer Key'
FROM    MATables.TACSWGOBW1R1NKAAGSASWebAdminis table2
        Inner join OC_DW.C_MSTR1 table1 on table2.C_ID = table1.C_ID
WHERE   table1.CINC_V >= 62000.0) table0;
CREATE TABLE WORK.null11 AS
SELECT (count(*)) AS DII_1 LABEL="
FROM    (
SELECT DISTINCT
table1.C_ID AS C_ID LABEL='Primary Customer Key'
FROM
        MATables.TACSWGOBW1R1MMAAFSASWebAdminis table2
        Inner join OC_DW.C_MSTR1 table1 on table2.C_ID = table1.C_ID
WHERE
        table1.CINC_V >= 52000.0) table0;
CREATE TABLE WORK.null11 AS
SELECT (count(*)) AS DII_1 LABEL="
FROM    (
SELECT DISTINCT
        table1.C_ID AS C_ID LABEL='Primary Customer Key'
FROM
        MATables.TACSWGOBW1R1LMAAESASWebAdminis table2
        Inner join OC_DW.C_MSTR1 table1 on table2.C_ID = table1.C_ID
WHERE
        table1.CINC_V >= 32000.0) table0;
CREATE TABLE WORK.null11 AS
SELECT (count(*)) AS DII_1 LABEL="
FROM    (
SELECT DISTINCT
        table1.C_ID AS C_ID LABEL='Primary Customer Key'
FROM
        MATables.TACSWGOBW1R1JOAADSASWebAdminis table2
        Inner join OC_DW.C_MSTR1 table1 on table2.C_ID = table1.C_ID
        WHERE table1.CINC_V >= 21000.0 ) table0;
```

There are 30 or so lines of SQL here, generated automatically from an easy-to-use graphical user interface, which empowers a marketer to generate a more effective marketing promotion while learning more about the selection process and the customer base from which customers are being selected.

INCORPORATING SUPPRESSIONS AND STANDARD EXPORTS

There are two major steps associated with every campaign activity that can be automated from the marketing automation campaign application: *suppressions* and *exporting the audience list* to the letter shop, call center, or other service agency.

Recall that suppression criteria are often standardized for every campaign; therefore a standardized query can be developed, scheduled for weekly execution, and the results incorporated into each campaign by adding a single icon (the Link icon). The same is common for exporting content for delivery agents.

Suppression criteria can be predefined as shown in Exhibit 16.12.

From this view the folder Suppressions has been selected, which contains several relevant criteria: *company employees, do not market,* and *dead.* The fourth criterion pertains to filtering customers who do not wish to have their name used by companies except for OurCompany, known as *opt-out.* This criterion would not be relevant to an internal campaign.

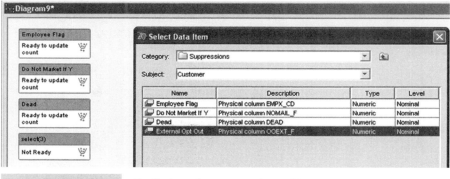

EXHIBIT 16.12   Defining Suppression Filters

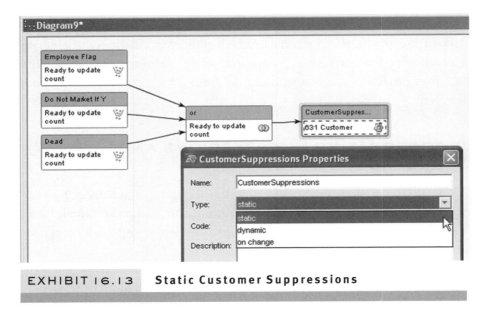

EXHIBIT 16.13   **Static Customer Suppressions**

The first three criteria can be joined using the logical OR icon. The combined criteria can be scheduled for periodic update, and to improve execution times the designation of the cell can be declared *static*, which means the query is not repeatedly executed for every campaign. The list of suppression candidates (customers) is updated weekly as a separately scheduled query (Exhibit 16.13).

As it is common to market to households, additional household-level suppressions can be defined separately and joined in the final campaign diagram.

The information map again makes it easy to identify the appropriate household exclusion information; it is incorporated in a separate folder (Exhibit 16.14).

For the marketer defining the household exclusion criteria, not all attributes are appropriate in every campaign, and multiple predefined exclusion queries may be necessary.

In Exhibit 16.14, on the left the folder containing the household exclusion items is highlighted, and on the right some of these exclusions are shown implemented in the selection criteria.

Test exclusions are another important exclusion criterion. All customers participating in test promotions are not necessarily excluded from

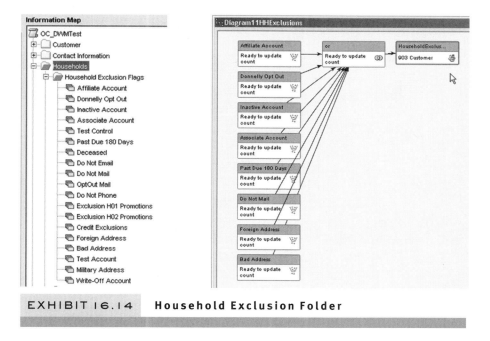

EXHIBIT 16.14   **Household Exclusion Folder**

all other promotions for the duration of a test, hence the need to be able to select test audiences (and controls) for exclusion. By incorporating the appropriate exclusions in a separate exclusions list, consistency and reliability of results are more likely. OurCompany has coded all their test activities for both control and test populations using a three-digit code as shown in Exhibit 16.15, so it is a simple matter to select those to be excluded.

Using separate exclusion filters provides more control for those circumstances where refining the filters becomes necessary.

There are several approaches available for incorporating exclusions; the most convenient is to establish the available target audience at the outset. This can be done through the link icons and specifying "Exclude this group from the audience." This results in a query that retrieves "everyone else." Alternatively, the initial selection criteria can be specified, which may result in a faster query. In the former case the marketer is more informed as to the available population at the outset. In the latter case, the marketer knows what proportion of the prospective audience was excluded. Both cases have interesting ramifications.

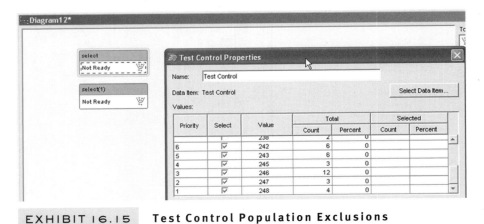

EXHIBIT 16.15   **Test Control Population Exclusions**

The only step required to change a "selection" to "exclusion" in the SAS Campaign Studio diagram (Exhibit 16.16) is to check the "Exclude Customer" box in the lower-left corner of the Selection window, as shown in Exhibit 16.17.

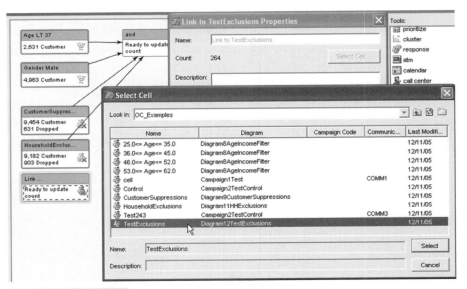

EXHIBIT 16.16   **Selecting a Base Audience Minus Exclusion Lists**

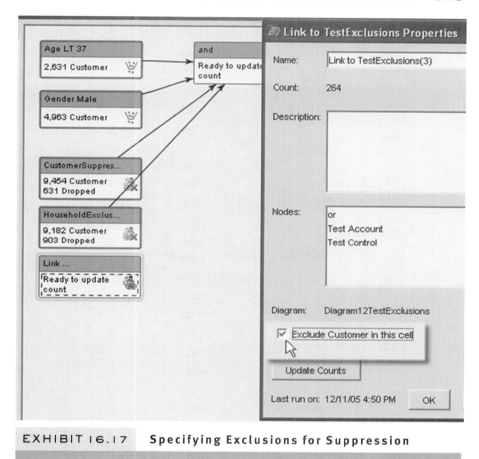

EXHIBIT 16.17   **Specifying Exclusions for Suppression**

The completed query requirements shown in Exhibit 16.18 are: "Select male customers less than 37 years old and Exclude any customers who are either in the Customer Suppression list, Household Exclusion list, or Test/ Control list" (Exhibit 16.18).

HOLDOUT AUDIENCE FOR RESPONSE TESTING

As noted earlier, it is important to validate response results by comparing customer response to that of a holdout sample of the same customers, who do

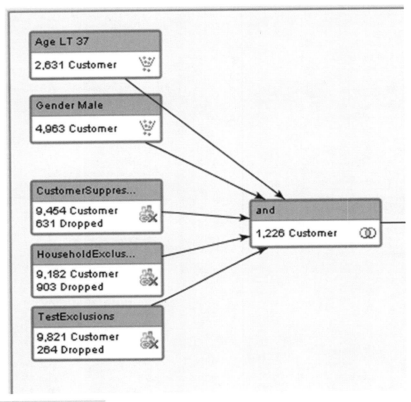

Age LT 37

2,631 Customer

Gender Male

4,963 Customer

CustomerSuppres...

9,454 Customer
631 Dropped

HouseholdExclus...

9,182 Customer
903 Dropped

TestExclusions

9,821 Customer
264 Dropped

and

1,226 Customer

EXHIBIT 16.18   Query Definition with Multiple Exclusions

not receive the communication (see Exhibit 16.19). Creating a holdout sample involves choosing a random group[2] of people from within the same population, and making the group available for sales analysis after the

---

[2]Comparing the response of the holdout sample with that of the promotional group is definitely a statistical analysis of some sophistication. This does not mean only a PhD candidate has the skills to do the analysis; it does mean that statistical concepts regarding results obtained from sampling must be respected in the analysis. The penalty for not paying attention to the realities of sampling results is either to lose money repeating a losing promotion or to miss an opportunity, both because the sample results were mishandled and therefore misinterpreted. Testing and sample audience selection is discussed in the next section. For this example, the holdout sample of 200 is wholly inadequate for most test purposes, unless the response rate can be expected to be above 50%.

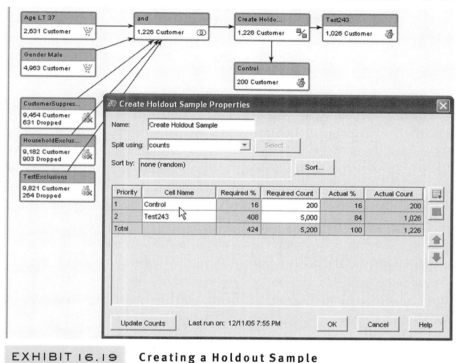

EXHIBIT 16.19   **Creating a Holdout Sample**

promotion is complete. The promotional group will be recorded in the *contact history* table; the ID codes for the holdout sample group will be exported to a *test/control* table for future analysis, when response to the promotion can be considered to be complete. Specifying the sample values, in this case "200" requires the population to be split. The Split icon provides the functional ability to split the audience by either percent or count, in addition to the "Split on Prior Value" used in the earlier example.

Further discussion on holdout samples and response testing is included in the testing discussion in Chapter 17.

Creating an Audience List for the Call Center or Letter Shop

At this point, audience selection for this simple campaign is complete. The next step is to transform the audience list into a format that can be transmitted to the call center, letter shop, email agent, or other service agency responsible for creating the deliverable content and delivering it to the recipients. A list intended for a call center will at least include the recipient name, address, and phone number; a list intended for a letter shop will include the same information plus additional personalization information intended to assist the customization of hardcopy content.

The finished output file is commonly referred to as a *campaign export* file. The file format and content are, to a certain extent, dictated by the vendor responsible for delivery. Each vendor will have unique requirements: The export file must be readable by their system; frequently their system is precoded to anticipate a particular file format and a certain ordering in the fields. Vendors will often charge additional setup fees to massage incoming data that is not in their requested format.

The following is an example of a campaign export file for direct mail, containing name and address information to be used by the letter shop in creating the mailable promotion content. This file sample is in *CSV* (comma-separated-values) form, with a header line that identifies the source field column names:

```
"C_ID","CLNM","CFNM","CTTL","CSTRT_N","CSTRT","CCITY_T",
    "ST_CD","CZIP"
10314,Sanger,Ed,"Mr",1347,MINNESOTA ST,Wiggins,MS,"39577"
10426,Kossmann,Howard,"Mr",260,CHANNEL ST,Kilbourne,LA,"71253"
11372,Cherry,Toni,"Ms",114,ELSIE ST,Billings,OK,"74630"
11919,Layman,Millicent,"Miss",120,SHANNON AL,Fort Smith,AR,"72901"
12189,McCann,Sorraye,"Miss",584,CHESTNUT ST,Maumee,
    OH,"43537"
12425,Vitron,Donna,"Ms",90,BOWMAN ST,Clinton,WA,"98236"
12706,Labianca,Simone,"Miss",66,LASKIE ST,Castle Hayne,NC,"28429"
13513,Swinson,S J,"Mr",1739,YOSEMITE AV,Chico,CA,"95926"
13864,Kernodle,Emma,"Miss",744,BROADWAY ST,Kirbyville,
    TX,"75956"
15051,Sheedy,Reuby,"Mrs",2085,19TH ST,
    Monument,OR,"97864"
```

The first field is the Customer ID, labeled "C_ID," which can be recalled from the information map discussion earlier. In this case the field name is used for exporting, not the information map name. The Customer ID is necessary to enable the marketer and vendor to match specific recipients.

In telemarketing, for example, the customer response will be directly to the telemarketer, and if an order is placed, the response data transmitted by the telemarketing vendor back to OurCompany will require the Customer ID in order to properly place the order.

The second field, labeled "CLNM," is last name followed by first name, title or salutation (Mr., Mrs. Ms., SSgt., or Dr., for example), street address number, street name, city/town, state (two-character code), and Zip code. The first record is:

```
"Mr. Ed Sanger, 1347 Minnesota St., Wiggins, Mississippi, 39577"
```

PERSONALIZATION

While this information is sufficient to address and deliver a promotion, it would be more likely to include additional customer-specific information in order to *personalize* the promotion content consistent with known attributes of the recipient. Age and family information could be used to tailor an email promotion, for example, to enable use of differing images that appeal to individual customer segments. A resort vacation promotion could make interesting use of the images in Exhibit 16.20, which appeal to unique customer segments.

Here we have images of a quiet poolside view from a comfortable lounge chair, a beautiful (and uncrowded) beach view, both of which differ significantly from the very active waterskier and volleyball scenes. Other views appeal to still different segments: family, couples (both older and younger), and friends.

The importance of customer attributes in personalization provides an interesting opportunity to further differentiate content presentation by recipient. The basic promotion offer may be simply a discounted resort vacation, while the images convey a vacation experience more consistent with what the recipient may consider an ideal vacation opportunity. The result should be higher response rates: The images communicate the sizzle and aroma of the steak dinner that is the promotion.

Using customer age and family information (as available) enables these and similar images to be promoted to individual groups or segments of customers, segments that might be characterized as young, or family, or

active in sports, or mature. On another dimension, the images identify different activities, which again may more or less appeal to different customer segments.

The goal is to present information—text and images—that elicits a positive response, which "sells the product," whatever the product might be. The export file is used to communicate the necessary personalization information that enables the promotion—in whatever form it happens to be—to be tailored (personalized) to different customer segments.

Of course, while the export file may be used to communicate customer attributes to a letter shop printer or email delivery engine, one should keep in mind that customers are unique people and segmentation is a generalization process, which presents an incongruity. Some younger recipients, generalized as "active and sports minded," whose email or letter is so personalized, may have been more receptive to the pool or quiet beach images as generalized in presentation to "mature" recipients. Testing should be done to ensure the generalizations and assumptions made about personalization content and customer segments in fact provide a lift to response.

AUDIENCE LIST DEFINITION AND MANAGEMENT

It would be advantageous if the marketers did not have to become involved in the interaction with letter shop or call center or email delivery vendors on the actual formatting of the audience list. The selection of specified fields, field ordering, and field formatting must be agreed on in advance of submitting a prospective audience list to a vendor. The call center has to program its computer to read the incoming list (e.g., to identify the phone number field).

It would be equally advantageous if the export file definitions could be stored and reused, as vendors should be participating in more than one campaign over time. And the export definition should be flexible enough to allow modification for specific campaigns to incorporate different levels and types of personalization.

SAS Marketing Automation includes a facility to define and reuse export file definitions, based logically enough on an export definition. Creating an export definition entails selecting the required fields, defining a format for the output content, a format for each field if necessary, and specifying the type of file for output, such as CSV (text-based, comma-separated values) or other types as shown in the drop-down list opposite the Output label, upper right in the Export Definition properties window in Exhibit 16.21.

In the bottom half of this window the list of available fields is shown on the left, and the selected fields, column names, and formats are shown on the right. In this example, the fields selected include the customer identification field, their name and address information, email address, and at least one field with personalization potential, Gender. Additional fields can be added for a specific promotion by selecting from the list on the left side, which is the same list used in the campaign selection process, being based on the same information map. Here again the value of the information map can be considerable.

This is an example of one export definition. This one is labeled "CustomerCSVEmail," representing a customer subject, a CSV (comma-separated-values) format, and an email channel. Multiple export definitions can be created to support different channels such as mail, phone, and email, as

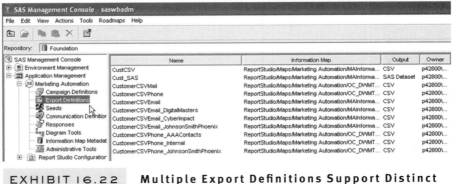

EXHIBIT 16.21   **Creating an Export Definition**

well as multiple vendor requirements in the same channel. In Exhibit 16.22, several channel-specific definitions are shown, followed by channel- and vendor-specific definitions. These latter definitions include the names of specific vendors (Digital Masters, Cyber Impact, and Johnson/Smith of

EXHIBIT 16.22   **Multiple Export Definitions Support Distinct Vendor Requirements**

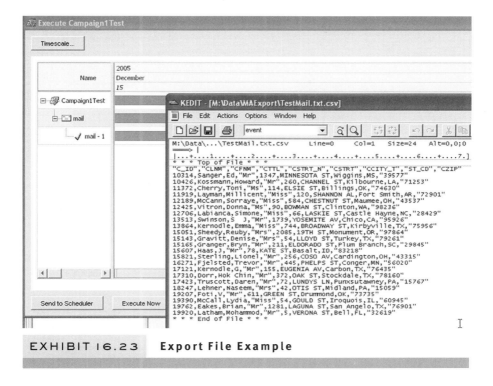

EXHIBIT 16.23   Export File Example

Phoenix), which enhances the ability of marketers to participate in the audience selection process.

To complete the discussion of export definitions, a sample output is shown in Exhibit 16.23, based on the export definition CustomerCSVMail.

The CSV file format is often used in exchanging Excel spreadsheet information between applications. The data values are separated by commas and the top row contains field labels, based on the database fields, not the information map data items. As shown earlier, the second row contains the first entry for this customer list, identifying contact information for Mr. Ed Sanger, customer number 10314, who lives at 1347 Minnesota St, in Wiggins, Mississippi, 39577, unambiguously the basic information for a mail campaign.

The export definitions are flexible, specific fields can be designated for particular campaigns, and content can be further personalized by including other customer fields (see Exhibit 16.24). To improve communication (and expected customer response), certain information could be provided for call center personnel, so the caller can anticipate the conversation based on some

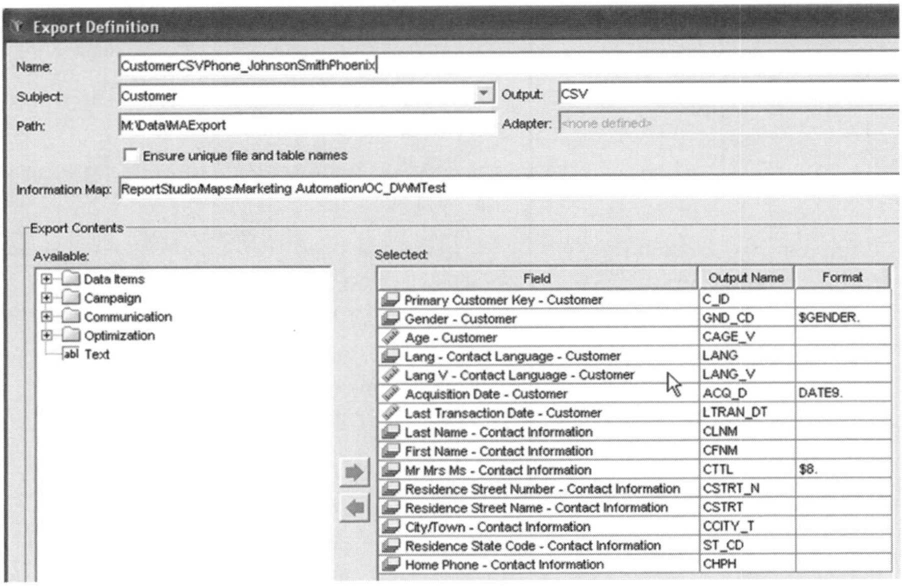

EXHIBIT 16.24   Call Center Export Definition, Enhanced for Personalization

attributes of the callee[3]: particularly language and customer longevity. From experience, personalization information has been advantageously used, and customers as well as vendors have appreciated the closer relationship made possible by some personalized information provided in advance. Fundamentally if the information can be used to enhance the customer experience and add value, the relationship between OurCompany and its customers will benefit: Customers will become aware of products that meet their unique needs, and OurCompany will generate higher sales.

In this export definition, recipient address information is included to create an opportunity to confirm name and address information when contact is made. In addition, a language indicator is provided as well as the acquisition date for the customer that differentiates newer customers from older, more

---

[3]There is some question here as to the risk or even liability associated with the transmission of personal information to outside services, particularly where a phone conversation takes place. The recipient may not appreciate that personal information has been communicated beyond the company or even that the company is using that information for marketing purposes.

established customers, and the customer's gender and age. The latter information can enable the callers to more effectively engage with the people whom they are calling. Assumptions based on this sparse information may not always be valid, and could occasionally be misleading, but more often it can be helpful for the caller and establish a more effective basis for the conversation.

The export definitions are repeatable as part of a campaign definition, which improves consistency of execution, minimizes the repeated effort of definition, and maximizes the effort of the marketers in focusing their effort on the creation of the campaigns and campaign content.

Export definitions are selected as part of the *communication definition*, as shown in Exhibit 16.25. In this case, a communication icon, "call center," has been added to the diagram. Opening the properties of the icon shows four tabs: Details, Export, Seeds, and Audience. The Export tab has been selected. Several vendor-specific definitions are available for this campaign: a generic call center definition, "CustomerCSVPhone," and three more specific definitions: "AAAContacts," "Internal," and "JohnsonSmithPhoenix."

By providing the definitions in advance through the export definition, the marketer is insulated from having to redefine the export content to the vendor-requested definition as well as from having to determine what the vendor requirements are in the process of defining the communication. This also ensures that the definition is consistent over time.

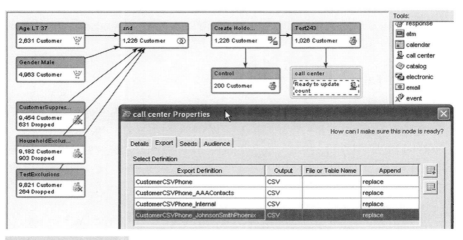

EXHIBIT 16.25   Selecting Call Center Export Definition for Communication

SCHEDULING CAMPAIGN EXECUTION

Having chosen the export file definition to be used in the campaign, in this case based on a specific vendor, JohnsonSmithPhoenix, the next (and almost final) step in defining the communication is scheduling the execution time. "Execution" refers to running the query against the customer database to select the audience. By "scheduling" execution, the query will be put in a queue with an execution date, and an operator can initiate the formal scheduling of the campaign. At the requisite time a software "scheduler" will automatically initiate the campaign. Ideally the audience should be selected as close as possible to the expected or specified vendor delivery time. This increases the accuracy of the information used in making the selection, and should improve the results of the promotion by ensuring recent customer activity is included in the selection criteria. An audience selection that relies on prior purchase activity will be best if prior purchase information is up to date.

Scheduling will also improve the use of IT resources, by allowing operators or DBAs to manage execution times according to resource availability and demand. One of the goals for marketing automation is to improve the coordination of resources used in the marketing process. Enabling the marketer to specify a desired execution date and allowing the operator or DBA to modify the execution time to fit the system demand schedule benefits both groups within the organization (Exhibit 16.26).

By providing easy-to-use, calendar-driven widgets, a marketer can initiate scheduling easily and confidently, well in advance of the actual campaign requirements.

Response Follow-up

The final step is closing the loop on the marketing communication to the re-cipient. In this example a recipient receives a phone call promotion. How will the recipient respond, and how will the marketer determine and implement the appropriate next step for the responder? If a purchase is made, there is an opportunity for a follow-up offer to be generated, such as a cross–sell or upsell promotion. If no purchase is made, an *incremental offer* might be appropriate.

The timing of the follow-up activity must be considered. When should the upsell or incremental offer be made? Seven days later? Two weeks later? Can the decision—and the promotion—be generated in advance, and can the timing of delivery be specific to each type of response?

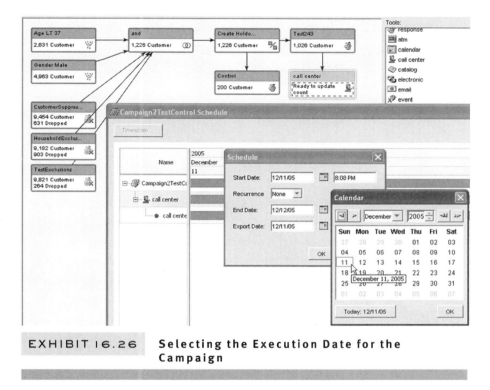

EXHIBIT 16.26   **Selecting the Execution Date for the Campaign**

By defining possible responses in advance, SAS Marketing Automation provides an ability to facilitate these follow-up steps. For example, the following responses are possible based on an initial telemarketed offer:

- Purchase.
- No purchase.
- No answer.
- Recipient is not available.
- Phone number is wrong.
- Recipient does not want to receive further calls and requests a "Do Not Call" listing.

The possibilities for marketing follow-up could be:

- **Purchase.** Upsell/cross-sell/order confirmation/incremental promotion

- **No purchase.** Incremental offer through another channel

- **No answer.** Incremental offer through another channel

- **Recipient is not available.** Incremental offer through another channel

- **Phone number is wrong.** Incremental communication through another channel

- **Recipient is annoyed and requests a "Do Not Call" listing.** Mailed confirmation

Under the Details tab of the Call Center Properties icon shown earlier, SAS Campaign Studio incorporates the *response* possibilities with the *communication* definition and enables the marketer to select follow-up actions based on selected responses. In Exhibit 16.27, the marketer has

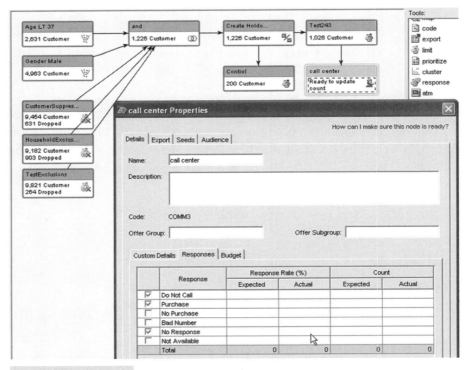

EXHIBIT 16.27   **Selecting Responses for Follow-up (Closing the Loop)**

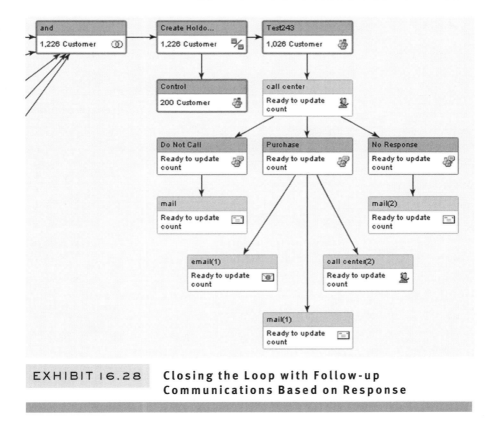

EXHIBIT 16.28   **Closing the Loop with Follow-up
Communications Based on Response**

chosen to follow up on "No Response," "Do Not Call," and "Purchase" responses by checking the boxes next to these predetermined responses.

Exhibit 16.28 is automatically updated showing new icons for the three possible responses, and the marketer has added three incremental communications: a direct mail follow-up to the request for Do Not Call listing to confirm this was done; a direct mail purchase confirmation for purchasers *plus* an incremental discount offer sent via email; *and* a "customer satisfaction" call to be scheduled following delivery of the purchase. For "No Response" recipients, an incremental promotion is to be created and delivered using direct mail.

All of these additional communications can be scheduled similar to the first communication and automatically executed at the appropriate time following delivery of the first promotion. If the marketer wished to add further follow-up activities (a follow-up to the follow-up), this would also be possible.

EXAMPLE SUMMARY

To summarize this example, the marketer has generated a fairly complex sequence of activities (see Exhibit 16.29).

Male customers aged less than 37 have been selected, suppressions have been applied for standard suppressions and test and control populations, a campaign promotion has been created for call center contacts, and follow-up contacts have been scheduled for responders, opt-out customers, and customers who were not able to be contacted by phone. The follow-up communications use both direct mail and email to provide additional offers and confirmation of purchases and opt-out decisions.

All of this has been accomplished by a marketer without consideration for database characteristics or use of SQL. It is arguable that this relatively simple campaign will be more reliably executed than the equivalent campaign managed manually using SQL-based selection criteria. Execution is scheduled automatically; it is not subject to "other priorities" or fire drills, as the database marketer can be. The syntax specifics of manual SQL logic are embedded in the execution of the flow, based on the diagram, and not subject to human error and inconsistency. The automated campaign still

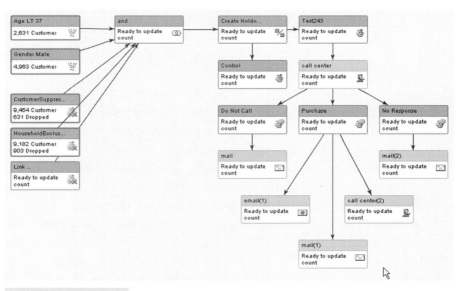

EXHIBIT 16.29   Completed Campaign with Follow-up

retains all the flexibility necessary to meet the variety of marketing requirements possible, given the availability and easy access to customer information provided by the SAS Campaign Studio application.

REFINING MARKETERS' CUSTOMER KNOWLEDGE

In the process of defining the promotion, the marketer may also have learned something about the characteristics of the audience (e.g., age and gender distribution) (see Exhibit 16.30).

This may suggest incremental marketing opportunities based on further review of the purchase characteristics of the audience, based on their age.

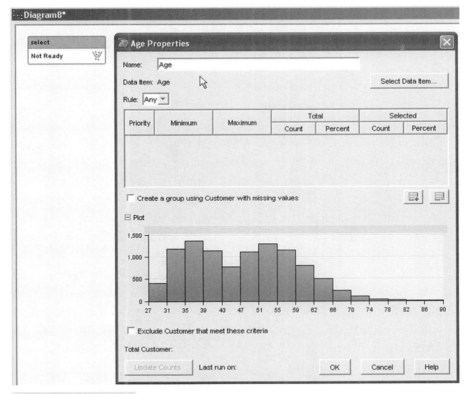

EXHIBIT 16.30   Age Distribution for OurCompany Customers

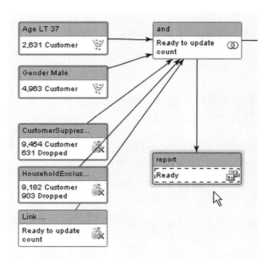

EXHIBIT 16.31   **Accessing Customer Information from a Diagram Icon (Report)**

SAS Campaign Studio anticipates this possibility through the use of the Report icon.

This icon provides an opportunity for a marketer to delve further into the attributes of customers in the process of building a targeted campaign, on an ad-hoc basis. It is not a substitute for in-depth analysis provided by other, reporting-specific applications; it provides immediate visibility into attributes specific to a particular campaign audience. In Exhibit 16.31, the Report icon is added to the campaign diagram and connected to the And icon.

The SAS Campaign Studio Report icon provides access to a number of different graphic presentation options, as shown in Exhibit 16.32, from scatter plots to bar graphs. Multiple views can be embedded in the Report results (see Exhibit 16.33), and the results of each view are integrated, so highlighting from one graph will also be displayed in the second graph and the table (see Exhibit 16.34).

In this example, people who have been customers of OurCompany for more than 9 years do not show a marked difference by age, other than that far fewer are younger than 29 years of age, which would be expected.

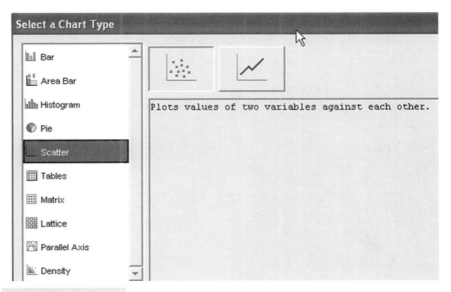

EXHIBIT 16.32   Report Icon Graph Display Options

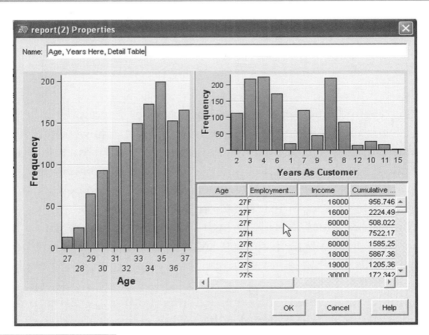

EXHIBIT 16.33   Multiple Views of Customer Attributes
with Report

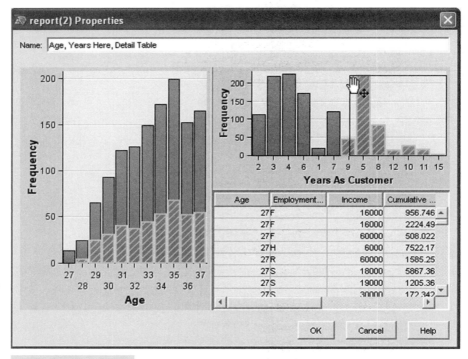

EXHIBIT 16.34   Integrated Graph Views

This type of limited ad-hoc investigation can be interesting. It helps to gain a better understanding of basic customer attributes; however, it can also provide valuable business insight. For example, if "Last Transaction Date" is monitored on a regular basis, customers who have been "good customers" in the past may not be such good customers now, as indicated by less frequent purchase activity, such as that shown in Exhibit 16.35.

This display shows a relatively high volume of customers with a most recent transaction date more than 60 days ago. In trying to assess how best to appeal to this group in a prospective offer, a comparison of age might be considered (see Exhibit 16.36).

In this example, the lagging transaction group (for age less than 37) is highlighted using a box. This makes the corresponding "people" in the Age histogram visible. From a marketing standpoint, it appears that lagging purchase activity is not focused in any one or two age groups; it is broadly distributed across all ages, from 27 to 37.

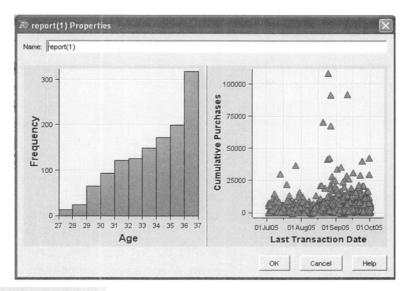

EXHIBIT 16.35   Using Report Node to Compare Customer Attributes

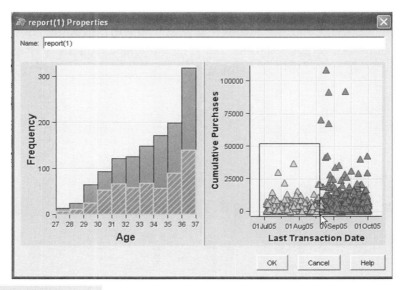

EXHIBIT 16.36   Using Report to Compare Attributes within Segments

Lagging purchasers could be good candidates for a *reactivation* promotion. Investment return is the important question here: how much to spend on the opportunity, what the likelihood of response is, and how best to invest in this situation. As an example, is this audience open to email or would direct mail be a better approach? Maybe there is a sizable audience potential for a phone contact. Is a discount promotion necessary? If it is, how large a discount? What products should be in the promotion? Might it be worthwhile to evaluate prior purchases by this group and tailor the promotion accordingly? Would that make a substantial difference, enough to merit the time and creative cost? Is *age* a good variable to use in differentiating the audience? Are there other variables that might be better, or used in combination with age?

All of these questions are appropriate to any new promotional consideration. The only way to resolve them is to try them and see. To avoid a long lead time in promotion, response and analysis of different combinations of channels and offers and presentation of multiple promotions might be worthwhile. This necessitates a smaller audience for each promotion. How small can the audience be? Will the results be repeatable? Assuming one of the promotions generates a significant (material) response, is that a reliable indication of future performance if the same promotion is "rolled out" to the entire population, now as well as in the future? Answering these questions requires testing, and the next chapter discusses marketing automation and promotion testing.

CHAPTER 17

Response Testing

J ust as marketing automation facilitates the creation and execution of a higher volume of increasingly targeted marketing communications, marketing automation also facilitates the testing process. Testing the results of campaigns ensures that the investment in marketing communications is producing a *better* return on the investment and marketing activities. Testing involves comparing the sales results of groups receiving different promotions as well as groups receiving no promotion at all. The difference in performance is attributed to the promotion and represents the return on the investment. By testing different promotions, marketing is able to improve response, as well as improve knowledge of customer differences and customer preferences.

For example, using the campaign developed in the previous chapter, a promotion is targeted to male customers under 37, and a holdout sample has been created, known as a *control*. The control group will not receive the promotion (see Exhibit 17.1).

At a suitable point after the promotion, and before the follow-up promotions, sales results of the two groups can be compared (Exhibit 17.2).

If the sales results for Promotion Test243 were evaluated alone, it would be tempting to trumpet a magnificent 6.5% response rate, and $9.87 per customer in sales results (Exhibit 17.3). However, by comparing results to a group that did not receive the promotion, the incremental sales are much more sobering. The increase in response is only 1.5%, and the sales improvement is only (9.87 − 7.49), or $2.38. If OurCompany were quite large, with millions of customers, an increase or *lift* provided by a promotion such as Test243 would be quite substantial: A

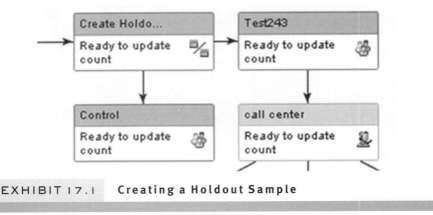

EXHIBIT 17.1   **Creating a Holdout Sample**

difference of $2.38 in sales over 5,000,000 people is a very sizable $11.9 million dollars.

Yet this promotion is still worthwhile for companies the size of OurCompany, with several hundred thousand customers. It is worthwhile because of the reasons outlined in Part One: It represents a positive (and material, as will be shown) return on a marketing investment. Going further, the return may be repeatable, and the incremental results will become available to generate additional promotions, which in turn may also provide positive and material returns of their own, provided that the returns of these incremental promotions—any promotion, in fact—are constantly and consistently evaluated for their positive benefit proportional to their cost.

Evaluating the return of the promotion against the investment requires a look at the profitability of the investment, as shown in Exhibit 17.4.

Since this is a test case, sales and profit are evaluated on a per-person basis. This could be done by dividing the total sales and profit by the number of responders, but this creates a problem for comparing results; therefore the

EXHIBIT 17.2   **SALES AND RESPONSE FOR TEST243 AND CONTROL**

	Control	Test243
Response Rate (%)	5.0%	6.5%
Sales Per Customer ($)	7.49	9.87

EXHIBIT 17.3   **TEST243 RESULTS WITHOUT CONTROL COMPARISON**

	Test243
Response Rate (%)	6.5%
Sales Per Customer ($)	9.87

total sales and total profit are divided by the *total* number of customers in each group. In this example, the Test243 promotion generated a small increase in the *profit per customer* of $1.24 ($4.24 – $3.00). Some of this increase may be due to sales of higher-priced items: The margin on sales for Test243 is 43% compared to the control of 40%.

Adding the cost of the Test243 promotion and creating ratios of the results completes the picture (Exhibit 17.5).

While the response rate increase of 1.5% seems small, it is substantial when expressed on a percentage basis. The terminology used in this ratio is called *lift*: Test243 generated a *response lift* of 30%, a similar *sales lift* of 32%, and a *margin lift* of 42%.

Finally, the marketing cost per customer was $0.097. There is no equivalent "marketing cost" for the control; as this is a *holdout* sample, it did not receive an alternative promotion. For a meaningful comparison, the marketing cost for Test243 must be factored into the return on investment calculation.

The *return on investment* (ROI) ratio is calculated as (Incremental Profit – Marketing Cost) divided by Marketing Cost. The result is a substantial 1,187% return.

Note that the profit figures are generated before overhead and all costs for the promotion are included, *except* the cost of the marketing and creative

EXHIBIT 17.4   **PROFITABILITY OF CAMPAIGN TEST243 AND CONTROL**

	Control	Test243
Response Rate (%)	5.0%	6.5%
Sales Per Customer ($)	7.49	9.87
Gross Profit Per Customer ($)	3.00	4.24
Gross Profit Rate (Margin) (%)	40%	43%

EXHIBIT 17.5   **RETURN ON INVESTMENT FOR CAMPAIGN TEST243 AND CONTROL**

	Control	Test243
Response Rate (%)	5.0%	6.5%
Sales Per Customer ($)	7.49	9.87
Gross Profit Per Customer ($)	3.00	4.24
Gross Profit Rate (Margin) (%)	40%	43%
Response Lift (%)		30%
Sales Lift (%)		32%
Profit Lift (%)		42%
Marketing Cost ($)		0.097
ROI (%)		1,187%

people at OurCompany who participated in the development of the promotion and its analysis. These latter costs would have been incurred even if the promotional test had not been run, so they are excluded. Any outside costs, however, such as call center costs, would be included in the marketing costs. If the call center is internal to OurCompany, it would be appropriate to include its direct cost but exclude its overhead costs. There would be an expected *opportunity cost* associated with use of their time for Test243: They could have been making (or receiving) other calls for other promotions.

These results appear quite good, but do they justify a rollout of this promotion to the customer population as a whole? Is there reason to expect that a similar response rate would occur if the promotion were to be given to all customers? These questions are often phrased as, "Are these test results repeatable?" meaning, "If the same promotion is made to 200,000 customers (all males aged under 37), will the response lift still be 30%?" Will the incremental profit actually be close to 200,000 times ($1.24 − 0.097) or $228,600?

Why would results *not* be consistent with the test? The test group is a random sample of OurCompany customers aged under 37, and the purpose of the random sample was to establish a reasonable expectation that the results *could* be repeated. And if the results cannot be reasonably expected to be repeatable, what is the point of testing at all?

There could be a reasonable expectation for repeatable results *if* the sample sizes of the test and control groups used in the test are sufficiently high to rule out a *chance* response result. This is a fundamental aspect of testing,

EXHIBIT 17.6   **TEST 243 RESPONSE FOR DIFFERENT POPULATION SAMPLES**

	Control	Test243-A	Test243-B	Test243-C
Response Rate (%)	5.0%	6.5%	5.2%	7.0%
Sales Per Customer ($)	7.49	9.87	8.10	10.24
Gross Profit Per Customer ($)	3.00	4.24	3.24	4.92
Gross Profit Rate (Margin) (%)	40%	43%	40%	48%
Response Lift (%)		30%	4%	40%
Sales Lift (%)		32%	8%	37%
Profit Lift (%)		42%	8%	64%
Marketing Cost ($)		0.097	0.097	0.097
ROI (%)		1,187%	152%	1,879%

and, while the theory and calculations used to describe it—statistical sampling theory—are not simple, the results of chance are easy to demonstrate by example: Using a simple calculation it can be shown that all of the results are statistically reasonable for Test243 (Exhibit 17.6).

In the initial case in the exhibit, now labeled Test243-A, the results were very positive. It would not be difficult to decide the test was successful and should be rolled out to the population as a whole. However, the results for Test243-B are really no better than the control, and the results for Test243-C are significantly better than Test243-A.

If the results for Test243 are used to influence business planning and determine how best to allocate investment funds for OurCompany, expectations for the business plan are difficult to determine based on these results: If Test243-B results are used, when in fact Test243-A is more likely, the investment will not be made at all and a significant profit opportunity is forgone: 200,000 × 1.24 = $248,000.

If Test243-C results are used to estimate plan profits based on a rollout to 200,000 customers, and results are more consistent with Test243-A, profit will be less than expectations by a substantial amount: The gross profit difference between Test243-A and Test243-C is $0.68, and 200,000 × $0.68 is $136,000. Instead of creating an incremental benefit for the company, the test backfires and creates a shortfall of $136,000 against Plan. The profit was still incremental, but not as high as the expectations created by the test results of Test243-C. Management is now forced to make up the difference in order to achieve the plan, and Marketing loses influence in decisions over how funds are to be allocated in the future. OurCompany in turn will lose an obviously beneficial investment channel in incremental marketing activities. Test243 seems to be a good incremental promotion, if expectations based on the test results can be resolved.

In order to better estimate expectations and rule out or minimize chance in the results, OurCompany could do this test several times, choosing several groups randomly from the overall population of male customers younger than 37 years old. The results could be averaged together, and this would not be an unreasonable approach to ruling out chance and increasing the likelihood that the averaged results would be more repeatable than any one of the sample groups alone. Using the cases above, the average gross profit expectation is $(4.24 + 3.24 + 4.92)/3 = 4.13$. Expectations would be set conservatively in this case, and results, if similar to Test243-A, would come in slightly better than expectations, creating a nice contribution over Plan.

However, using more sample groups in the test increases the cost of the test, and, if the promotion in fact generates lower results or lower profit per customer, the test could in fact cost OurCompany twice: first in the cost of doing the test over multiple sample groups, and second in the cost of lower results in each group. Incremental marketing test promotions will never provide consistently higher results; there will be some winners and a good proportion of losers. Testing will minimize the impact of the losers, but repeated testing of losers to demonstrate their negative impact should be avoidable.

Instead, statistical theory can be applied to design the test effectively and minimize the expectation that the results are not repeatable, or their variability is too ambiguous to merit a decision to roll out the promotion. In other words, good test design can *minimize* the level of chance surrounding the results. The results of the rollout may still not match exactly the results of the test, but the expectation will be higher that the results of the rollout will come close to the test results.

Statistical sampling theory states that results for samples of the entire population will differ from the result of the population as a whole by a range that is related to the size of the sample. If the entire population is used—all male customers under age 37—there is no sampling variation from repeated tests, as the entire population is used. Testing uses smaller groups to minimize cost, and the smaller the sample, the greater the range of possible response rates based on sampling theory alone. For an expected response rate of 5%,

95 out of 100 tests using 10,000 customers could generate a range of response rates from 4.6% to 5.4%, using a simplified calculation.

Applied to the example of Test243, where the expected response rate was the same 5%, the response rate of 6.5% is well beyond that level, and beyond the range attributed to chance, 4.6% to 5.4%. In fact there is less than 1 chance in 1,000 that a 6.5% response rate would occur by chance. From this statistical observation, a marketer can conclude that the promotion gene- rated the incremental result and is the sole driver behind the higher response rate. OurCompany can be confident that the rollout will generate a response close to the test result.

Is it also possible to calculate a reasonable expectation for the rollout, and choose a "good number" for the business plan? Using the same logic and calculation, a 0.5% *range of expectation* could be assigned to the test response rate of 6.5%. For business plan purposes, or in establishing an expectation for results of a rollout, the lower figure of 6.0% could be assumed for the response, with some likelihood of achieving the higher figure.

SAMPLE SIZE IMPACT ON RESPONSE RATE TESTS

For a rollout to a large population, this range of $\pm 0.5\%$ could have significant ramifications in presenting a very large profit impact from choosing the higher or lower figure. A 0.5% variability around the 6.5% expected rate seems high, almost 10%. This would be particularly true if the breakeven value for the promotion hinged on achieving a higher rate, one closer to the conservatively expected 6.0% rate. What if the variability in expected results caused the broad range of the test result to overlap that of the breakeven point? How would marketing make a decision to roll out in such a case? Could the test be structured to improve the likelihood of making the correct decision?

This can be done by choosing an appropriate sample size. Assume the result for the control is still expected to be 5%, and the lift needed to justify the rollout is 12% above 0.05 or +0.006 (5.6%). The range around the control sample of 10,000 customers was 0.004, and a similar range would be expected around the test result of 6.5%. To ensure that both ranges do not overlap and minimize the possibility that results are due to chance alone, the control *and* test sample sizes can be increased by a factor, from 10,000 to

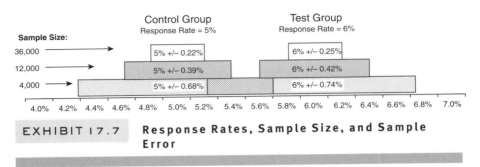

EXHIBIT 17.7   **Response Rates, Sample Size, and Sample Error**

12,000. The range around the results, known as a *confidence interval*, will then be narrow enough to rule out chance if the test achieves a response rate better than 5.4%, and minimize the chance of overlapping results.

This concept is illustrated graphically in Exhibit 17.7. The different bars represent the confidence intervals around the control response rate, on the left side, and the response rate of Test243. The two bottom bars represent the interval range based on a sample size of 4,000. The two bars which have narrower ranges than the bottom bars, are based on sample sizes of 36,000, nine times that of the initial sample. The bars show substantial change in the spread of chance results. With a sample size of 12,000, the two bars don't overlap at all in the middle of the graph. In other words, the chance likelihood of a response from a control sample falling in the range of the test result is exceedingly small. The same can be said for the Test243 results: The chance of a response rate falling into the range of the control is equally small.

What about the difference in the sales value noted in the example? Does that compound the impact of the test or even suggest the response rate could be lower and still merit a rollout? This is correct, and a confidence interval can be generated to ensure the test value for sales is also not due to chance. In fact, the test could be structured with exactly the goal of increasing average price, regardless of a notable lift in response (unless the lift is negative, of course). However, remember that the initial test was suggested by the lagging response from a sizable group of customers, the "under-37 male customer" population. If a response can be generated, the goal is achieved; if the price is higher than average, then the benefit is increased above the goal.

In that case it may be worth considering extending the promotion to a broader population, to generate sales at higher price levels. A test could confirm this. Instead of just selecting a test group of younger male inactive customers, additional sample groups could be added with specific demo-graphic attributes. Each test group would require a sufficiently high volume to minimize the impact of chance in the results. Hence the overall test strategy could benefit by including more expansive group criteria in many tests, to confirm the impact of certain promotions on populations outside of the range of the primary target group.

Another option might be to include a sample of the general population in the test. It might be believed that this group could be used to analyze the response of specific segments within the overall population. However, as soon as smaller "segment-specific" groups are selected for analysis from this "general population sample," the implicitly smaller size of the "segmentation" sample being analyzed encounters the influence of chance in the results. As the "segment" becomes more defined by specific customer attributes, the number of people in the sample having these attributes becomes smaller and smaller, particularly for groups having combined attributes: Gender + Age + Income + Region, for example. Such a subsegment might be too small in the test results to generate reliable results. Recalling Exhibit 17.7, as the test group becomes smaller, the range of chance response broadens considerably.

To offset this impact, the number of people selected for the "general population test group" needs to increase. As a result, the cost of the test increases as well. Because of the range of results possible through sampling, specific focus on particular groups and offers should maximize the value of results while minimizing the cost of testing to achieve such results.

CANNIBALIZATION AND PURCHASE TIMING

One final note on evaluating simple test results, which applies equally to the more complex case discussed in the next section: Any promotion can have a longer-term *negative* impact by motivating buyers to act now instead of at a near-term future date, which will result in higher sales during the promotion period followed by lower sales after the promotion, an impact known as *cannibalization* or moving sales forward. A discount-based promotion can have the additional impact of providing an existing buyer with a lower price point, which would lower sales dollars (revenue) during the period of the promotion as well as later, due to the combination of the lower price point and cannibalization of future sales.

Therefore, analysis of the promotion results must extend beyond the promotion period to capture the effect of any cannibalization and average price fluctuations from promotion discounts. For example, if the promotion period is two weeks long, the analytical period might extend another two or even four weeks forward. No harm is done from the extended analytical period, other than time and resources spent evaluating results over a longer period of time. If anything, business results will be improved by ensuring the test promotions in fact net a positive gain over the entire period, and not just a short-term lift and corresponding fall, or a lower price point longer term accompanied by lower profitability.

In conclusion, then, the sample size of the test and control groups should be determined based on the level of discrimination needed to ensure the results will be repeatable, and that they are not determined based on chance. The size of the sample will be dictated by the expected response rate and the level of discrimination desired, based on the lift. A lower response rate will generally be associated with higher sample sizes for better discrimination of smaller lifts, while a higher response rate will enable smaller test groups for equivalent discrimination. And last, the evaluation period for analyzing sales results should extend beyond the period of the test and normal response, to ensure near-term gains are not offset by an equivalent decline in sales in the period following the promotion period.

MULTIPLE TEST GROUPS AND MIXED RESULTS

Earlier it was suggested that multiple tests could be performed in parallel to assess the impact of using different channels, price points, and creative presentation at the same time, rather than trying repeated tests in sequence, which would usually take quite a bit of time.

Marketing automation can facilitate the test setup process by enabling easy splits for test audiences. The Split icon was used in the prior example to create a holdout sample as a control population. Response for the holdout group would be compared to the promotion group to identify the lift provided by the promotion and demonstrate the benefit of the promotion (see Exhibit 17.8).

The split function can be just as easily used to create many test cells, as shown in Exhibit 17.9, which generates a control plus six test cells.

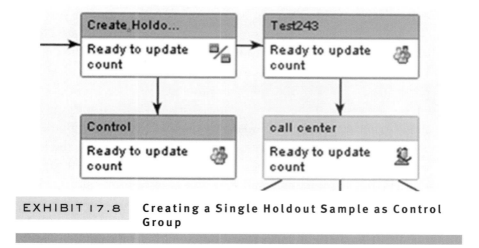

EXHIBIT 17.8   Creating a Single Holdout Sample as Control Group

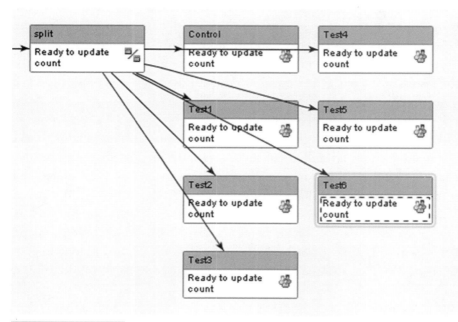

EXHIBIT 17.9   Creating a Control and Multiple Test Promotion Cells

In either case, the Split icon can make it easy to allocate all or part of a group to individual cells. In this design, it is also common to allocate a fixed group for the control and each test, and the balance of the population to the "standard" mailing. The test promotions are referred to as *challengers*. Once the separate groups are identified in their individual cells, a cell code is used that will become part of the distribution list created for transmission to a letter shop or call center. The cell code identifies the individuals with the test promotion they are intended to receive. The cell code is used by the letter shop or call center to identify the promotion content intended for this individual. Hence the initial separation of the population is followed by a regrouping together by channel or delivery agent, if multiple call centers are used, for example. Each "cell" label, such as "Test 1," "Test 2" (see Exhibit 17.9), would be included in the export file before it is sent to the promotion delivery agent. The population and cell code are saved in a *contact history* table to facilitate (in fact enable) follow-up analysis of results.

There are two types of test audience, one that receives a test promotion and one that does not. Both will exist in the test process. In the previous "Test243" case, a holdout group was created that did not receive the promotion, and whose response was recorded during the period when the "Test243" group was receiving and responding to the promotion. The two groups will otherwise be identical, and that is an important consideration for the results of the test. The decision to roll out the test to the population as a whole will be based on the sales lift associated with the group that received the promotion, as described earlier.

Using multiple test cells—different offers, offer presentations, and channels—creates an additional level of complexity in analyzing results, even though the primary interest remains in the comparison of each test cell to the holdout sample, the control group.

Multiple test cells may have similar results for response and sales. How does a marketer decide which response is best? Worse, response rates and price points may vary by cell in different directions. For example, which of the test promotions shown in Exhibit 17.10 is the preferred promotion? Test 3 has a much higher average profit, $13.69, over the control of $9.99, but the Test 3 response rate is significantly less than the control (see Exhibit 17.10).

And as with any test, there is a concern for the *repeatability* of the results: If this test were run several times, would the results be the same? More important, if a particular test promotion is rolled out to the population as a

EXHIBIT 17.10	RESPONSE RATE AND PROFIT/RESPONSE FOR CONTROL AND FIVE TEST CELLS

Test Group	Response Rate	Average Profit/Response
Control	10.6%	$9.99
Test 1	12.8%	$8.22
Test 2	13.6%	$7.43
Test 3	8.8%	$13.69
Test 4	10.5%	$11.25
Test 5	11.6%	$12.55

whole, will the results to the population as a whole match or be similar to the test results?

In the example in Exhibit 17.10, there are five tests and a control group. The sample sizes are all the same. Test 2 has the highest response rate (13.6%) but the lowest profit per response ($7.43). Test 3 exhibits the best profit per response ($13.69) but the lowest response rate (8.8%). Which result was best? How can the right decision for a rollout be made for this case?

First, multiplying the response rate times the average profit per response provides an *expected value* for each promotion, and reduces the comparison of each test from two variables to one. Sorting the results by highest expected value also simplifies the presentation and is shown in Exhibit 17.11.

Test 5 now clearly provides the best expected value of $1.46, which is $0.40 better than the control and substantially better than the closest test, which is Test 3 (see Exhibit 17.11). Tests 3 and 4 are very similar, but they are radically different in response rate, while Tests 1 and 2 with higher response rates suffer from the lower price point and fall to the bottom.

EXHIBIT 17.11	RESPONSE RATE, PROFIT, AND EXPECTED VALUE

Test Group	Response Rate	Average Profit	Expected Value
Test 5	11.60%	$12.55	$1.46
Test 3	8.80%	$13.69	$1.20
Test 4	10.50%	$11.25	$1.18
Control	10.60%	$9.99	$1.06
Test 1	12.80%	$8.22	$1.05
Test 2	13.60%	$7.43	$1.01

How do we know if Test 5 results are significant enough to be better than chance? The response rate for Test 5 is only nominally better than the control; it is the high profit level of $12.55 that is driving its lift over the control. And how might results for the other tests be compared systematically to the control, to indicate quickly, easily, and *unambiguously* which of these tests holds promise for OurCompany in the future?

This can be done in two stages using a statistical test that assesses the differences between the groups and their average response rate and average profit per response. The test, known as a *difference of means* test, can be very useful in ensuring that many tests can be executed in parallel to maximize the availability of information in the shortest period of time, and that the results will be useful in determining which tests are worth considering for rollout.

Using a difference of means comparison, the acceptance rates for Tests 3, 1, and 2 differ significantly from the control, as shown by the shading on the left side of the table in Exhibit 17.12. Response rate for Test 4, control, and Test 5 are effectively the same, statistically speaking. This means the promotions for Tests 4 and 5 had no apparent effect on customer purchase activity when compared to the control population.

The same comparison applied to the average profit per response in Exhibit 17.13 shows that Tests 2 and 3 still are significantly different from the control, this time at opposite ends of the table: Test 3 has the lowest response but best profit, while Test 2 is the exact opposite, having the best response but least profit.

Based on the table of expected value per promotion, Test 3 shows the best combination of response, profit, and *statistical significance*, while the higher response rate for Test 2 is not sufficient to overcome the very low profit point

	Response Rate
Test 3	8.8
Test 4	10.5
Control	10.6
Test 5	11.6
Test 1	12.8
Test 2	13.6

EXHIBIT 17.12   **Difference of Means Test for Response Rate**

	Profit / Response
Test 2	7.43
Test 1	8.22
Control	9.99
Test 4	11.25
Test 5	12.55
Test 3	13.69

EXHIBIT 17.13   **Difference of Means Test for Average Profit per Response**

of Test 2, which is $7.43, fully $1.56 or 16% below the control, and $6.26 below Test 3, nearly 46%.

The above is generally sufficient to evaluate response and profit potential from test results and ensure that the decision to roll out a promotion based on test results is well informed.

EXPANDING TEST ANALYSIS

It is essential to record the test goals, test audience selection criteria, and various other information so that the test results are analyzed in the context of the test, and the test is not misinterpreted as to purpose in light of results. The additional information can also ensure that the assumptions behind the test plan are in fact demonstrated in the test results. The additional information can also provide valuable leads in understanding results, particularly in cases where results deviate significantly from expectations. Analysis of test results is a unique opportunity to examine many aspects of the business in a fairly controlled environment. Much more information should be captured for test analysis than simply "purchase/no purchase" customer response.

For example, direct mail promotions are manufactured and delivered using a variety of mechanical and manual means. Actual delivery for third-class mail may not be knowable without an established seeding process to confirm delivery, at least on a sampled basis. If a substantial volume of promotions does not reach the intended recipients, or delivery is delayed, test results could be misleading: Response would be lower than expected.

Without information that can confirm delivery, a marketer could conclude the test did not work, when in fact it could have worked quite well with those receiving the promotion.

In one experience, freight delivery of a large quantity of test promotions was lost in a flood, which substantially lowered all results, not just the test results themselves. In another case, four test mailings were packaged (inserted) by operations on four separate, sequential days. Coincidentally, each day corresponded to a different region of the country. To simplify the insertion process, operations grouped the four different promotion packages by day. As a result, the package for Test 1 was only sent to the Northeast, the Test 2 package went to customers in the Southeast, Test 3 to the central United States, and Test 4 to the West Coast, primarily California.

Following delivery, response results were tallied for evaluation. After several days of analysis there was simply no accounting for the distorted results of Test 4. Although regional customer information was available, test results were not typically tallied by region—they were simply summarized nationally by test and compared, using a technique similar to the means comparison above. It was only after results were summarized by region that the error was identified. Had the test results not included the customer "region" code, the explanation for the distorted results might never have surfaced.

Recommended Test Information

The following information is recommended for capture at the start of every test to gain significantly greater understanding of the business and ensure results can be analyzed fully, particularly where unexpected and significant deviations are noted:

- Description of test
- Primary test goals
- Number of test cells
- Average response rate
- Average response value (profit, not revenue)
- Minimum lift acceptable
- Minimum cell size

- Manager
- Target population description
- Exclusions
- Snapshot requirements (variables required at start of test)
- Start date of test (audience selection)
- Export file transmission
- Duration of test period

The test outline should also list the reports requested, which should include the standard control versus test evaluation shown earlier, and the comparison of means, if more than one test is involved. But just as significant, an assessment should be made of other impacts on customer response. These other impacts include:

- **Customer attrition.** Telemarketing may result in customer cancellations or "Do Not Phone" requests.
- **Inactive customer response.** A test may activate previously inactive customers.
- **Customer retention.** An increased level of communication may increase the volume of customers who are active longer based on the increased frequency of communication between customer and company.
- **Channel usage.** Banks frequently try to motivate branch customers to use the less expensive ATM channel for transactions.
- **Purchase margin or product purchases.** Consumer companies may induce customers to purchase higher-margin products, or products that have been slower moving and have accumulated excess inventory.

Any test can be evaluated along these and similar purchase patterns for unintended or unexpected results in these areas.

The test outline should include the reports requested as well as the Distribution List and Report Frequency. Weekly analysis for most promotions may not be necessary but it cannot hurt to have automated reporting on a weekly basis. In fact, if the volume of testing increases, which is likely with the campaign management functionality provided by marketing automation, the automated generation of test results reports becomes mandatory in order to keep up with the volume of information being generated from the tests themselves. The availability of automated reporting, provided from the customer warehouse in conjunction with the test database, will ensure ease of access to results on an ad-hoc basis, which will make weekly reviews possible as well as easy. The above discussion suggests that more and more frequent tests will become common, and having tests in progress with limited results analysis will frustrate marketers interested in test results for timely decision making. Lack of test results is no better than lack of tests.

The following report criteria are suggested for each test cell as well as control:

- Cell number
- Cell description
- Mail date
- Channel (direct mail, email, phone, newspaper, etc.)
- Offer/promotion (by cell)
- Population description
- Copy/creative (PDF or other graphic format)
- Recommended cell count
- Actual cell count
- Response by media type (opens and clicks for email, shopping cart abandons, purchases)
- Total revenue
- Total returns
- Net revenue
- Product cost
- Gross profit
- Cost of promotion
  - Setup costs
  - Nonrecurring costs (creative, setup, freight, list costs)
  - Recurring costs (media cost, delivery costs)

- Net profit after promotion
- ROI
- Lift versus control by test cell

This information is no different from the information acquired and reported for any marketing campaign. It simply has more detail on a cell-by-cell basis to support analysis of the test results.

Given availability of automated reporting and many tests to be evaluated, caution is advised in evaluating results. Reports implemented in the form of a table with significant differences highlighted can be easily read and absorbed, but they can just as easily support the wrong conclusions based on cursory review. Caution is advised in jumping to conclusions, particularly for complex multiple cell tests.

It is also worth reemphasizing the value provided by creating and analyzing holdout and control group performance, to create a baseline to measure the true impact of marketing promotions. The calculation of return on marketing investment makes a convenient assumption that customer purchases *are the result of* a marketing promotion, which is a fallacy. Examining the actions of customers over time can demonstrate a level of purchase activity that exists almost independent of marketing activities. It may be tempting to conclude that customers who have not purchased in six months will *never* purchase. But in fact some *will* purchase, regardless of the marketing activity, and this is the reason for using a control population for almost any promotion, test. The goal is always to identify the *incremental* impact provided by the marketing investment.

Analysis for incremental impact should also include *incremental cost*. The cost of some customers may be high relative to others. This might be demonstrated by evaluating the long-term activity of reactivated accounts compared to a control group of similar, nonreactivated accounts. Follow-up analysis over a longer period of time may demonstrate that a proportion of reactivated accounts return rapidly (immediately) to inactivity; in fact their only substantial response is based on repeated reactivation promotions. These thinly reactivated responders may have other, less positive attributes, such as higher returns and higher account maintenance. A reactivation promotion may have the incremental effect of attracting such high-maintenance accounts, which may be less profitable for the business. The availability of the control population enables follow-up analysis in these areas, whereas without the control, the evaluation of long-term performance after reactivation becomes more difficult.

The corollary for this situation is a filter to be developed through modeling the reactivated accounts against their purchase activity and maintenance costs. This filter would be used to minimize the volume of potential low-performance–high-maintenance accounts selected for reactivation in the next and succeeding promotions.

FORECASTING TEST RESULTS

Earlier it was cautioned that cannibalization risks required evaluation of postpromotion sales results before deciding on a rollout. Ideally this is a good, conservative approach; however, a given test may involve similar promotions, all of which may have similar cannibalization impact. In the meantime, delaying the decision to roll out a positively performing test may create an opportunity cost. Is it possible to evaluate preliminary results and make a decision before the promotion is complete?

Such a decision could be based on a *forecast* of expected results. A good, consistent, and reliable forecast could result in an earlier promotion rollout to the larger population and net higher revenue earlier in the business cycle, which could be advantageous at the end of a challenging business quarter or business year.

One approach to forecasting results is based on the same reporting framework, using extrapolated values. Performance of extrapolated values can be compared to actual over time to assess the reliability of the estimates done at incremental time periods in the course of a promotion's response cycle.

The forecasting technique is initially based on a promotion *sales curve*. This curve assesses the sales percentage complete for the promotion, based on incoming responses. In Exhibit 17.14, at approximately 4 weeks, the promotion is about 20% complete; at 9 weeks it is 60 to 70% complete; and at 17 weeks it is 90% complete. At approximately 26 weeks, sales attributable to the promotion are 100% complete.

If response is fairly consistent, these percentage complete figures can be used to estimate potential total sales for a promotion. "Estimate potential" is conservatively overstated. From personal experience, sales performance on a

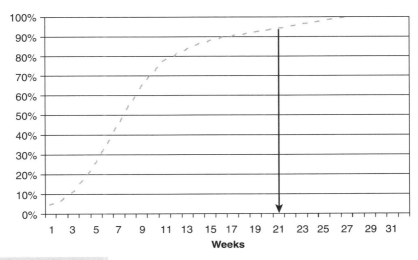

EXHIBIT 17.14   **Sales Curve Showing Percent Complete**

time basis (by week over 25-week periods) exhibits very high variability. Seasonality, month-end timing, shipment delays, mail delays, competing offers, and overlapping promotions all combine to induce a lack of consistency in response from promotion to promotion. The lack of consistency affects the data used to derive the percentage values as well as the promotion whose results are being estimated.

That being said, the technique may have merit nonetheless. Using the percentage complete references by week, total sales estimates would be made at the same time. For example, the two curves in Exhibit 17.15 represent an average promotion response compared to a test. In this case the test is underperforming the average. The sales estimate (connected curve) is estimated based on the last cumulative sales figure (dotted curve) and the figures are expressed in cumulative sales dollars. Profit could be used as well, based on margin estimates.

Using a previous percent complete sales curve, the total sales expected in the next 10 to 15 weeks can be forecast for the test (see Exhibit 17.16).

The estimated total of $772,000 is significantly lower than the promotion average of $1,072,000. Such a significant shortfall estimated at the 7-week point, about 25% complete, suggests the test will underperform the average

Test 243 Actual (In progress) vs Average Sales Promotion

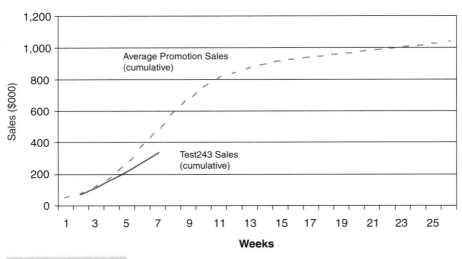

EXHIBIT 17.15   Forecasting Response—Initial Actual
Response

Tes 243 Estimate vs Average Sales Promotion

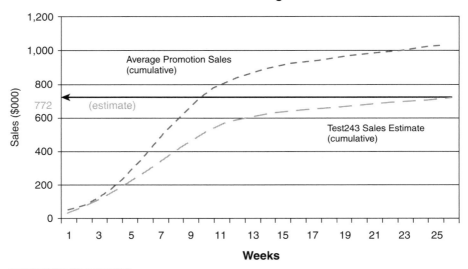

EXHIBIT 17.16   Forecasting Response—Forecasted
Expectation

promotion. It may also signal an operations issue in processing sales, a vendor issue in executing delivery, or a presentation problem with the creative. It would be appropriate to check these aspects of the promotion before assuming that the test failed (to better the average promotion).

The advantages of forecasting results based on prior experience are several: It may warn of operations issues enough in advance to ensure monthly financial performance is not affected; it may warn of execution issues or vendor-related problems, particularly with new vendors or new channels; it may warn of an inconsistency in creative presentation. And, if the test instead does well, it may provide an opportunity to roll out earlier, and bring the sales in before the end of a quarter or year.

CHAPTER 18

Modeling

odeling customer response and applying the model results to a campaign can provide a significant cost savings as well as surface new promotional opportunities, based on the ability of models to aid in targeting likely responders and reduce marketing costs. By identifying more likely responders, some promotions may become profitable enough to roll out, where previously the inability to identify the appropriate audience resulted in a predictably high promotion cost to mail a large audience, and the significantly lower customer revenue available from the small audience receptive to the promotion.

A customer response model is developed based on response to prior promotions. Customer attributes associated with responders and nonresponders are the components of a model. The model itself is an equation that brings these attributes together and summarizes the result as a number. In modeling likelihood to respond, the higher the result from the equation, the higher the likelihood to respond; a lower figure equates to a lower likelihood to respond.

This information can be used to determine whom to mail and whom not to mail (promote). If the *expected value* of the promotion is higher than the cost of the promotion, it is a good idea to make the promotion. This is called the breakeven point for the promotion. The marketer can calculate the relationship between likelihood to respond, cost to promote, and value of response. Any customer with a model score above breakeven is worth promoting.

The curve in Exhibit 18.1 shows the distribution of customers against response scores from zero to one. It is similar to the sales response curve

Population Distribution to Response Score

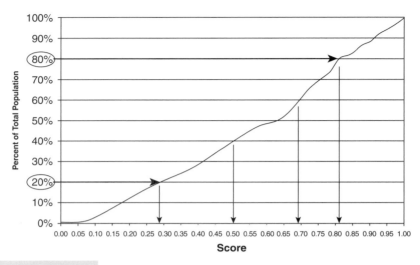

EXHIBIT 18.1   **Modeling and Response Scores**

(e.g., 20% of the customers have a score below 0.28, 40% have a score below 0.50, 60% below 0.69, and 80% below 0.81). Of course, 100% of the customers have a score below 1.0. Taken in reverse, 80% have a score higher than 0.29, 50% are higher than 0.50, and 40% are higher than 0.69. If *0.69* is the breakeven score, then the promotion mailing would go out to only those whose score is above 0.69, or only 40% of the population, representing a 60% cost savings.

The latter approach is used in applying the score to a business situation. The breakeven score is what is used to select the population to receive the promotion. Typically each customer must have a score *above* that figure.

For example, assume the score shown in Exhibit 18.1 is used to filter a selected audience for a promotion that costs $1.00 to produce and deliver. Let us say this is a direct mail promotion. Each response is expected to net $8.00 profit. The typical response to similar promotions is 10% and expectations for this example are no better than 10%, based on prior experience.

If the total population is 250,000 people, the total cost of the promotion is $250,000. A 10% response will generate 25,000 × $8.00 profit or $200,000. This equates to a loss of $50,000 for this promotion.

If the score values are applied and a suitable audience selected, the promotion can be set up to generate a sizable profit. What if there are in fact only 25,000 people who will respond, and nothing that marketing could do would generate a higher response? To make this campaign profitable will require fewer people in the mailing.

If no more than 50,000 promotions are mailed, then the campaign could generate a $150,000 profit:

$$25,000 \text{ Response} \times \$8.00 \text{ Profit} = \$200,000 \text{ Gross Profit}$$
$$\underline{50,000 \times \$1.00 \text{ Cost} = \$50,000 \text{ Cost}}$$
$$\$150,000 \text{ Net Profit}$$

If 25,000 of 50,000 respond, that is a 50% response rate. The campaign will net $200,000 gross profit, less $50,000 for the cost of the promotion, a net of $150,000 profit, compared to a $50,000 loss before the score values were applied as a selection filter.

Choosing the 50,000 people for the mailing can be done based on the score and population percentages in the graph: Selecting 50,000 people means selecting 20% of the total population of 250,000. From the graph, a score of 0.81 equates to the cutoff for the top 20% of this population, 50,000. The assumption is that a score of 0.81 or better *equates to a high likelihood to respond*.

If this were a perfect predictor of response, then a score of 0.92 or so, representing the top 10%, would identify the 25,000 people who would respond. Unfortunately, the score is not a perfect predictor; some people selected will not respond, and some people not selected *would* have responded to the promotion. The score only represents a possibility, a *likelihood*.

Calculations can be done to estimate the likelihood of choosing the nonresponsive people and not choosing the responsive people, but in general, selecting a breakeven point as a score cutoff can be adequate for establishing a good score filter.

To compensate in part for the imperfect model, slightly more than the best 50,000 customers can be selected by reducing the score filter value from 0.78 to perhaps 0.70. This small reduction in score value—0.78 to 0.70—will double the population from 50,000 to 100,000. This increases the possibility of capturing more responders; however, it also increases the likelihood of nonresponders. If a model accuracy of 95% is assumed, then 5% of the people in the selected group with a score greater than 0.70 may not respond. The net expectation is therefore 25,000 minus 5%, which is now 23,750 responders times $8.00 or $190,000 profit, less $100,000 cost for the promotion, a net of $90,000 profit for this promotion. A $90,000 profit compared to −$50,000 before the application of the model scores—such can be the value of modeling.

There are a number of caveats to the use of models. A model of population A can be used to predict response for people who are similar to population A. The same model cannot arbitrarily be applied to other populations. A good example would be a model developed from a population of male customers aged under 37. Such a model could not be applied to female customers or male customers aged over 37. It may work, in that positive results are found, but such results would be coincidental and may not be repeatable unless it can be demonstrated that the model generates equivalent results for this second population, which is certainly possible.

Models are sensitive to missing data for the variables used to develop the model. The reliability of the model can be reduced either by missing data, because available information is less, or by interpolation, where a value for missing data is guesstimated from other records. Interpolation may distort results by creating or reinforcing a relationship where in fact none exists.

The development of models can be a very sophisticated process and rely on highly skilled specialists making use of advanced statistical concepts in creating the score values. The score values themselves are maintained along with other customer information in the data warehouse. The models that generate the scores are periodically reevaluated, and the customer scores themselves are recalculated to take account of new information, such as recent purchases.

Models that marketers use in improving audience selection for maximum sales impact can be implemented through the data warehouse process using an information map, which serves the same purpose as for customer data in general: It presents the marketer with an understandable, natural-language-based description of the model score, and it is available directly from the Campaign Studio interface, like same as all other customer data items.

A score filter can be added to the previous example of male customers aged under 37 by adding a new selection criterion and connecting the new attribute to the And filter that already exists.

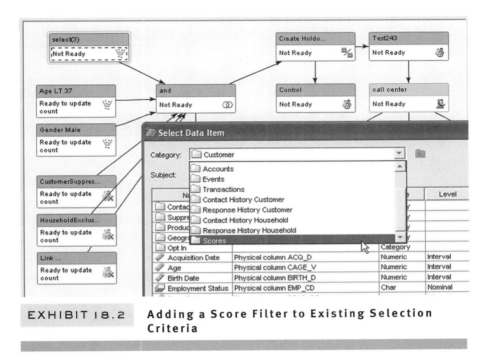

EXHIBIT 18.2   **Adding a Score Filter to Existing Selection
Criteria**

Scores are selected from the Scores folder shown in Exhibit 18.2, and there are several scores available within this folder (see Exhibit 18.3).

The *response score for personalized mail* is selected, which displays a histogram (Exhibit 18.4). The selected start value will be 0.7, which provides a count of 3,137 customers.

Using this approach, simply adding a filter that measures likelihood to respond could reduce the cost of this promotion by over 50% and increase the profit significantly as a result.

While the marketer's view of models can be limited to knowing which model to choose, selecting the appropriate breakeven value, and determining whether the remaining population is sufficient to earn a material profit, there can be considerable sophistication involved in model development and deployment.

In Exhibit 18.5, the model was deployed by having a score table updated by batch-run applications (jobs) that prepare the data and execute the arithmetic calculations underlying the score itself. The score is updated to a single table for each customer and each score. The table itself can have many

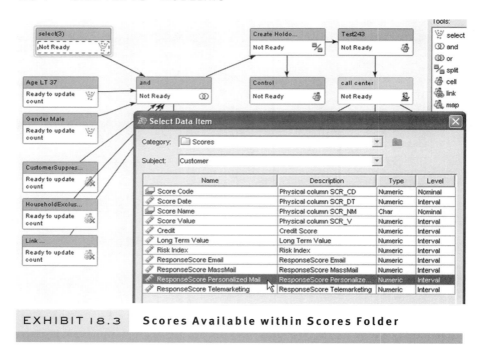

EXHIBIT 18.3   **Scores Available within Scores Folder**

scores for each customer: The view of the Scores folder showed at least seven scores available, from *response likelihood for different channels* to *credit risk* and *long-term value.*

It is also possible to execute a model score on the fly by embedding the calculation in a *calculated variable*, a variable that is created from the values of other variables *on demand*, when the marketer selects the value. This is an interesting approach, and could incorporate the most recent available information in the score calculation. A batch calculation approach cannot do this unless the entire population is rescored and the model results recalibrated. The batch calculation will usually lag real customer activity by some period of time.

The value of the model, whether batch or executed on the fly, is in refining the audience and improving the response rate. This provides a significant cost reduction for the campaign and higher profits. From a marketer's standpoint, it opens up possibilities for further promotions, promotions that would not be profitable without the benefit of a score in

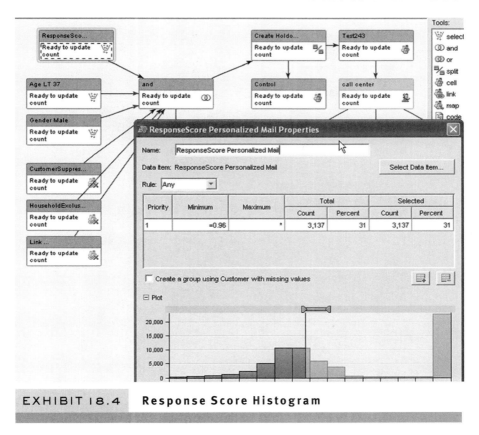

EXHIBIT 18.4   Response Score Histogram

filtering out likely nonresponders. The higher volume of communications to smaller groups of people should net higher overall profits.

PART TWO SUMMARY

Part Two has provided an overview and examples of marketing campaign implementations using a marketing automation application from SAS. The fundamental customer database and database query steps have been identified, and a simple example of their implementation through an information map and campaign management software application has been provided.

The campaign example was used as a starting point for a discussion of testing, sample size, and the impact of modeling. The latter topic could be developed much further through a detailed discussion of modeling

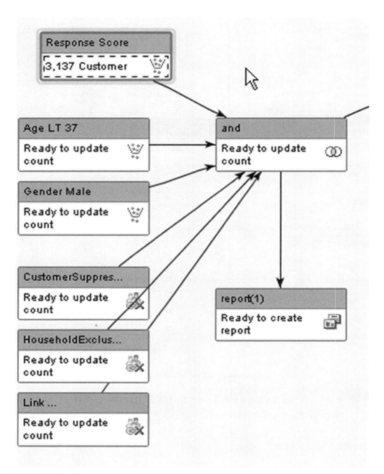

EXHIBIT 18.5   **Implementing a Score Filter with Selection Criteria**

techniques, but this would go beyond the scope of the marketing focus of *Pragmatic Marketing Automation*. What is important for marketers is to recognize the ability to integrate model scores into an environment that enables them to select appropriate scores as audience selection filters for campaigns, to improve promotion response and reduce the cost of campaign promotions.

PART THREE

Advanced Topics

I n this final part of the book, several topics of a more advanced nature are addressed. The preceding chapters discuss and demonstrate the advantages provided by a customer data warehouse, information map, and campaign management application. These capabilities alone will enable marketers to direct more and more frequent promotions to increasingly smaller and more targeted audiences.

However, these communications and the process of development and execution do not address several fundamental issues:

- Strategic contact management
- Optimizing the choice between multiple contacts and/or resource constraints
- Model management
- Customer interaction management
- Strategic marketing

These areas provide an opportunity to refine the marketing processes, relying on the marketing automation infrastructure already discussed. Refining the marketing processes becomes necessary, for the reasons discussed below, in order to maintain response rates and revenue growth.

CHAPTER 19

Optimizing Contact Strategy

Increasing the level of communication between company and customer will result in a higher level of customer contacts. Each contact is recorded appropriately in *contact history*. Contact history records expand dramatically as more communications are generated. A need arises to address the best use of this information; if left alone its accumulation will become unwieldy and useless. *Strategic contact management* will reduce the volume of unnecessary information as well as identify and improve the use of the relevant information.

As more marketers are enabled to communicate with customers within the same organization, there is a risk that the best customers will be increasingly targeted for a disproportionately high volume of promotions, and existing resources for contact execution will be taxed to the point of exhaustion. This will be detrimental in several ways, and attempting to filter messages is difficult; there is no facility discussed so far to determine which of several competing messages is best. Campaign response will be reduced and profit will not be maximized. Marketing messages to the same customer need to be optimized based on likelihood to respond and value maximization, as well as in the context of resources available to make the contact. Management of this process is referred to as *marketing optimization*.

STRATEGIC CONTACT MANAGEMENT

Strategic contact management does not, in this section, refer to the frequency of contact, channel selection, or other promotion management strategy considerations, which are discussed further along. In this section, strategic contact management refers to the management of the contact history records—how this potentially voluminous amount of data can be reduced and summarized to provide a contact strategy resource instead of just taking up volumes of disc space.

Contact history is maintained for each promotion distributed. This is necessary for establishing the metrics on response as well as follow-up analysis for modeling and improving response. Contact history data accumulates rapidly, which makes it increasingly difficult to extract meaningful information. For example, two years of promotion to 250,000 people can cumulate almost 30 million records. Assume 250,000 customers are contacted on average two times per month using batch-based communications. Assume two more targeted communications are generated each month, on average, for half the population, across different channels. Assume further that event-based, customer-specific communications are generated at least once per month to half the customer base, and one ad-hoc contact is made per month to each customer. In the course of a year there will be:

$$
\begin{array}{r}
250,000 \times ((2 \times 12) \\
+ .5 \times (2 \times 12) \\
+ .5 \times (1 \times 12) \\
+ (1 \times 12)) \\
\hline
13,500,000 \text{ Contacts}
\end{array}
$$

At the end of the second year the total contact records will be 27 million, and in the third year over 40 million. How is this data best organized? By customer and contact? By channel? By year and month? How might it best be retrieved? Is all of this information even relevant? Over time, is all of the information *still* relevant or does it fade in importance after 12 months, even after six months? Is there a useful approach to reducing this level of detail to something more meaningful and relevant to ongoing promotions?

Several initial summary measures are very relevant. Total number of contacts during specific windows of time is very important. As noted earlier, as marketers evolve in their ability to exploit marketing automation and modeling and begin to craft incremental communications, there is a risk that the best customers will become inundated with promotions and their response will decline from saturation. There will be too many offers for any one or two or three to maximize their relevance; each successive offer beyond the saturation point will further dilute the effectiveness of even the best offers. Worse, the best customers may begin to feel saturated themselves, and begin to ignore successive communications regardless of relevance.

Therefore, the first measures to create from contact history are records of the communications made during prior time periods such as 24 hours, 48 hours, 72 hours, 1 week, 30 days, 60 days, 90 days, and 6 months. This information is used to manage the contact *frequency* to all customers. The level of communication appropriate to any one customer along different media channels must be determined from testing and/or perhaps company policy. Telemarketing is very intrusive, while email is lightweight and less expensive. This is still an assumption on a per-customer basis. Satisfied customers may appreciate a phone call; the challenge is modeling to find them.

The other factor to test is the time period between contacts along a particular channel. From prior experience, for example, a dormant customer offer made via telemarketing was followed by a management-declared waiting period of six months. A flag on the database,[1] known as a dormant flag, was set with each dormant promotion and cleared after six months. All dormant selection queries used the "dormant flag" along with other selection filters.[2]

The summary record(s) of communications volume can include the channel for the offer to fine-tune control of the volume of email, mail, and telemarketing actions taken and provide a reference point for evaluating channel effectiveness by customer.

---

[1] A "flag" is a binary variable (field) in the database. When equal to one, the flag is "on"; zero is "off." Examples of flags include "Do Not Market," "Write Off Account," and "Foreign Address."

[2] There is an interesting supply/demand business tradeoff implied in this example. The supply of inactive customers will change based on the number of customers reactivated, the number who cancel or do not respond, and the number of newly inactive customers. If the reactivation program is more successful than the supply, the reactivation program will generate declining revenue over a period of time. Management or Business Plan expectations may be inconsistent with declining revenues; the balance between level of effort in reactivation and ongoing supply must be evaluated on an ongoing basis.

After creating summary contact frequency measures for specific time periods, the next step in strategic contact management involves data reduction: Instead of maintaining a detailed record for each communication to each customer, a summary record is created that captures essential offer and channel information for the prior N contacts, by customer. This record captures the sequence of offers made during the prior period, which may provide additional insight into offer sequencing based on the analysis of the success of specific sequences in maximizing revenue.

These are customer-based summary records and not "campaign" summary records. The latter summarize the total number of contacts for a specific campaign or set of campaigns/promotions. The former summarize customer contacts made on a per-customer basis.

The number of contact references to be maintained is related to the length of the "prior period," which must be determined from analysis. This may be a time-based figure or based on number of contacts. For example, one analysis demonstrated that a record of the prior nine promotions was useful in predicting response likelihood for more active customers, and not every customer received the same number of promotions in a given window of time.

Communications that took place prior to the most recent nine communications were largely irrelevant, at least in relation to current likelihood to respond. The prior nine communications were coupled to a record of the prior nine responses. This summary of promotional activity was useful in summarizing customer response by offer and the variety of purchases made. The data also demonstrated that the specifics of each contact—promotion, channel, media—were less relevant than that a contact was made.

Analysis is necessary to determine the number of promotions to maintain in the sequence record, and the actual number of relevant contacts could change over time. The relevant count has a significant impact on the number of records to maintain in the detailed contact history. It will signal whether detailed history should extend 6 months, 9 months, 12 months, or more. Clearly the volume of contact history will be dramatically smaller and easier to access as well as maintain when it is known just how much promotional information is relevant.

Once the summary information is initiated, the detailed data can be archived as required.

Marketing Optimization

Strategic contact management records will clearly help in managing absolute contact frequency and help marketers prevent saturation of the best customers with too many promotions. What it cannot do is aid in determining which of several competing offers in a short window of time should be made to which customer. With marketing automation in place, marketing teams will be empowered to maximize the volume of communications and the corresponding level of sales. However, when there are two similar and competing offers, how can the best combination of competing offers be directed to the customers who provide the highest likelihood to respond, and how can profit be maximized? When there are two competing offers through the same channel, but less capacity to make both contacts, how can the best combination be selected in the context of channel capacity?

Marketing optimization provides the ability to manage competing offers as well as competing offers in the context of limited resources. "Resources" can be channel capacity as well as marketing budget. Marketing optimization combines the expected value (estimated value for a response) for each offer through each channel, together with likelihood to respond, and, through a sophisticated algorithm, optimizes the revenue/profit combinations and selects the best combination of customer, channel, and offer.

For marketing process, this capability can represent a significant departure from the previous discussion, which involved marketer-driven selections and batch execution. Instead of several marketers each creating their own initial selection filters and, in the spirit of cooperation, determining who has the best opportunity for revenue contribution, each marketer tries to maximize the total volume of communications, targeted or otherwise, regardless of competing offers. Assuming the response models are reasonably accurate, marketing optimization will create the optimal combination.

Assume two marketing teams, A and B, each select several hundred thousand recipients for a promotion, Team A for telemarketing and Team B for direct mail. One of the customers, Bob, is selected by both teams, but the company has a rule that dictates only one contact in the same period of time. For the first campaign Bob has a response likelihood of 0.35, the value of the promotion is $20 profit, and the combination yields an expected response value for this campaign of $7.00 (0.35 × $20.00) (for Bob alone).

For the second campaign, Bob's response likelihood is 0.40 and the campaign value is $15.00. The expected value of the second campaign is therefore $6.00 (0.40 × $15.00), which is less than the $7.00 of the first campaign. Because there is a requirement for only one contact per person in a given time frame, the decision as to which of these campaigns to deliver to Bob is easily made in favor of the first because of the higher expected value.

Assume a slightly more complicated scenario. Assume a third campaign is being activated on the telemarketing channel. There are ten telemarketers available and they can make only so many calls per day. This is what is meant by limited capacity—this is a *resource constraint*. Assume only one call can be made, and two recipients are eligible for the call, Bob and Helen, and Helen has been selected for only one of the three active campaigns, while Bob has been selected for all three.

Assume Helen's response likelihood for the third campaign is 0.30 and the value of the campaign is also $20.00, which means Helen's expected value for the first campaign is lower than Bob's (0.30 × $20.00, or $6.00). Bob's expected value is $7.00, as calculated above. It would appear that Bob should receive the first campaign and Helen should not be contacted at all. See Exhibit 19.1.

However, this yields a lower total profit for the company: If Bob is selected for the first campaign, the expected gain is $7.00. However, Bob has an optional opportunity to be contacted through the second campaign from Marketing Team B. His expected value from that campaign is $6.00. Therefore, if Bob receives the second campaign and Helen receives the one available telemarketing call, for an expected gain of $6.00, the total profit for the company increases from $7.00 to $12.00.

EXHIBIT 19.1   MARKETING OPTIMIZATION EXAMPLE

	Bob			Helen		
	Value	Response	Exp Value	Value	Response	Exp Value
Team A TeleMkt	$ 20.00	0.35	$ 7.00	$ 20.00	0.3	$ 6.00
Team B Dir Mail	$ 15.00	0.4	$ 6.00		(not selected)	

This is exactly the scenario that marketing optimization is designed to manage. And this is why marketing strategy would change with use of marketing optimization. The application will determine the best contact when there are competing offers on the table to the same customers. As a result, marketing can generate more offers, and the application will ensure the contact frequency will be respected as well as channel constraints and budgetary allocations for each promotion.

This raises a practical question: If two marketers each develop respective campaigns that map some of the same people for contact, but the actual contacts are made on the fly using a computer program run shortly before the promotion is delivered, how much product is ordered for the respective promotions, or how many contacts can be committed to the call center? This information is not and will not be known until the selections are done for the respective promotions. However, the additional cost incurred is small compared to the gain provided by the higher expected value of response.

Not every promotion need be optimized and subjected to *optimization filtering*, in which case the campaign will be delivered according to plan. Optimization is important where channel constraints, budget constraints, competing offers, and contact frequency limits are encountered. Some promotions may be considered *standard*, to be delivered without regard to other promotions.

CUSTOMER INTERACTION MANAGEMENT

Campaigns developed initially on an ad-hoc basis may become part of the yearly campaign process, based on batch selection and execution techniques: June campaigns will be reexecuted every June and results compared to prior years. However, events that take place between customer and company outside of the normal "promotion/response" sphere may provide valuable signals for marketers to initiate further contact. Batch-based campaigns, even if based on an automated weekly selection process, will lag the contact-suggesting-event in time. As more time passes between the customer action and the marketer's response (and lack of response), response likelihood declines and the relationship weakens. Enabling *trigger-based campaigns*, which are executed very close to the actual event, can reduce the time lag and improve response.

There is also a type of event that is not directly related to customer transactions, marketer contacts, or customer/marketer contacts. These events are referred to as *state changes* and can be quite broad in definition. A basic state change would be when a customer's purchase (or other) activity falls below a recognized level determined from prior experience, such as three-month average purchases. The state change is from "active" to "less active." By building state descriptions and establishing the attributes of specific states, such as level of activity (a purchase), scale of activity (number of purchases), and duration between events, changes can be recognized and proactive steps taken to restore a previously more favorable state. Recognizing state changes relies on the ability to evaluate many events in the context of time and time duration.

Marketing automation applications that are able to generate both trigger-based signals as well as state-based signals for marketer action and reaction enable a broader set of customer communications that are more closely aligned with events or state changes. Campaigns developed through campaign management can be preestablished to respond according to these situations, both customer action (trigger) and state derived.

Batch-driven campaigns have a fundamental weakness that reduces response rates: By definition these campaigns do not address *events* in the customer/company interaction process. If customer Bob purchases Product X, there is typically no *marketing* signal that the purchase event occurred. Instead a sales record is inserted in a sales file and eventually Bob's customer record will be updated to record his purchase. Eventually, when the marketer executes a campaign for an upsell to customers like Bob, who purchased Product X, Bob will receive a promotion based on his purchase. When Bob receives the promotion will depend on how the marketer schedules the campaign. The time between Bob's purchase and the promotion could be a week, a month, or several months.

Typical marketing promotions will always lag purchase or similar events for most customers. Response will likely lag in proportion to how much time transpires from the purchase event to the promotion. For some customers the lag will be very significant depending on how often the marketer chooses to run a particular promotion. The falloff in response can be expected to be similarly significant.

Ideally, whenever a customer purchased Product X, a signal would be generated that triggers a follow-up communication. The communication would be generated on an optimal channel: email, phone, or direct mail. To do this requires that each customer transaction be evaluated in real time and a promotion developed and delivered accordingly.

This occurs already at supermarket checkout counters: As one printer is printing the purchase receipt details, a second printer is generating coupons, some of which are driven by product purchases and some of which are simply automatic.

Customer Interaction software works in the same way: It filters every transaction that has a digital record and creates the relevant signals when specific transaction signals cumulate to specified criteria. "*Cumulate* to specified criteria" is significant: By combining purchase activity with other information maintained in a "customer signature," a more complex trigger decision can be enabled, a decision based on more information than simply "Product X purchased 5:24 P.M. on January 12." The combination of a customer signature containing information relevant for event-driven promotional decisions and the event record itself enables the software to generate a marketing trigger when the right *combination* of event and signature is found.

The customer signature is developed based on all relevant *real-time* and *time-based* filters. The signature is updated for all transactions selected for real-time interaction monitoring. In addition, the signature is updated for time-based events. A time-based event can be relevant to the real calendar ("June 12") or based on time duration ("14 days before policy renewal" or "47 days since last purchase").

In addition, customer information can be combined and evaluated together with events and time duration–based updates and marketing promotions determined as appropriate:

"Forty-seven days since last purchase"

+ "Previous purchase $50–$100"

+ "Current high-value customer"

+ "Prospective customer value reduction to Medium"

+ "Prior purchases of Product X"

+ "Email channel preference"

= "New promotion Z"

The definition of *high value* or *medium value* can also be determined in real time based on a combination of events and customer information: total purchases in a 2-week or 30-day period, average weekly purchases over 6 months, maximum purchase value greater than a specified limit, top 10% of customers for a given period. Any of the above or combination of the above could be used to determine a value classification for customers.

The goal is to treat the best customers better and try to maintain their status as best customers. Enabling promotions that are both real time and timely can contribute to a better dialog. *Timely* means more than simply real time; it means the appropriate time between the juxtaposition of events and information that signal an action and the time in which the actual promotion or other marketing action should take place.

This approach suggests many more frequent communications to smaller groups of people in order to address the lag-induced falloff in response rates. This may suggest higher setup costs to accommodate the more frequent communications, and this is a valid criticism. However, setup costs can be mitigated by running the campaign as any equivalent wave-based campaign would be run, with smaller volumes at each wave.

The optimal purchase/response period for types of customers will be determined with testing, for now the events are evaluated and the signals collected in a table of events. The table—or tables—can be structured in a variety of ways to manage IT resources best; the important consideration is that the events themselves are abstracted from the primary customer database and made available directly from an "events table," which may be structured in a variety of ways. The events table is used as the source for event-driven communications.

For a typical batch-driven campaign, every time the promotion is run there will be IT costs incurred to find those customers who have purchased Product X in the past 10, 30, or 90 days. Unless unique flags are used to signal "Product X purchase on January 12," all sales records must be searched.

By abstracting the event or event combination in real time and building a small summary table of event-significant records, the equivalent IT resources to execute the same evaluation using batch processes are conserved, resulting in a savings in IT by driving promotions in real time.

The end result will connect promotions more closely in time with the event triggers themselves, thus creating an opportunity for overcoming response falloff due to the promotional lag associated with batch-driven campaigns.

MODEL MANAGEMENT

As models become further integrated in the process of refining audiences, a need arises to enable management of the scoring process and the model update process. Model performance is monitored on a regular basis, scores are refreshed, and models are updated. The modelers need to have access to applications that facilitate the update process and provide some measure of control, a process known as *model management*. Marketers will benefit from being able to continue to use models and scores that are carefully managed behind the scenes.

Utilizing a systematic approach to model management is effective when more than one person is developing models and several models are active in production. There is no formula for determining the exact numbers that would dictate when model management can or should be implemented. Model management helps the modelers by managing some of the overhead of development and deployment; therefore modelers managing more than a few models would find model management helpful.

Modeling is typically done in a controlled environment; the finished model is a small computer program that prepares the data and performs a calculation. The controlled environment consists of a computer, statistical software for modeling, and sample data. The computer can be a personal workstation or a more powerful server or even a mainframe. The sample data can be system driven or derived by the modelers themselves, as most are very skilled in data manipulation.

The resulting computer program must be moved out of the modeler's controlled environment and into a production environment to create the model scores. The production environment enables the software to be executed on a planned and repeated basis to update scores as well as score new customers; it protects the model from the risks associated with residence in a single person's environment such as a desktop personal computer (PC). The production environment ensures the best use of information technology (IT) resources: The scoring process is another production process to be scheduled for execution on scarce resources.

Models are company assets and need to be preserved and protected no less than the application software that drives operations and finance. If a model process—the computer program—is lost or becomes corrupted, the corresponding scoring job will fail and marketers will no longer be able to identify those customers most likely to respond. Without consistent and up-to-date scores, the campaigns will continue but response will decline as increasing numbers of poorly selected customers are targeted for promotions that are less likely to find favor.

The scoring process is not a one-time process. While models can be stable, customers are not: Scores have to be updated on a regular basis to reflect changes in customer status and customer activity. This requires an ongoing effort by the modeler to retest the scores and compare the results against sample response data.

When the model is reevaluated, small changes might be made. These changes need to be reflected in the version of the model that is being used in production. Both of these criteria—updating scores and updating the model—will involve new production execution of the model to update the customer scores.

To ensure the ongoing integrity of the production version of the model, a process of change management should be used. Change management enables a copy of the production model to be used by the modeler for testing while ensuring the production version of the model is "frozen" and cannot be modified, by the modeler or anyone else, intentionally or in error.

When the modeler has completed testing, if there are changes made to the model—the score calculation or the data preparation—the modeler copies the new version of the model into the production environment and identifies the new version with a *version number*. The version number uniquely identifies each version of the model, and a copy of each version of the model should be saved. This ensures that previous versions can be restored to production if there is a problem with the latest version. This also helps the modeler maintain a history of model changes to facilitate comparative performance analysis and to understand in what ways the model is evolving.

In production the scoring process may always invoke the newest version of the model, or continue to use a fixed version until the job that initiates the scoring process is manually updated for the newer version. Ongoing model performance evaluation and production versioning for model updates ensures that marketers will always use the correct score or score content. The infrastructure for managing model updates and production deployment is called model management.

Model management provides an infrastructure for the modeler to facilitate production deployment of models and the ongoing protection of the assets (the computer programs). New models are developed and existing models are refined and improved over time; sometimes a model is refined and replaced by two or three models. As the number of models grows, it becomes increasingly difficult and time consuming for the modelers to manage the information and production deployment without a more rigorous infrastructure.

CHAPTER 20

Strategic Marketing

The last topic in this part, strategic marketing, addresses the life cycle of the customer–company relationship, from inception to growth to stability and then to potential decline and attrition. A batch-based promotion process, even a batch process complemented by trigger-based communications, ignores the customer life cycle—the progression of events between the time a customer first makes contact with a company (or is first contacted), purchases are made, accounts are opened and the eventual decline in the effectiveness of the relationship, when the customer transitions to either inactive or dormant, or moves to a competitor.

Recognizing that the relationship is progressive suggests a strategic marketing approach that takes advantage of the time aspects of the relationship. This approach improves the duration of the relationship by recognizing and managing the succession of states that make up the life cycle. Instead of relying on batch-calendar-based promotions and trigger events, a marketer may be proactive in generating communications based on first purchase or contact and developing additional communications proactively, communications that anticipate *stages* in the relationship. The combination of batch- and trigger-based communications capabilities provides the necessary infrastructure for a strategic marketing–based approach to managing customer communications.

The key element behind strategic marketing is a plan for *proactive* communications based on an *expectation* for customer behavior within a cohesive *relationship development framework*.

Proactive means the marketing communications, as a sequence, are planned in advance and will be executed based on customer behavior over time. The sequence is flexible; it is not a hard-and-fast Comm01, Comm02 sequence. The communication pattern is planned in advance because the marketer has an *expectation* for customer behavior at different points of time, based on the passage of time as well as the sequence of communications. The sequential pattern of communication possibilities is determined based on a *framework* that attempts to develop a *relationship*.

This is very different from batch-based communications repeated year after year: Spring campaigns, June campaigns, Back-to-School campaigns. The relationship development framework recognizes the relationship stages: beginning, middle, and end. There is an attempt to couch the communications in this context of *development*. The expectation of strategic marketing is for a *longer, more profitable relationship.*

For example, recognizing that a new customer may know little about the company's breadth of product offering, it makes sense to follow a purchase with a catalog and a discount coupon. It would make sense to select a subset of products from the 250-page full catalog and mail a small introductory promotion, more similar to a cross-sell or upsell offer than a catalog presentation. It would be cheaper, it would be logically connected to the customer's first purchase, and it leaves the door open for follow-up and equally less costly communications as well as promotional offers.

Comparatively, mailing the full catalog at the outset would be an expensive one-shot deal. What does the marketer do next—mail another catalog, and another, and for how long?

This becomes a "Love-me-or-leave-me" proposition, all or nothing. There are many opportunities for the customer to acquire a negative mindset, which now must be overcome by future mailings. Instead of taking advantage of positive momentum, the marketer must overcome negative resistance.

The framework is important to provide a logical flow to the pattern of communications over time. The flow moves from beginning to end and proactively establishes company and product positioning at specific points of time.

The framework is helpful in planning suitable communications that anticipate customer activities in the future. The framework is based on an expectation that there is a *life cycle* to the relationship between customer and company. Strategic marketing addresses the life cycle of the customer and company relationship and is aimed at creating a proactive set of communications specific to the *stages* of this life cycle. The proactive communications are time based, customer activity based, and event based.

Strategic marketing–based communications and offers exist in parallel with more standard company- and product-specific campaigns; they do not supplant them or augment them. Strategic marketing–based communications are an incremental marketing program.

The infrastructure to deliver strategic marketing–based campaigns includes *batch-*, *trigger-*, and *state-based communications*. Therefore the infrastructure is not an element of strategic marketing; the infrastructure of marketing automation makes strategic marketing possible, a capability to plan communications in advance as proactive steps, in the context of marketing to successive life cycle stages. Execution of these life cycle–targeted communications is planned and scheduled in advance, and delivery is automated through marketing automation.

While it would be tempting to anticipate continued growth in individual customer spending (i.e., the same customers spending more money this year than last), it is important to recognize that growth in the business can come from two additional sources: new customers and a longer term relationship with existing customers.

The advantage of marketing to existing customers longer was also discussed in Part One of this book. Higher revenue from current customers maximizes the return on the acquisition costs, which enables higher spending on acquisition based on the higher return on the acquisition investment. It is a truism that it costs 10 times more to acquire a new customer than to achieve higher revenue from an existing customer. It is not necessary (and could be self-defeating) to anticipate and pursue the Platinum spenders. There are not that many of them to go around and the competition for Platinum spenders is stiff; more marketing effort must be extended to sustain that relationship. On several counts it makes great business sense to invest marketing dollars in extending the customer relationship.

Extending the relationship in a noncommodity business requires targeted promotions and communications that serve to reinforce and maintain the relationship. It is helpful to describe the stages in the customer life cycle using terms that would describe almost any relationship, without intending the terms too literally. The terms support the concept of a framework for crafting promotions and communications that derive at least part of their definition from this concept of a relationship. Instead of a constant stream of "Buy *this!*" promotions or repeated catalog mailings, the customer is given communications that introduce, expand awareness, educate, reinforce, and add value.

In that sense, then, these are suggested terms for the stages in the *customer life cycle*:

1. Inception[1]
2. Introduction
3. Exposure
4. Reflection
5. Evaluation
6. Second step
7. Reinforcement
8. Reemphasis
9. Repeatability
   - Renewal
   - Revitalization
10. Substitution
    - Win back, restoration
11. Stagnation
    - Loss of value
    - Decline
    - Fade
    - Cancellation

In a strategic marketing program, communications begin after the first contact, such as first purchase. After inception of the relationship, the company provides a communication to introduce itself in a broader context to the customer. Incremental communications follow that further expose the company and its products, followed by a period of reflection and an evaluation of whether to extend the relationship. The second step, an

---

[1]It is obvious that the missing term at the beginning is *courtship*, referring to acquisition marketing, an ongoing effort distinct from customer relationship marketing.

incremental purchase, is—and should be followed with—reinforcement, a reemphasis of the value of the relationship. Incremental purchases may then depend upon the repeatability of this value message. When the relationship flags or there is competitive substitution—purchases decline or stop—there is a need for renewal of the value message and a "win back" or restoration effort. Eventually the relationship may give way to stagnation and loss of mutual value. Sometimes this stage can be recovered; sometimes it is inevitable. The key item for a relationship of any duration is stage 9, repeatability. If a customer cannot anticipate repeatable added value, then the door will open to stage 10, substitution—a competitor—or stage 11, stagnation and corresponding loss of value.

The emphasis here can be placed on creating a perception of value between company and customer. There are alternative marketing approaches, approaches that push the typical buttons of seasonality and *Sale! Sale! Sale!* The emphasis on value is expected to protect profit margins as well as form a basis for a longer-term relationship and corresponding incremental sales and return on the marketing investment. Sale and related discount-based promotions are still important, but endless repetition dilutes effectiveness, and repeated *Sale!* messaging does not differentiate the company from competitors or provide incremental value.

Inception is the event that initiates the relationship, following the footnoted reference to *courtship*. The first event is typically a customer's first purchase, but it could also be the first time a contact is made that is mutual: The customer walks into the store, visits the web site, or places the first call, or the company makes the first call or email, which generates a neutral or positive response.

Based on the first purchase or information gathered from the first contact experience, the new customer may provide signals as to future or prospective preferences. By comparing these signals with those of previous customers, the new customer may fall into one or more initial segments that suggest or stipulate successive marketing actions. The segments—and actions—will have been derived from analysis of the behavior of other customers, their behavior *following* the first purchase or contact and the success or failure of follow-up communications or promotions.

The first communication following the inception of the relationship between customer and company provides an *introduction* to the company, its products, and possibly its employees and vision. From the first purchase or other contact, the customer has signaled her needs and the company introduces solutions or products to meet those needs. The company is in this for the long term; hence the introduction, as the first proactive communication, does not have to include the entire product catalog. This is just an introduction. The choice of presentation may also be predicated on the initial purchase or first experience.

Following the introduction, the company can extend the introduction by *offerring* the broader product line, as well as provide further information on the company and its product, to attempt to build a broader value equation between itself and the customer.

After the initial exchange of information, a period of *reflection* takes place; the customer reflects on the previous experiences and the information that the company has provided. Reflection is followed by *evaluation:* The customer asks himself, *Do I go back?* Should I make an incremental purchase? Is there a reason not to go back? From a marketing standpoint, a *reinforcement* promotion could be introduced to tip the scales, and a soft discount offer would not be surprising.

If a favorable decision is made following the question *Do I go back,* the *second step* would follow: The second purchase is made. The second purchase could double the available information on the customer, which can provide additional communication opportunities: upsell or cross-sell offers, related product opportunities, and/or recognition messaging.

After the second purchase, the challenge is to repeat the process and create opportunities that generate a third and fourth sale. *Reinforcement, reemphasis, and repeatability* describes the process of maintaining the relationship in the long term.

Of course, if the initial messaging is successful at the outset, there may be a need for only a light level of reinforcement. Customers can independently determine the value of the relationship without it being hammered home by more or less aggressive marketing actions.

Following the second purchase, the level of customer activity can be observed to establish a pattern relative to other customers. The pattern could be simply *Low, Medium*, and *High* purchase activity. The initial classification is to establish transition points. This enables communications intended to *transition* a customer to a higher level, or respond to customer *transitions* to a lower level. Transitions, as noted earlier, can be monitored using interaction management.

Renewal and revitalization are the steps necessary to rejuvenate a flagging relationship.

Substitution is a stage where the relationship more or less abruptly stops because a competitor has successfully interrupted the relationship. Substitution can be reversed through efforts to *win back* and *restore* the relationship.

Stagnation is always possible due to declining value, lack of communication, or lack of originality in both products and communications. This leads to and is signaled by declining sales, fading activity on the web site, or a falloff in response to email. It eventually concludes with "cancellation" or "termination" of the relationship in the customer's mind. Efforts to restore the relationship are similar to substitution: win back and rejuvenation.

The latter stages require marketing communications that are aimed at reemphasizing the value of the relationship, which, of course, calls into question whether there is in fact sufficient basis to rejuvenate the relationship. Some honest soul-searching may be necessary before throwing good marketing dollars after older customers, dollars that might be better spent on establishing new relationships. Fundamentally, a company's product line may not have the depth or breadth of value to sustain an indefinite relationship.

MARKETING COMMUNICATIONS BY LIFE STAGE

The description of relationship life stages provides an interesting perspective for marketing communications. It creates a reusable pattern for promotions, a pattern that can be tested, refined, and perfected over time. It also provides a perspective of continuity, bringing almost the entire sequence of marketing communications into a single view. The life stage descriptions can be used to orient promotions and create a sequence of unique positions, an improvement over the repetition of *Sale! Sale! Sale!*

The pattern also provides a background for response analysis that can shed light on the constantly impending threat of stagnation in communications. By comparing performance of customer groups at similar life stages, the prospective value of different groups may be forecastable. This means that a group of customers in their second stage can be compared to a similar but older group at their second life stage. If the younger group's cumulative sales are higher, it may signal higher long-term potential value. In reverse, if the life stage value is less, it signals an impending shortfall in sales that may require remedial action.

In banking circles, this concept of life stage is expressed as "vintage," and vintage refers to the year or business cycle in which the customers were first acquired. Vintage analysis is done on a regular basis, and forecasting of results includes revenue as well as credit risk.

From the earlier discussion, a significant number of communication contexts are suggested that correspond to the life stage descriptions provided. Since the implementation is sequential with expectations of repeatability, analysis of comparative impact can be made to improve response: How did communication 4 response compare to communication 3; what is the cumulative impact of 3 to 4 to 5 compared to similar or different groups?

The life stage approach is just one dimension. The communication sequence will not take place at the same time of the calendar year for every customer. Seasonal activities can overlay the life stage promotional theme, which creates another dimension for promotions. The age of the customer, if known, provides another dimension, as may other demographic attributes. Segmentation analysis may reveal unique customer segments, which again provide a dimensional view for promotional variety.

In summary, Exhibit 20.1 demonstrates a considerable variety possible in time, season, and customer attribute–based marketing content.

	Contact Frequency	Best/Worst	Transitions	Product Groups	Seasonal	Events	Age	Segment	Other Attributes
1. Inception 2. Introduction 3. Exposure 4. Reflection 5. Evaluation 6. Second Step 7. Reinforcement 8. Reemphasis 9. Repeatability 　Renewal 　Revitalization 10. Substitution 　Win Back, Restoration 11. Stagnation 　Loss of Value 　Decline 　Fade 　Cancellation	Higher — Derived Analytically Point Based — Lower	Based on Customer Purchase Activity	Based on Changes in Purchase Activity	Based on Product Purchase Patterns	Based on Time of Calendar Year	Based on Customer Events (Purchase or other Contact)	Based on Customer Age Groups	Based on Analytically Derived Segments	Selected Attributes Derived from Testing

EXHIBIT 20.1   Customer Life Cycle and Strategic Marketing

IMPLEMENTATION OF STRATEGIC MARKETING

Using the life cycle stages as well as marketable attributes and dimensions as a guideline, appropriate and relevant marketing communications can be planned. More than one communication can be planned for each stage. The plan will include conditional communications, particularly communications that address changes in customer purchase patterns, from low to high (worse customers moving up to higher levels) and high to low (platinum customers whose purchase frequency or value declines).

Tools that facilitate the planning of a connected sequence of promotions that combine batch, seasonal, event, and sequential promotions are not now available; therefore the plan will be cast in a spreadsheet program or word processing application. A complex plan will be more difficult to manage as a result, but not impossible.

The most difficult area to plan is the cycle of communications that establish repeatable added value, the middle point of the customer relationship. The challenge is to extend the relationship; however, challenges arise, such as product limitations. Just how many CDs can I be expected to purchase? Is my demand for Product X conceivably insatiable? By analyzing customer purchase patterns, a number of ideas may be generated that may not be intuitive or immediately obvious, classic "diapers-and-beer" combinations.

Different product combinations can be analyzed using market basket analysis, which may create opportunities for combined product discount offers as well as sequential product-based promotion opportunities.

The plan must address contact frequency, and Exhibit 20.1 outlines more frequent promotions and communications early in the relationship. This is followed by analytically derived promotion frequency, which can take two forms. Based on scoring, a customer is selected more or less frequently for promotions. Based on guidelines derived from testing against purchase patterns, less frequent purchasing merits less frequent promotions. Even a simple Low-Medium-High classification can significantly reduce promotional costs, particularly as the relationship declines in value.

Toward the end of the relationship, even one or two annual promotions may continue to be worthwhile, such as a seasonal product offer during the holidays or an aggressive sale offer of slower-moving inventory. The selection of customers for these purchases is also filtered based on likelihood to respond, particularly as the volume of less active (or inactive) customers increases over time. This group could also merit occasional testing of special promotions. And again testing can confirm whether this is worthwhile and to whom it is most worthwhile.

Strategic Marketing Execution

Implementing the plan involves establishing the life cycle stages in terms of customer signals that in turn can initiate marketing communications. This is effected through a combination of batch-, time-, and event-triggered communications. The plan provides the basis for implementation using marketing automation campaign management capability. Marketing automation planning capabilities in fact make such complex marketing decisions possible, with a reasonable number of people applied to the effort.

Creating 20, 30, 40, or more new promotions is daunting in both creative and query selection terms. However, as discussed in Part Two, marketing automation campaign management provides many features that simplify execution. This is precisely what marketing automation was designed to support. The original premise is an increased volume of communications and promotions to smaller groups of people for improved response rates, lower cost, longer relationships with customers, and higher profits. The infrastructure to accomplish this is marketing automation.

Strategic Marketing Results

The increased volume of communications creates a significant challenge for the analysis of results. Results generation must be automated and the presentation format must accommodate the connected nature of the communications: Single-point-in-time summaries are no longer adequate to assess the effectiveness of the plan in generating incremental profit. The cumulative purchases derived from a sequence of communications must be evaluated.

However, this is not without precedent. As noted earlier, banks have been doing vintage analysis for many years. Once the data has been cast in a form to support vintage analysis, the cumulative purchases at points in time can be fairly easily evaluated. Results from the implementation of a strategic marketing plan will need to be compared with a holdout sample, the control group. And the incremental volume of communications will in turn generate a significantly greater volume of tests, which in turn require their own analysis.

The most significant challenge will be keeping up with the sheer volume of information generated from higher communication and promotion volume derived from multiple customer segments. It is essential to provide the executive summary–level information (are we doing better than Plan; are we doing better than prior year) but equally essential to provide access to the details that explain the variances—improvement or decline—against Plan and prior year.

Marketing automation can provide this level of detail beneath the summaries, surfaced through manual drill-down flexibility, but the volume of information will likely be simply overwhelming. Coping effectively with the management of a dramatic increase in marketing communications will require analytical applications that provide insight to the variances that underlie the summary figures.

However, this is nothing more than an extension of the financial rate/volume analysis discussed in Part One. Instead of a set of campaigns being the denominator, the view is changed to a dimension or a number of dimensions. The underlying analytical calculations are no more complex than the equations shown in Part One. The automated execution across several hundred possibilities is done effectively, with suitable variances highlighted for further review.

These dimensional attributes comprise the KPIs (key performance indicators) for marketing, and can be complemented with other metrics such as survival rates, attrition rates, total sales per customer over time, average purchase value, average profit per store visit, and so on. The metrics, accumulated over time, become the basis for trend graphs. Trends beget another set of metrics: trend analysis. Trend analysis can also be supported with automatic reporting of underlying activities that explain variances as required, over time.

Unfortunately or not, the utility provided by marketing automation in supporting significantly greater opportunity to communicate and promote to customers brings along its own challenges in managing the increased level of complexity in marketing. The standard "batch" approach of June campaigns followed by Summer Savings followed by Back-to-School Sales comprising the marketing year, repeated year after year, has the attraction of simplicity. But the earlier argument voiced in Chapter 7 (Modeling) that demonstrated the value of increased promotional activity to smaller groups of people revealed a significant and previously untapped profit potential. Yes, there is additional complexity; however, the full breadth of the potential is expected to take several years to approach. Time will be required to develop the incremental opportunities, to test into the appropriate models and promotions. Time will be required to develop a strategic marketing framework similar to the customer life stages presented earlier. The volume of communications will increase *over time* and the skills of the marketers participating in the evolution will develop *over time* in managing the additional levels of complexity. Over time, their effectiveness in creating an extended relationship will be reflected by increased value from each individual customer. The increased value improves the return on the acquisition effort that generates incremental profit for continued corporate and marketing investment.

Conclusion

A broad range of topics have been addressed in the preceding pages: financial business management in the form of the operating management reports, return on investment and investment proposal presentation, marketing financial information, return on marketing investment (RMI), customer information and information management (data warehousing) for storage and retrieval, the use of customer information in modeling, campaign management, and more advanced marketing possibilities afforded by a marketing automation system.

The practical aspects of these topics have been addressed from a marketer's perspective in the context of the opportunities available from a marketing automation system. Some of this material is addressed in other books, often in great detail, but often in detail tedious for a marketer to absorb or exploit. This is not said in derogation of most marketer's capabilities. The details behind a successful data warehouse project, for example, involve a level of database sophistication that is not in the marketer's experience. The same can be said for modeling, where many practitioners hold advanced degrees in mathematics or statistics. It would be a rare single individual who could wear all of these hats successfully.

A marketer, however, is on the front line in crafting customer communications, and marketing promotions can have a significant positive impact on profits. The application of marketing automation on behalf of marketers has a significant potential for amplifying marketing's impact and increasing profits. The implementation of a marketing automation system, however, is not a small project, and successful implementation involves financial systems, customer information, information management, and the integration of response models of customer behavior. Marketing needs to be involved and to influence the implementation to ensure the marketing goals are met.

The preceding discussion has provided further details in these areas, with the goal of exposing and expanding their relevance for marketing and marketers. Sufficient detail has been selected to assist in the discussion of the central components of marketing automation between marketers and others in a business organization, primarily finance and information technology management. Marketing needs to be in a position to motivate and participate in the design and implementation of marketing automation with these business groups. Marketing needs to be aware of the positive impact of financial information, ease of access to customer information, and the role of modeling in customer selection if they are to influence their implementation into the marketing process.

Several areas in the customer marketing process such as database queries were identified that limit the ability of marketers to take a stronger role in that process. Marketing automation capabilities and functionality have been shown that overcome these barriers to participation. With the complement of a campaign management system, marketing is in a strong position to play a more direct role in the evolution and production of marketing campaigns. The ability to play a more direct role will enable the marketing group to increase the production of more specifically targeted communications to customers, targeted communications that will elicit stronger response.

Many organizations already have a few individuals familiar with the customer database and skilled in the development of customer selection using Structured Query Language (SQL). The demands on their time and skills are a limiting factor in the marketing organization's attempt to exploit customer information. A campaign management system based on an information map can open the customer data to the broader marketing audience. A graphical user interface in place of queries based on SQL in turn enables marketers to build communication audiences, increasing the number of people able to exploit customer information.

Increasing marketing's participation in the process of audience selection provides the increased resources necessary to effect more communications to customers. Effective incorporation of response and contact history in audience selection ensures that customers do not receive more junk mail and may in fact receive communications of increasing value.

The variety of opportunities for more promotions is still in the marketers' hands. Marketing automation does not generate automatic communications. Marketing's understanding of product value and customer interest, their creativity in presentation, and their effective use of multiple channels for communication offers are still demanded to create the value of the communications. Their success will be quickly measurable from the feedback provided by the marketing automation system.

Index